Marquette's Explorations:
The Narratives Reexamined

Marquette's Explorations:

The University of Wisconsin Press
MADISON, MILWAUKEE, & LONDON

The Narratives Reexamined

RAPHAEL N. HAMILTON, S.J.

1970

Published 1970
The University of Wisconsin Press
Box 1379, Madison, Wisconsin 53701

The University of Wisconsin Press, Ltd.
27-29 Whitfield Street, London, W. 1

First printing

Printed in the United States of America
Pantagraph Printing, Bloomington, Illinois

ISBN 0-299-05570-1; LC 78-121768

TO DISCOVERERS

TABLE OF CONTENTS

LIST OF ILLUSTRATIONS

PREFACE

WHILE writing this book, I have felt very much like a detective reporting the evidence for the solution of a case concerning a friend. My earliest teaching was done in a school close to the place where, in 1673, Louis Jolliet with Fr. Jacques Marquette entered the Mississippi River. A Jesuit myself, I quite naturally took an interest in the Jesuit member of the exploring party. Later, in my chosen field of American colonial history at Marquette University, I read and taught much about him. Thus in 1960, when a monograph by Reverend Francis B. Steck attacked the traditional presentation of Marquette, I read it with more than ordinary attention. The author said his studies had led him to believe that the documents supporting Marquette's place in history had been faked.

My own reading about the French regime had acquainted me with travel journals which were counterfeits. Well known to historians of the period is *Dernieres Découvertes . . . par M. le Chevalier Tonti*. It tells the adventures which de La Salle's lieutenant is said to have encountered from 1679 to 1687. De Tonti was alive when it was published (1697) and he repudiated it as a brazen fabrication. Was there a possibility for similar fraud in Marquette's narrative?

I went through Steck's work again and found that, with some notable exceptions, he rested his proof heavily upon reprints of materials from foreign archives, such as those edited by Pierre Margry, Reuben G. Thwaites, and others. I realized that my own knowledge of Marquette came from these same sources. Both Margry and Thwaites employed long-hand transcriptions in compiling their volumes. Aware that transcribers sometimes transpose, summarize or omit passages, I decided to obtain photocopies of the manuscripts themselves to see what they might reveal. My findings proved so exciting to me that I went far beyond what I had first intended to do. Journals by other seventeenth- and eighteenth-century explorers, many rare books of the era, maps by colonial cartographers, French, Spanish, and English, all these supplied me with material relevant to my topic. My notes became ponderous.

In pursuing my clues, I found that many different sorts of people were interested in the answer to the question I was endeavoring to solve. Dwellers along the route of his explorations had erected monuments to Marquette and eulogized him; now they asked me whether they had been indiscreet. Students were curious to find out if any error could turn up in Steck's book. Clergymen wondered why it suggested that Marquette was an unordained missionary. My teaching colleagues prodded me to be on with my work because they hoped it might prove to be an impartial evaluation of one so often popularly memorialized. To all of these, the present book is my response, and if the ordinary detective story appeals to most of us, this one should fascinate the many who have desired a solution of this biographical mystery.

Before ending these introductory remarks, I should like to add a word for the professional historians. My long standing admiration for the man whose case concerns me and my membership in the Jesuit Order to which he belonged should, in justice, cause the reader to look for bias on my part. The historian in me has been aware of the threat to my objectivity in discussing such a person; hence, I believe I have been more cautious than ordinary in drawing conclusions. On the other hand, the Jesuit in me made me think of places where I might find evidence about my man, which might not have been suggested to one not belonging to the Order. Indeed, this acquaintance with the Jesuit technique of living and writing opened so many new aspects related to seventeenth-century New France that I have tried to explain how it affects the understanding of a single individual, in the belief that it will supply an unaccustomed approach to the study of other individuals and of the wider field of French colonial history.

Just as my manuscript was ready for the press, Joseph P. Donnelly's *Jacques Marquette, S.J. 1637–1675* was published. It is a biography which defends the traditional presentation of the missionary-explorer. It does fortify the approach to this position with new material, but it omits a specific discussion of the authenticity of the original Marquette documents. My work is primarily concerned with such an investigation. Anything included in the following pages is there to supply evidence bearing on the validity or invalidity of the primary sources relating to Marquette. To weigh this evidence is the purpose of this book.

The Marquette documents were written at a time when French scholars had not yet adopted a standard form of excellence in spelling and accentuation. A fundamental aid in this direction was the *Dictionnaire de l'Académie Française,* first published in 1694. In an effort not to tamper with the original manuscripts in any way, their spelling and accentuation is transcribed here just as it was found. The same holds true for French books listed in the Bibliography. My aim with regard to them has been to copy exactly what appears on their title pages without correction of spelling or accentuation.

A grant from the Marquette University Committee on Research has enabled me to collect the needed material and secure expert assistance at various stages in the production of my manuscript. The Provincial of the Jesuit Province of Wisconsin, Very Reverend John J. Foley, gave me permission to publish in 1963.

Special collections in the Library of Congress, the New York Public Library, the Newberry Library, and the Cornell University Library have been placed at my disposal. The Library of Congress, the Bibliothèque Nationale and the Archives Nationale in Paris, and the Public Library of Nancy, France, have graciously furnished me photocopies from their manuscripts with permission to print them. From the Archivum Romanum Societatis Jesu and the Fondo Gesuitico Societatis Jesu, by the kindness of Fr. Joseph Teschitel, archivist, and through the interest of Fr. Ernest Burrus of the Institutum Historicum Societatis Jesu in Rome, I have received microfilms of documents connected with Marquette after these experts had gone through these two depositories, looking into all the files where their experience suggested such materials might be found. In like manner, Fr. Paul Desjardins, archivist of the Collège Sainte-Marie, Montreal, and Fr. Georges-Emil Giguère, then a member of its history department, supplied photographs of unique Marquette documents available only in Canada. Fr. Lucien Campeau, professor of church history in the Collège de l'Immaculée Conception, Montreal, allowed me to summarize his studies about watermarks in the paper of these documents and others in Europe. The advice and encouragement of Fr. Hugues Beylard, archivist of the Jesuit Province of Champagne, France, were helpful. Fr. Joseph Dehergne, archivist of the same Order's Province of France, not only furnished microfilms from the rich supply of seventeenth-century documents under his care at Chantilly, but went himself to Parisian depositories to unearth their treasures and have them reproduced.

The staff of Marquette University Library, together with those of many other libraries contacted, have favored me with the unselfish cooperation traditional in their profession. The monotonous task of preparing my notes for printing was cheerfully carried out by several helpers: Mrs. Ernst Baumeister, Miss Karen J. Bellman, Mrs. Floyd Christensen, Miss Bernice Doucette, Mrs. Ceil MacDonald, and Miss Susanne Reading all deserve thanks for such work. I am especially grateful for the expertise by which Miss Mildred Mary Holly transformed the residual amalgam into a clear typewritten version. The illustrations were prepared by Mr. Stanislaus Ratajczak, photographer in the Department of Biology at the University.

R.N.H.

Milwaukee, Wisconsin
January, 1970

Marquette's Explorations:
The Narratives Reexamined

LIST OF ABBREVIATIONS

Archives

ACSM Archives du Collège Sainte-Marie, Montreal. (These archives have been moved to the Jesuit house of studies in Saint-Jérôme, P.Q., Canada. Their title is "Archives S.J. Canada-français"; shelf numbers will not change.)

AMU   Archives of Marquette University, Milwaukee

APF   Archives de la Province de France, S.J., Chantilly

ARSJ Archivum Romanum Societatis Jesu, Rome

ASH   Archives du Service Hydrographique (Dépôt des Cartes et Plans de la Marine), Paris. Historical material formerly in this depository has been transferred to the Archives Nationales, but retains its call title.

BN   Archives de la Bibliothèque Nationale, Paris

Periodicals

M-A   *Mid-America*, Loyola University, Chicago

RAPQ *Rapport de l'Archiviste de la Province de Québec*

CHAPTER 1

The Discoverer

T HE Père Marquette documents to be explored in the present study are those manuscripts relevant to the man commonly known as the discoverer of the Mississippi River. He was a seventeenth-century Jesuit. When Ignatius of Loyola founded this Order, he wrote the *Constitutiones Societatis Jesu* to direct its members in accomplishing their purpose. One provision he incorporated therein was a requirement for superiors, in charge of individual communities, to inform their higher superiors frequently about the success or failure of the apostolate with which they had been charged.[1] Until 1581, when Ignatius'

1. *Constitutiones Societatis Jesu Latinae et Hispanicae cum Earum Declarationibus* (Matriti, 1892), p. 232, pars 8, cap. 1, no. 8 and no. 9. The highest superior of the Jesuits has the title of general. A provincial is an intermediary official, between the general and the rectors of individual communities. In mission lands, the superior of the whole mission area has control of all Jesuits working there, but he must report to that particular provincial who supports the area with funds and men.

third successor died, there had been a lack of unanimity in carrying out this rule. This year, in accord with another precept of the *Constitutiones,* an assembly of delegates, known as a General Congregation, met in Rome to elect a new major superior. At such time, the *Constitutiones* empowered these representatives to legislate for the whole Society. In 1581, they chose Claude Aquaviva to be the general and, among other decrees, specified the time at which news should go to the provincials and the form which such communications should take. Each year, the rector of each house was to send in a short catalog, as it was called, in which every individual under his care was listed with his duties and status in the Order. At the same time a fuller evaluation of what these men were accomplishing was to be written out in what came to be known as the annual letter. It was the duty of each provincial to forward the catalogs of his province to the Jesuit headquarters in Rome and he was expected to accompany them with a compilation of news drawn from the annual letters.[2] Such material, from all over the world, has come to rest in the Archivum Romanum Societatis Jesu where, along with the Fondo Gesuitico, a collection of correspondence from Jesuit colleges and missions, it is today.[3] In a search for Père Marquette docu-

2. *Institutum Societatis Iesu* (Florentiae, 1892-93), III, 41-45, "Formula Scribendi." Because the first Congregation had decided never to change the wording of Loyola's *Constitutiones,* all amendments to them are published in a separate codex entitled *Institutum Societatis Iesu;* see ibid., II, 161, Cong. I (A.D. 1558), post elect., titulus II, decree 15.

3. E. J. Burrus, "Monumenta Historica Societatis Jesu," *Woodstock Letters,* LXXXIII (1954), 158-68, relates the almost miraculous means by which the Jesuit archives in Rome were saved from destruction during the suppression of the Order, 1773-1814, and how in 1870, when Giuseppe Garibaldi again threatened them, they were spirited away to Valkenburg, Holland, where they remained for almost fifty years, before they were returned to Rome once more in 1939.

ments, this Roman depository seems the most logical with which to begin.

The Archivum Romanum Societatis Jesu actually houses thirty-eight seventeenth-century handwritten catalogs in which Marquette's work is mentioned. In both it and the Fondo Gesuitico there are other manuscripts valuable for the present research. The first catalog of interest comes from the province of Champagne in 1654 and tells that Jacques Marquette was born in Laon, in the northeastern corner of France, on June 1, 1637.[4] He attended the Jesuit university at Reims and, while there, he made up his mind to become a member of the Order which was deeply involved in educational work at home and missionary work abroad. He entered the Jesuit novitiate at Nancy, near Laon, on October 7, 1654.[5] There he and his companions began their preparation for the religious life by making a thirty-day retreat.[6] After the Council of Trent, 1545–63, when the essential dogmas of Catholic theology were

4. L[udovicus] Carrez, *Documenta ad Historiam Societatis Jesu in Gallia Concinnandam, Catalogi Sociorum et Officiorum Provinciae Campaniae Societatis Jesu* (v.p., 1897–1914) [cited hereafter as Carraz, *Catalogi*] V, 61–62, reprints this catalog and others dealing with Marquette's European career are published in subsequent volumes. After 1666, when he started work in the New World, his assignments quoted in this book are taken from the original manuscripts; see Sec. I of the Bibliography, "The Marquette Documents."

5. Ibid., the new novices are announced, "Renatus le Sevre, Claudius Nicolas, Petrus Chifflet, Edmundus Poissenot, Joannes Bordois, Theodoricus Thuret, Nicolaus de Lettres, Jacobus Marquette, Petrus-Joseph Amé, Rudolphus Rigault et Petrus Beguin."

6. During this month, under the direction of an experienced priest, five hours of each twenty-four are devoted to meditation drawn from Ignatius' book of the *Spiritual Exercises*. Here the young men are made to review the meaning of Christ's career. The retreat, reduced to eight days, becomes an annual event for all Jesuits and the daily order in Jesuit communities allots the members an hour each day for contemplation.

epitomized in catechetical form, teaching these truths to the
children of the neighborhood became a regular practice for
the novices; so, with his long retreat finished, Marquette
worked on the preparation and delivery of such instructions.
He also took turns with his fellow novices at preaching practice sermons. Twice a year until he took his final vows, he
spent three days of recollection under a spiritual director,
taking inventory of his progress.[7] Noviceship ends by taking
simple vows of poverty, chastity, and obedience, whereupon
the young Jesuits are sent to teach in a college of the Order.
At this stage of his career, Marquette was twenty-one years old,
and there is a letter in the Roman Archives which testifies to
his having already asked to be sent to the foreign missions. It
is from the general and refuses his petition; so, in 1658, he
became a teacher like the rest of the young men who had entered the Society of Jesus with him.[8]

In the seventeenth century the lowest class in a Jesuit college
was the sixth. Thence, boys progressed to the first and then
entered humanities, which was on about the same level as the
present college freshman year. Marquette's first assignment
was to the college at Auxerre where he taught Fifth Class. Then
he moved up to the University of Reims, where he spent
twelve months as regent, or teacher, of Fourth Class and then
took over Second Class for the next year. The autumn of 1661
brought him to the college at Charleville. Two years later, he
was in Langres teaching First Class. The next year, 1664–65,

7. *Institutum S. I.,* II, 10–11, Examen, cap. 4, no. 14 and no. 11;
also II, 302, Cong. VI (A.D. 1608), Decree 29, no. 1.

8. ARSJ, Epist. Gen., Camp. 8, pt. 2, 257, "P. Oliva ad Jacobum
Marquette (4 Feb. 1659)," in Gilbert J. Garraghan, "Some Hitherto
Unpublished Marquettiana," *M-A,* XVIII (1936), 15. Here, Garraghan calls the general who wrote Marquette Father Oliva. This is
not quite so. In 1659, Fr. Goswin Nickel still held office, but his
infirmity required an assistant. Fr. Paul Oliva held this position
until he became general on Nickel's death, 1664. Marquette's letter
to Father Nickel has not been found.

was to be his last as instructor. He spent it at the University of Pont-à-Mousson, where he was listed among the faculty as "M. Jacobus Marquette, professor humanitatis." [9] This summary calls attention to the progress of a successful educator: year by year he had been promoted to more difficult classes until he was handling college work. Furthermore, the catalog for 1665 contains the information that Marquette had acquired the higher degree of Master of Arts. Of the nineteen scholastics who had finished regency and were his companions at Pont-à-Mousson, only five others had the M.A. Only those who gave extra time for special studies during the teaching years merited this honor.[10] The next step for the young Jesuit was a formal course of theology.

Six years as a pedagog had not weakened Marquette's eagerness for foreign mission work. In 1665, as he was about to become a student again, he renewed his request for it. Mentioning the general's previous answer, "I had received a response that I must make a course in theology," as cause for the refusal of his first petition, he proposed a reason for not tarrying so long by saying, "I feel less qualified by nature and entirely indifferent by temperament toward getting up the speculative science." He wondered if he might not, now, go on the missions, "without finishing or even beginning theology, since I have already been considering cases of conscience [moral theology]," and was twenty-eight years old. After a few more sentences, his final one comes back to his motive, "zeal and fervor worthy of a true son of the Society," which he believes is better "for seeking these souls, whereas specu-

9. Marquette's teaching assignments are set down in the yearly catalogs of the Champagne province of the Society, see, Carrez, *Catalogi,* V, 81, 161, 170; VI, 26, 45.

10. ARSJ, Camp. 11, 208v. This information is found only in the special catalog sent from each province to Rome triennially, see *Institutum S. I.,* III, 45, par. 32–35, "Formula Scribendi." The title "scholastic," derived from *schola* ("school,"), is applied to Jesuits still in their studies.

lative sciences have little value in winning them to Christ."
He ends by asking the general, Fr. Paul Oliva, to pray for his
progress toward becoming such a true son.[11]

To one unacquainted with the normal program by which a
seventeenth-century Jesuit made his immediate studies for
ordination, the tenor of this letter might seem to express a
willingness to forego the priesthood; a word about this period
of preparation will remove any such misunderstanding. As
soon as the ordinary young Jesuit had put his schoolmaster's
mantle in mothballs, he shoved his knees under a desk and
went to work on a survey of philosophy in a class for the
Repetentes ("Reviewers").[12] At the end of twelve months, a
successful examination would promote him to the study of revealed truth. Ignatius had prescribed that six years be devoted
to this field. In the first four, all of speculative theology was
to be covered: creation, justification, escatology, and the attri-
butes of God. When this was finished, all of the men were
ordained. Those who had done well were to add to their final
vows of poverty, chastity, and obedience a fourth, which
promised readiness to employ their knowledge anywhere the

11. Gilbert J. Garraghan, "Some Newly Discovered Marquette
and La Salle Letters," *Archivum Historicum Societatis Jesu, Rome,* IV
(1935), 284–85, reproduces the entire letter from Fondo Gesuitico
Societatis Jesu, Rome, Indipetae, Busta 26 [changed, since his visit, to
Indipetae 757], no. 126. All translations were made by the author.

12. ARSJ, Franc. 23, 17, names the three classes of philosophy,
Logici ("Logicians"), *Physici* ("Physicists"), and *Repetentes* ("Reviewers"). The review of philosophy is required by *Institutum S. I.,*
II, 328, Cong. VII (A.D. 1615–16), decree 33, par. 1. In the
twentieth century, young Jesuits usually complete all three classes of
philosophy before any teaching. In the seventeenth century, the teaching ordinarily took place after the boys had finished the year of
Physicists. Marquette, together with all his fellow novices, followed
this pattern, see Carrez, *Catalogi,* V, 61–62 and VI, 14, 63. Gilbert J.
Garraghan, *Marquette, Ardent Missioner, Daring Explorer* (New
York, 1937), p. 6, had the twentieth-century sequence in mind when
he suggested that Marquette began studying theology in 1665.

pope might send them. They were known as professed fathers.[13] From among these, the men who had demonstrated conspicuous talent formed a chosen group, who continued their studies, and Ignatius had written "research, suitable for the doctorate degree, will be undertaken by those, who are thus advanced," with the hope that, after two additional years, they might become eminent scholars, ready to step in to bolster European Catholicism wherever it might be wavering before the then new danger of the Protestant Reformation.[14] While the founder was still at work on his *Constitutiones,* missions beyond the ocean sea had begun to claim his men. Concomitant with the first royal demand for Jesuit missionaries came the first princely offer to endow a college for lay students, if Ignatius would supply the teachers.[15] Preparing men for these entirely divergent fields required courses different from those appropriate for making doctors of theology. Loyola met the challenge. He drafted new programs. They were approved by Pope Paul III in the brief *Exponi Nobis* of 1546, which is directed to the general superior and his successors. It reads, in part, "We . . . concede the right and faculty . . . to you, that in future, you may have priests who will assist you in spiritual things and secular persons who do so in temporal things and in the domestic duties of your houses." [16] In the *Constitutiones,* the founder outlined curricula for those who would specialize in secular learning and missiology; in administration and plant

13. *Institutum S. I.,* II, 87, Const., pars 5, cap. 2, no. 1–no. 2 and declaration B, lists the requirements for profession. The formula of the vows taken by the professed is available, ibid., II, 89, Const., pars 5, cap. 3, no. 3. The necessity for their being priests before profession is stressed, ibid., II, 2, Examen, cap. 1, no. 8.

14. Ibid., II, 80, Const., pars 4, cap. 15, no. 3. Candidates for the doctorate are called "Repetentes theologiam."

15. Ludwig Koch, *Jesuiten-Lexikon Die Gesellschaft Jesu Einst und Jetzt* (Paderborn, 1934), col. 1206 and cols. 1007–8.

16. *Institutum S.I.,* I, 12–13, Paul III, *"Exponi Nobis."*

maintenance.[17] The latter were the "temporal coadjutors." They took no designated courses in theology and their vow formula distinguished them from priests just as it is the vow formula which distinguishes one religious group from another —in the Dominican Order preaching is stressed, while among the Franciscans simplicity of life is emphasized—though all take substantially the same vows of poverty, chastity, and obedience.[18] On the other hand, the spiritual coadjutors were to be raised to major orders after two years. During these, the candidate is told, "He should be content with a study of Humane Letters and a short course in Logic, which will enable him to understand the lectures in Cases of Conscience."[19] They did not take the special vow to the pope, because they were to be specialists, not in evidences of religion, but in a particular field of education or administration for which they would be trained.[20]

When Ignatius divided his Company of Jesus into these platoons, he called each one *gradus* ("a grade"). This caption does not imply that there are steps in the Order by which one makes progress from a lower to a higher level. The "Examen

17. Ibid., II, 62–63, Const., pars 4, cap. 5, no. 1–no. 2 and declarations C and D.

18. Ibid., II, 28, Const., pars 1, cap. 2, no. 2–no. 3 and declaration A, outline the temporal coadjutors' preparation. Their belonging to the laity, "ad sacros Ordines non promoti [without being in holy Orders]," is stressed, ibid., II, 19, Examen, cap. 6, no. 1. Their vow formula is spelled out, ibid., II, 91, Const., pars 5, cap. 4, no. 3.

19. Ibid., II, 19, Examen, cap. 6, no. 1, requires the priesthood, "Coadiutores . . . spirituales quidem qui Sacerdotes sunt [Spiritual Coadjutors, also, who are priests]." Since moral theology was finished in two years, this amount of time was the maximum theological requirement for the spiritual coajutor, ibid., III, 159, Ratio Studiorum, Regulae Provincialis, no. 12 and ibid., II, 208, Cong. II (A.D. 1565), decree 69.

20. Ibid., II, 29, Const., pars 1, cap. 2, no. 5–no. 13, outlines the studies. The special vow formula of the spiritual coadjutor is found, ibid., II, 90, Const., pars 5, cap. 4, no. 2.

Generale" which is to be pondered thoroughly by all who apply for admission, underscores the permanence of status once a grade is selected. For example, it warns, "Let him not for any reason seek to change from the state of Temporal Coadjutor to the state of Spiritual." [21] Behind this is Paul III's brief, *Exponi Nobis,* which created the divisions. It is a prescription of personal papal law (Jus Pontificium); hence it can be changed only by the pope, because canon law of the Catholic Church limits the dispensation from ecclesiastical decrees to him who has the same or greater authority than the original law maker.[22] For Catholics no one has greater ecclesiastical authority than the pope and, in 1956, Fr. Anthony de Aldama, Roman expert concerning the *Institutum Societatis Iesu,* presented findings of Jesuit commentators on the rule of the Order from Francisco Suárez in the seventeenth century to Edward Fine in the twentieth century for his authority that this dispensation had never been conceded by any pope.[23]

Because Marquette had taught the more advanced classes and had a master's degree, there was every probability he would be told to pursue the cirriculum of the professed fathers. After five to seven years of apprenticeship, he might end up occupying the chair of theology at a university in Europe and never get to the foreign missions. This is why he emphasized his

21. Ibid., II, 19, Examen, cap. 6, no. 5–no. 6.

22. *Codex Juris Canonici Pii X Pontificis Maximi Iussu Digestus, Benedicti Papae XV Auctoritate Promulgatus* (Westminster, Md., 1944), Canon 80, n. 2, sets forth the history of church decrees limiting the power of dispensation.

23. AMU, N. Amer., Fr. Reg., 16, Ant. de Aldama, S.J. to Ernest Burrus, Roma, May 23, 1956, calls as witnesses, "F. Fine, *Juris Regularis Tum Communis Tum Particularis Quo Regitur Societas Iesu Declaratio* (1909), pars I, cap. 5, no. 21; F. Suarez, *De Virtute et Statu Religionis* (1625), vol. IV, tract. 10, lib. VII, cap. II, no. 12; V. Magioni, *Syntagma Juris Universi Societatis Iesu* (17th century), tit. V, cap. 1, no. 2; A. Oswald, *Commentarius in Decem Partes Constitutionum Societatis Jesu* (1895²), Quinta pars, cap. 2, no. 380."

willingness to forego "speculative sciences." By dropping them, he could become a spiritual coadjutor and his zeal for the apostolate would be fully equipped to function after only two years. To this purpose, he told the general his eagerness in devoting his study to "cases of conscience," which are the subject of this curriculum.[24] What he said about being ready to start overseas, without "finishing or even beginning theology," can mean either of two things. One, he was willing to follow the short course of theology in a Jesuit-staffed mission seminary on the scene in Canada or India.[25] Two, he was ready, if the general wished to interpret it that way, to accept immediate ordination in France. In the seventeenth century it was not uncommon to bestow major orders whenever a bishop saw fit. The Council of Trent in its decree on seminaries was concerned with the surroundings and discipline of the men preparing for the priesthood rather than the time they should devote to study of speculative theology; hence, no decree of the Council stood in the way of his immediate ordination.[26]

24. Garraghan, "Newly Discovered Letters," pp. 284–85.

25. Reuben G. Thwaites, *The Jesuit Relations and Allied Documents, Travels and Explorations of the Jesuit Missionaries in New France, 1610–1791* (Cleveland, 1896–1901) [cited hereafter as Thwaites, *Jr*] L, 327, transcribes a manuscript which mentions that the Jesuit, Philip Pierson, missionary at St. Ignace in 1673 studied all of his theology in Quebec and was ordained there in 1669. How Thwaites edited this series of Jesuit documents will be considered in ch. 3. For the seminary in Goa, India, see Ludovicus Carrez, *Atlas Geographicus Societatis Jesu in Quo Delineantur Quinque Ejus Modernae Assistentiae . . . Necnon et Veteres Ejusdem Societatis Provinciae Quadragintatres cum Earum Domiciliis Quantum Fieri Licuit* (Paris 1900), p. 5 and map, ibid., p. 42.

26. H. L. Schroeder, *Canons and Decrees of the Council of Trent, Original Text with English Translations* (St. Louis, 1950), p. 446, Sessio vigesima-tertia, De Reformatione, Die XV Julii, MDLXIII, "Forma Erigendi Seminarium [Directions for Establishing Seminaries]." St. Charles Borromeo, one of the most ardent reformers at the Council, returned to his see of Milan in 1563 and set up three curricula of theology. One lasted 4 years, the others were completed in much less

Probably because he knew the rules in the *Institutum Societatis Iesu* forbade any Jesuit to be advanced to holy orders without satisfactorily passing an examination in "Cases of Conscience," he tells, in his letter, of his efforts to be prepared for this.[27]

True, there was a Tridentine decree, which warned bishops to decide the adequacy of preparation on the part of those whom they ordained, but Pope Gregory XIII in 1582, issued a bull giving them faculties to raise Jesuits to the priesthood, even without the special studies which the Council of Trent required, if they were presented "by the general of the aforesaid Society of the time or those delegated by him." [28] This dispensation from common law was intended to free the prelates from the burdensome duty of following the frequent moves of Jesuit candidates to verify their competence. It enabled them to place the responsibility on the local provincial, whose office obliged him to know about his men. By virtue of this privilege, in 1666, Godefred Thierry, who had begun the review of philosophy in the company of Marquette in 1665, was to receive ordination. Another colleague, Jean-François Vignolles, was made a priest at the end of his scholastic teaching in 1667, and put back as an instructor of a class in the autumn of the same year, without attending any formal lectures in theology.[29]

---

time, see Servinus Binius, ed., *Concilia Generalia et Provincialia Graeca et Latina Qvotqvot Reperiri Potvervnt . . .* (Coloniae Agrippinae, 1618), IV, pt. 2, 523–30.

27. *Institutum S.I.,* III, 275–76, "Regulationes Generalis." Fr. Everard Mercurian, general from 1573–80, required the test in moral theology and also bade provincials to make sure that the men to be ordained would be prudent in approaching the problems which confront pastors of souls. In 1665, Rome had been notified by the triennial catalog that Marquette might be relied upon to show sufficient prudence in making such judgments, ARSJ, Camp. 11, 239v.

28. *Institutum S.I.,* I, 85–86, Gregory XIII, *Pium et Utile,* September 22, 1582.

29. Carrez, *Catalogi,* VI, 79, 97, 83.

Despite all the possibilities which existed in 1665 for satisfy-
ing Marquette's request for immediate assignment to the lands
overseas, in the reply to his letter of request Oliva approved
the "ardent desire . . . to go on the foreign missions," but
evaded the main issue with a noncommittal, "I am writing
Fr. Provincial to ascertain his judgment." [30] When in the fall
of 1665 classes were resumed, the young man was told to take
up his books as Repetens and begin the review of philosophy
like those who were preparing for the long course in speculative theology. His wishes seemed to have been completely
overlooked.

In December, 1665, the annual letter about the events in
New France for the previous twelve months reached Father
Oliva. There he learned how Fr. Claude Allouez was in the act
of starting a new mission at the far end of Lake Superior,
among Indians numbering a hundred thousand warriors. Monsieur de Tracy, viceroy for Louis XIV in his American posses-
sions, had sent the Ottawa presents and urged the Jesuits to
speed their conversion before the trader's brandy became an
obstacle. Priests were sorely needed.[31] On December 29, 1665,
the general wrote a letter to Fr. Nicolas Roger, Marquette's
provincial. In it, he said, "The Canadian mission has great
need for a reinforcement of workers . . . [Your Reverence]
has, among others, Master Marquette who can be dispatched
upon the first occasion." [32] The first occasion would be in the
spring, when the ships would start their annual westward
voyage to New France. Father Roger acted immediately. Marquette was separated from the Repetentes and told to devote

30. ARSJ, Epist. Gen., Camp. 8, pt. 2, 428v, General Oliva to
Jacques Marquette, April 28, 1665, in Garraghan, "Unpublished Marquettiana," p. 17.

31. Thwaites, *JR*, XLIX, 240–51.

32. ARSJ, Epist. Gen., Camp. 8, pt. 2, 428v, General Oliva to
Provincial Roger, December 29, 1665, in Garraghan, "Unpublished
Marquettiana," p. 18.

his full time to moral theology.[33] After a few months at this, he was able to handle cases of conscience in a way which satisfied his examiners. At Toul on March 7, 1666, he was ordained by Bishop André de Saussay.[34]

Almost before the oil of Marquette's priestly anointing was dry, he was on his way to Paris. Fr. Jacques Brotier, provincial of the Province of France, had his headquarters there. Since the Canadian mission was his responsibility, Father Marquette was loaned to him.[35] On May 31 in a letter to Oliva from La Rochelle, the young missionary, waiting to go aboard his boat, put in writing the joy he felt over what had happened. He admitted that, "up to the present, I had been indifferent to any particular mission, now, after it has been decided [about my going to Canada], every fiber of my soul longs for it . . . I follow God's call, who will not permit me to be tried beyond my strength, especially since I believe this whole venture has been brought to fruition by the Blessed Virgin. I now ask only one thing of Your Reverence, namely that you give me your blessing . . . so that I may show myself a true son of the Society of Jesus." [36]

33. ARSJ, Franc. 14, 172, the triennial catalog for 1669 takes cognizance of Marquette's preparation thus, "Tempus studiorum, 2 phil. theol. morali aliquot menses [length of studies, two years of philosophy and several months of moral theology]."

34. For a full discussion of the controversy over Marquette's ordination, see Appendix I. The episcopal archives of Toul disappeared during the French Revolution. Today, the see is joined to Nancy, where the episcopal records begin with the nineteenth century. Diocesan histories establish de Saussay as the ordaining bishop, AMU, Univ., D-2, 2.

35. ARSJ, Camp. 19, 88, "Catalogus Provinciae Campaniae, 1667 Exeunte," under the heading "Extra Provinciam, in Nova francia [Outside the Province n New France]," one finds "P. Theodororcus [sic] Beschefer, P. Ioannes Pierron, P. Iacobus Marquet." Father Marquette's provincials are listed, C. Van De Vorst and J. B. Goetstouwers, *Synopsis Historiae S. J.* (Lovanii, 1950), col. 668–75.

36. Garraghan, "Newly Discovered Letters," p. 286.

In the short catalog sent to Rome in 1666, the provincial of the Province of France tells of Father Marquette's assignment to the mission of Canada. He writes, "Fr. Jacques Marquette studies the language of the Montagnais at Sillery." [37] The North American Jesuits had made up their minds that the only way to convert the Indians was through the medium of their own language; hence, Marquette was supposed to learn some of the Algonquin dialects before everything else. The Indian parish, close below Quebec, was conducted by experienced missionaries; so it was chosen as a suitable location to commence such training. But, in 1666, Fr. Gabriel Druillettes, who was one of the most accomplished linguists, had been moved to Three Rivers and Marquette followed him there, almost as soon as he set foot on the soil of New France. That he remained there for two years becomes evident from the catalog for 1667, which says, "Fr. Jacques Marquette assistant at Three Rivers on [Cap de la Madeleine], and he is studying languages." [38] By following the statements of the short catalogs of the Province of France, as they exist in the Archivum Romanum, the major events in Marquette's missionary life can be summarized.

In 1668 his appointment reads, "In the mission of the Holy Spirit of the Ottawa . . . Fr. Louis Nicolas, Fr. Jacques Marquette are the missionaries." This indicates that his progress in native dialects was considered sufficient for him to begin active missionary life among the Algonquin tribes dwelling around Lake Superior.[39] He settled down among the Chippewa, at the rapids by which Superior drains into Lake Huron.[40] Next

37. ARSJ, Franc. 23, 218v–219, "Catalogus Provinciae Franciae, 1666 Exeunte."

38. ARSJ, Franc. 23, 232, "Catalogus Provinciae Franciae, 1667 Exeunte."

39. ARSJ, Franc. 23, 245, "Catalogus Provinciae Franciae, 1668 Exeunte."

40. Raphael N. Hamilton, "Jesuit Mission at Sault Ste. Marie," *Michigan History,* LII (1968), 128.

year, the catalog reported that a missionary who had been at the far western end of Lake Superior went to a new field, and that Father Marquette succeeded him at what was known as the Mission of the Holy Spirit at the Point. Fr. Claude Dablon took Marquette's place at what is now Sault Ste. Marie. There, Dablon was delegated by the superior in Quebec to direct the mission expansion in the West. "Mission of the Holy Spirit among the Ottawa. Fr. Claude Dablon, Superior, Fr. Claude Allouez, Fr. Jacques Marquette, Louis Le Boême takes care of the missionaries' temporal needs."[41] There is no indication of a change in Marquette's status in 1670. The catalog says: "In the residence of the Holy Spirit among the Ottawa. Fr. Claude Dablon Superior, Fr. Claude Allouez, mission of Algonquin and Huron language, Fr. Jacques Marquette, mission in Language of the Algonquin territory, Fr. Gabriel Druillettes, mission of Algonquin language, Fr. Louis André, mission of Algonquin language. Louis Le Boême helps the missionaries in temporal affairs." [42]

In the year 1671 Marquette's name does not appear in the catalog. One possible explanation for this may be drawn from the list of assignments for 1672, where it is recorded "Fr. Jacques Marquette takes care of the Huron and Algonquin mission of St. Ignace with two *donnés.*" [43] He must have been on the move during the time when the superior was gathering the news for the previous catalog. In the summer of 1671 the Sioux drove the Indians of the Mission of the Holy Spirit at the Point from their homes. They fled eastward until they finally settled at the site of the present St. Ignace, Michigan,

41. ARSJ, Franc. 23, 261, "Catalogus Provinciae Franciae, 1669 Exeunte."

42. ARSJ, Franc. 23, 275, "Catalogus Provinciae Franciae, 1670 Exeunte."

43. ARSJ, Franc. 23, 301–301v, "Catalogus Provinciae Franciae, 1672 Exeunte." A *donné* (literally, "given") was a layman who helped the missionaries, serving without pay.

on the Straits of Mackinac.[44] This was the mission at St. Ignatius, which Marquette was caring for in 1672. What he was to do the next year is described in the short catalog for 1673: "Fr. Jacques Marquette takes care of the Algonquin mission of St. Ignatius with a donné, he has undertaken a journey this spring toward the Pacific or Chinese Sea with French and Algonquin companions." [45] This announcement is provokingly simple and lacking in detail. There is no definite destination assigned for the journey's end. There is no indication of the method to be used in travel. The Mississippi River is not mentioned. However, this much is made certain, Marquette did spend the summer of 1673 in an exploration of the unknown West.

One might have wished that the catalog for 1674 had told about the success or failure of the discovery which Marquette set out to make in the direction of the "Chinese Sea" during the spring of 1673. This was not its function. It only told what the men were to do as missionaries. In 1674, this one was to set up a mission somewhere among the Illinois Indians.[46] The brief announcement is "Fr. Jac. Marquette Fr. Ant. Silvy are opening a new mission toward the central sea [Gulf of Mexico] where recently many tribes were found." [47] Next year, the short catalog is silent about Marquette. Why this should be becomes

44. The events of this year are analyzed in ch. 6.

45. ARSJ, Franc. 23, 320, "Catalogus Provinciae Franciae, 1673 Exeunte."

46. The data surrounding the establishment of this mission are considered in ch. 5.

47. ARSJ, Franc. 23, 337, "Catalogus Provinciae Franciae, 1674 Exeunte." Antoine Silvy did not accompany Father Marquette to Illinois. Father Dablon, superior of the Canadian Mission who wrote the appointment in the catalog, sent a letter on October 25, 1674, to the French provincial, which says he was conditioning the departure for the new foundation on the need for priests at St. François Xavier on Green Bay. Apparently Silvy's work at the latter place necessitated his remaining behind. See Thwaites, *JR*, LIX, 68–69.

clear from consulting the official death notices of Jesuits gathered each year in the Roman Archives of the Order. Bound among the other obituaries, in the volume for 1675, is "Lettre circulaire du P. Jacques Marquette," dated from Quebec, October 13, 1675.[48] At the age of 38, the young priest-explorer was dead. He could no longer be appointed to labor among the Indians of North America.

The documents used thus far, in giving a summary of Father Marquette's missionary life, were unknown to historians from the seventeenth century until they were discovered by two twentieth-century Jesuits doing independent research for histories of widely separated provinces of the Society of Jesus. Between 1897 and 1914, Fr. Louis Carrez devoted what time he could to the compilation of data concerning men and events in the province of Champagne, France. He prefaced his completed work by telling how the custodian of the general archives of the Order, then in Holland, copied for him the short catalogs of this one province. In ten volumes, he edited them with the biographies of a number of the men who were mentioned on their pages as active between the years 1616 and 1714.[49]

The catalogs of the province of France were uncovered in 1935, when Fr. Gilbert J. Garraghan was at work upon a history of the American Jesuit province begun at Florissant, Missouri, in 1818.[50] He knew of Carrez' publication and visited Valkenburg to look for source material about the men who had come from Europe to found the Missouri province. Marquette was the first Jesuit to enter the area, so Garraghan had an incidental interest in him. The letters dealing with

48. ARSJ, Gal. 110, pt. 2, 195–196v, "Lettre circulaire du P. Jacques Marquette."

49. Carrez, *Catalogi*, I, ii.

50. Gilbert J. Garraghan, *The Jesuits of the Middle United States* (New York, 1938).

Marquette and some of the catalogs which had been sent to headquarters by Parisian provincials of the seventeenth century and which had rested among the papers of the Archivum Romanum for two hundred and fifty years or more were brought to light, along with the volumes of personnel assignments and letters more pertinent to the nineteenth century of Garraghan's concern. Since he was not writing about the early Jesuit activity in the Mississippi Valley, he made no further study of the cataolgs he found.[51]

Long before the discoveries of Carrez and Garraghan pointed the way to the Marquette manuscripts in Europe, American historians had placed this missionary among the discoverers of their country. This was owing to what they knew from other manuscripts, coming from Quebec in Canada, which chronicled in detail activities of his only hinted at in the short catalogs. These exciting narratives of Father Marquette's exploits are the documents which the present work intends to study.

51. Garraghan, "Newly Discovered Letters," pp. 284–85.

CHAPTER 2

Documents of Discovery

THE Mississippi Valley has been called the "Valley of Democracy." [1] The designation is a natural one if one considers the effect its settlement had on late-seventeenth- and early-eighteenth-century Europe. When the way was first opened into the rich interior of North America, vast opportunities were presented to allow a common man to raise his status from dependence and poverty to independence and property; the common man began to do just that along the Mississippi River. Even before 1700, French *habitants* had permanent settlements in the Illinois country opposite the site of St. Louis, and their farms were producing wheat for all of New France with enough left over for a profitable export trade with Europe. The

1. John D. Barnhart, *Valley of Democracy, The Frontier versus the Plantation in the Ohio Valley, 1775–1818* (Bloomington, 1953), p. viii, agrees with John H. Finley and Meredith Nicholson that "Valley of Democracy" applies best to the *whole* Mississippi Valley, though his book only attempts to demonstrate the applicability to one section.

treaty of Paris in 1763 ceded the new town of St. Louis to Spain, but it continued to develop and became the center of all the Western fur trade before the French Revolution of 1789.

When, in 1783, the young United States acquired what had been the colonial back country extending to the Mississippi River, Americans began spilling over the Appalachians so rapidly that a crisis was created by their immediate need for free access to foreign markets. Thomas Jefferson, third president of the Republic, found the solution in persuading Congress to appropriate funds adequate to complete the Louisiana Purchase; this was accomplished by 1804 and Spanish control removed from the mouth of the Mississippi River. French and Spanish settlers were terrified by these events.

To preserve law and order among the alien dwellers in the new empire bought by President Jefferson, Captain Amos Stoddard was sent to St. Louis to act as first civil and military commandant. There, Stoddard accomplished the cession of old Louisiana to the United States in a manner which won the respect and goodwill of the whole population whether French or Spanish by descent. In a few months his mission was completed and he was reassigned to New Orleans. However, within this short time, his experience had convinced him that so few of his countrymen appreciated the value of the rich domain which had been purchased primarily to afford them an outlet to the sea that he put into writing what he had learned about the history and geography of the Mississippi Valley.

Stoddard began by informing his readers that he had worked on the spot, while he was "destitute of books," but he would let them know what he had seen himself or heard from "respectable men" who had furnished him "such local and other information as they possessed." His work was published just as the War of 1812 broke out and, owing to its sources, was erroneous in some respects. For example, Stoddard was told that the French explorers of the Mississippi, Louis Jolliet and Fr. Jacques Marquette, were "two missionaries of Canada." [2] Unaware that the former was a layman, he passed the word on to his American readers in a way which by its very vagueness was to whet their curiosity for more knowledge about these first comers to the West.

The early nineteenth century was an epoch when travel books dominated the market and were eagerly read. If Americans of those times were not too sure whether they had received a bargain by the purchase of 1804, they quickly manifested a propensity to investigate the merchandise. Many went to have a look for themselves. There, they were charmed with the Old World atmosphere of New Orleans and by the quaint French villages and plantations along the Mississippi. Those with literary talent supplemented Stoddard's book with descriptions of what they saw, enlivened by snatches of local folklore as they heard it. For a long time Marquette and Jolliet appeared on the pages of such books as characters belonging to the river folklore, and a quarter of a century passed before they took their place in history.

John Bradbury's narrative of Louisiana was on sale five years after Stoddard's had appeared. It promised to tell of the French regime "as far as may be gathered" from Creole habitants. All Bradbury learned from them about Marquette and Jolliet concerned the route of these explorers to the upper Mississippi River. It was one proceeding "along the [Great] Lakes and descending the Illinois or Miami rivers." [3] In 1820, Henry Schoolcraft had found an English translation of an eighteenth-century Jesuit journal which included a boatman's

2. Amos Stoddard, *Sketches Historical and Descriptive of Louisiana* (Philadelphia, 1812), pp. vi–viii and 14.

3. John Bradbury, *Travels in the Interior of America, 1809, 1810, 1811, Including a Description of Upper Louisiana, with the States of Ohio, Kentucky, Indiana, and Tennessee, with the Illinois and Western Territories, and Containing Remarks and Observations Useful to Persons Emigrating to Those Countries*, in *Early Western Travels, 1748–1846*, ed. Reuben G. Thwaites (Cleveland, 1904), V, 257–58.

legend of "Father Joseph [*sic*] Marquette."[4] In 1826, Timothy Flint, who for ten years had been making excursions into the Mississippi Valley, wrote a book about it. Of its discovery, he knew no more than to say it was "first explored by adventurers from Canada" without mentioning their names.[5] Two years after this, Gabriel Richard expanded the accumulating tradition by adding to it what *voyageurs* and Indians had told him from their legends.[6] The same year, Giacomo Beltrami, who made his way to the headwaters of the Mississippi, said "Fr. Marguette [*sic*]" was sent, in 1673, "by the governor of Canada" to seek gold and thus became its discoverer.[7] At last, in 1829, a history of Louisiana written by François X. Martin cited a book by Melchisedech Thevenot, published eight years after Marquette's exploration of the Mississippi, as the source for an account of the event. Martin also drew upon the eighteenth-century journal used by Schoolcraft in his discussion of the missionary's death.[8]

Thevenot's book purported to be a contemporary account of the 1673 river trip derived from Father Marquette's own

4. Henry Schoolcraft, *Narrative Journal of Travels through the Northwestern Regions of the United States, Extending from Detroit through the Great Chain of American Lakes to the Sources of the Mississippi River in the Year 1820,* ed. Mentor L. Williams (East Lansing, Mich., 1953), p. 27. The author of the journal he cited was Pierre F-X. de Charlevoix, see ch. 2, n. 14.

5. Timothy Flint, *Recollections of the Last Ten Years Passed in Occasional Residences and Journeys in the Valley of the Mississippi from Pittsburgh and the Missouri to the Gulf of Mexico and from Florida to the Spanish Frontier . . .* (Boston, 1826), p. 351.

6. [Gabriel Richard], "Lettre de M. Richard, Missionnaire au Detroit à M***," *APF,* III (1826), 336–49.

7. Giacomo C. Beltrami, *A Pilgrimage in Europe and America, Leading to the Discovery of the Sources of the Mississippi and Bloody River, with a Description of the Former and of the Ohio* (London, 1828), II, 116–17.

8. François X. Martin, *History of Louisiana from the Earliest Period* (New Orleans, 1827–29), I, 70–78.

report. The author was a Parisian scholar who attracted to himself the group which in 1666 received official sanction as the French Académie des Sciences.[9] In 1684, Thevenot became *Maître* of the Bibliothèque du Roi. He died October 29, 1692.[10] His best title to fame was the editing of a series dealing with the French journeys, something after the manner employed by Hakluyt's chronicles of English explorers. A volume, finished in 1681, called *Recueil de Voyages de Mr Thevenot,* contains articles about worldwide discoveries. The first of these dealt with the Mississippi trip of 1673.[11]

The eighteenth-century journal, quoted by both Schoolcraft and François Martin, had been written by Pierre François-Xavier de Charlevoix, a Jesuit scholar who, in 1715, had gained acclaim for a book about Japan. It was probably because of this book that Louis-Alexandre, Duc de Bourbon, minister of the colonies, became acquainted with Charlevoix and learned

9. *Le Grande Encyclopédie Inventaire Raisonné des Sciences, des Lettres et des Artes* . . . (Paris, 1887), I, 199.

10. L. G. Michaud, ed., *Biographie Universelle Ancienne et Moderne ou Histoire, par Ordre Alphabetique, de la Vie Publique et Privé de Tous les Hommes Qui Se Sont Fait Remarquer par Leurs Ecrits, Leurs Talents, Leurs Vertus et Leurs Crimes* (Paris, 1811–45), XLV, 377. The Bibliothèque du Roi is now the Bibliothèque Nationale, Paris.

11. [Melchisedech Thevenot], *Recueil de Voyages de Mr Thevenot. Dedié au Roy* (Paris, 1681). During Thevenot's lifetime, his book was reprinted in 1682, 1687, and 1689. On the verso of the title page is a table of contents. The first caption is "Decouverte dans l'Amerique Septentrionale par le P. Marquette Jesuite [Discovery in North America by Fr. Marquette, Jesuit]." "Découverte" which is applied to the trip made by Marquette and Jolliet will be translated in the present book as "discovery," despite de Soto's earlier contact with the Mississippi. See Wilcomb E. Washburn, "The Meaning of 'Discovery' in the Fifteenth and Sixteenth Centuries," *American Historical Review,* LXVIII (1962), 15, who finds Spanish, French, and English authors employ the word to mean "find by chance," "uncovering," or "exploring."

that as a young man he had spent some time in Canada.[12] The Court had decided to send a Jesuit to New France, ostensibly to survey the missionary scene for the king, but actually to investigate the rumor of a vast bay which was supposed to penetrate deep into the American continent from the Pacific coast.[13] In 1720, de Bourbon summoned Charlevoix from his armchair travels through the Orient and by July had him aboard a sailing vessel buffeting the Atlantic on his way to the West Indies in search of the Western Sea.

Just before Charlevoix started, Madame Louise-Bernardine, Duchesse de Lesdiguières, who had included the Parisian Jesuits in her substantial charities, asked him to keep her informed of the adventures which she was sure he would encounter. Respect for a patroness forced compliance to her demand. Thus, Charlevoix's journal took shape in the form of letters addressed to her. In the first of these he protested his inability to think of anything of interest.[14] However, during

12. Pierre Margry, ed., *Mémoires et Documents pour Servir à l'Histoire des Origines Françaises des Pays d'Outre-Mer. Découvertes et Établissements des Français dans l'Ouest et dans le Sud de l'Amérique Septentrionale, 1614–1754* (Paris, 1879–88) [cited hereafter as Margry, *Découv. et Étab.*], VI, 531, "Charlevoix au Comte de Morville, Ministre et Secrétaire d'État (1 avril, 1723)."

13. [Louis Armand Lahontan], *New Voyages in North America by Baron Lahontan*, ed. Reuben G. Thwaites (Chicago, 1905), I, 193–95; Jean Delanglez, "A Mirage: the Sea of the West," *Revue d'Histoire de l'Amerique Française*, I (1947–48), 567–68, may be consulted concerning the rumor's beginning and end. In 1683, Lahontan, the seventeen-year-old orphan son of a bankrupt nobleman, was a soldier in Quebec. Until 1690, he fulfilled Canadian assignments which took him into the wilderness, even beyond Michilimackinac. When he returned to France, intrigue and his independent disposition led to the probability of his condemnation to the Bastille. He fled his country and in 1703 published his *New Voyages* in London. See Gilbert Chinard, *Baron De Lahontan, Dialogue Curieux entre l'Auteur et Un Sauvage de Bon Sens Qui a Voyagé* (London, 1931), pp. 5–18.

14. [Pierre F.-X. de Charlevoix], *Journal of a Voyage to North*

the next spring a forced delay in his westward quest tied him down at the mission "in the meadow de la Madeliere [Madeleine]" near Montreal. There, conversing with "some old missionaries who had lived a long time among the Indians," he acquired new understanding of "the different nations inhabiting this immense continent." [15] Thereafter Indian lore filled his correspondence with the Duchess. Lest this common fare become monotonous, anecdotes which he picked up as he pursued his search for the phantom sea were served as appetizers. It was one of these which Schoolcraft drew upon and François Martin repeated. As Charlevoix was being paddled along the east shore of Lake Michigan, his voyageurs pointed out the mouth of a stream which they called "Father Marquette's river." The story they told him about it is included in his twenty-second letter as "the constant tradition of all our travellers." They said, "The Fr. Joseph [*sic*] Marquette" had died there, just after celebrating Mass. Their tradition mistook the missionary's Christian name and the circumstances of his passing away. It did identify him as the discoverer of "the Mississippi which he entered with Sieur Joliet" and explained that they kept track of the spot because the boatmen considered him a "servant of God . . . [and] The French . . . never fail

---

America Undertaken by Order of the French King, Containing the Geographical Description and Natural History of that Country, Particularly Canada together with an Account of the Customs, Characters, Religion, Manners and Traditions of the Original Inhabitants. In a Series of Letters from the French of P. De Charlevoix (London, 1761), I, 61; reprinted with "corrected spelling," [Pierre F.-X. de Charlevoix], *Journal of a Voyage to North America. Translated from the French of Pierre Francois Xavier De Charlevoix*, ed. Louise P. Kellogg (Chicago, 1923). The great wealth and high station of the Lesdiguières family is a topic included in [Louis de Rouvroy, Duc de Saint-Simon], *Mémories de Saint-Simon, Nouvelle Édition*, ed. A. de Bois-lisle (Paris, 1923–30), III, 15.

15. Charlevoix, *Journal of a Voyage*, I, 272.

to call upon him when they are in any danger on Lake Michigan." [16]

The next addition to stories about Marquette's discovery came in 1830, after a young Virginian, Benjamin Franklin French, arrived in New Orleans and began publishing a series of reprints from narratives written in the era when Louisiana and Florida were colonies of France and Spain. He came upon a variant of Thevenot's version of the Marquette-Jolliet exploration in a seventeenth-century book by Fr. Louis Hennepin, a Recollect missionary who was associated with Robert Cavelier de La Salle, when, in 1679, he established Fort Crèvecoeur, his first post in the Mississippi valley. In 1683, the friar printed the story of his own adventures. This edition did not mention any previous explorations of the Mississippi, but it attracted so many readers that several new editions were issued in the next few years. In an early revision, the 1673 discovery was incorporated.[17]

In 1839, Jared Sparks, president of Harvard College, included Marquette in a biographical library of American heroes

16. Ibid., II, 95. This eighteenth-century translation turns the French "voyageurs" into "travellers." In the context, it is clear Charlevoix was speaking of the Canadian boatmen, who paddled their canoes over the rivers and lakes and knew the legends connected with these inland waterways.

17. Benjamin F. French, ed., *Historical Collections of Louisiana Embracing Many Rare and Valuable Documents Relating to the Natural Civil and Political History of that State, Compiled with Historical and Biographical Notes and an Introduction* (New York, 1846–53), II, 279–97, transcribes the account. The first edition of Louis Hennepin, *Description de la Louisiane Nouvellement Decouverte au Sud Oüest de la Nouvelle France, par Ordre du Roy. Avec la Carte du Pays: les Moeurs & la Maniere de Vivre des Sauvages* (Paris, 1683), did not mention Marquette. A German edition, six years later, contains the Thevenot account. See Ludwig Hennepin, *Beschreibung der Landschafft Lovisiana Welche auf Befehl des Koenigs in Frankreich, Neulich Gegen Sudwestern Neu-Frankreichs in Amerika Entdeket Worden* (Nurenberg, 1689), pp. 353–425.

which he was editing. He told his readers that he would add very little to Thevenot's work because it was supposed to be based on the missionary's own story.[18] These works were constantly presenting Marquette to a wider audience, but it was George Bancroft's *History of the United States,* begun in 1834, which made his part in the discovery of the Mississippi commonplace information to people even beyond the borders of the United States.[19] De Wolfe Howe, a biographer of Bancroft, says the influence of his "history can hardly be measured in terms of comparison with any work of a similar kind appearing in this latter day; for it would be difficult to name such a work passing so rapidly into many editions." [20] During the forty years required to write the entire history, frequent reprints of the separate volumes were made. Volume 3 tells the story of Marquette. It went into nine printings during the twelve months immediately after its first appearance in 1840. It had numbered twenty-three issues before the last volume of the set came out for the first time in 1874. After this, many full editions from American, English, Dutch, French, German and Italian presses, were exhausted before the close of the nineteenth century.

It was not a mere coincidence that, up to the date when Bancroft first printed his third volume, none of the original documents concerned with Marquette and Jolliet had been used by the nineteenth-century historians who wrote about the seventeenth-century exploration. Such archival material was no longer in the Jesuit college of Quebec. British troops had turned the building into a barracks after the conquest in 1763.

18. Jared Sparks, *Life of Father Marquette,* in *Library of American Biography,* ed. Jared Sparks (New York, 1839; new ed., New York, 1865), X, 273.

19. George Bancroft, *History of the United States from the Discovery of the American Continent* (Boston, 1834–74), Vol. 3.

20. M. A. De Wolfe Howe, *The Life and Letters of George Bancroft* (New York, 1908), II, 105.

The library had been dispersed.[21] The hope of finding such data elsewhere was faint. The suppression of the Society of Jesus, in 1773, had exposed Jesuit writings in Europe to confiscation.[22] Quantities of unprinted tracts and letters were burned on the spot. Sheafs of folios were sold for scrap paper. The few treatises which were retained were buried in state archives to which scholars had no easy access in the early nineteenth century.[23] The Order was restored in 1814. However, until the 1860's, the destitution and struggle for existence of its members was such that they could only begin to reestablish their book collections.[24]

In the 1830's, the confrères of the seventeenth-century missionaries seemed unable to make any contribution to the knowledge of what had been done by the Jesuits of earlier days, but it was not long before this situation changed. In 1842, Bishop Ignace Bourget of Montreal had asked some French-speaking Jesuits, dependent on the New York Province, to open a college in his city, and that year they announced their readiness to accept scholars at such a new foundation, the Col-

21. *La Compagnie de Jésus au Canada, 1842–1942, l'Oeuvre d'Un Siècle* (Montreal, 1942), pp. 17–18.

22. Ludwig Koch, *Jesuiten-Lexikon die Gesellschaft Jesu Einst und Jetzt* (Paderborn, 1934), cols. 119–29. For more details, see Sydney F. Smith, "The Suppression of the Society of Jesus," *The Month,* XCIX (1902), 113–30, continued in each issue through 1903, vols. C, CI, and CII. Ten years before the suppression, France exiled the Jesuits from her shores and colonies.

23. *Catalogue des Livres de la Bibliotheque de la Maison Professe des Ci-Devant Soi-Disans Jesuites* (Paris, 1763), prices 7,252 books from the Paris library of the Order; and promises a bargain list of manuscripts soon to be offered for sale. Gilbert J. Garraghan, *A Guide to Historical Method* (New York, 1948), pp. 68–69, takes time to warn researchers of the obstacles to be surmounted in getting at the documents in European state depositories. It was more difficult to gain admission to these places before World War II.

24. Gilbert J. Garraghan, *The Jesuits of the Middle United States* (New York, 1938), I, 29–34.

lège Sainte-Marie.[25] One of the faculty, Fr. Felix Martin, received instant recognition as a pulpit orator. On July 31, 1844, he was appointed superior. Thereupon a local historian and public official, Jacques Viger, sought his aid in collecting transcripts of original manuscripts dealing with the history of Canada. He wished to publish these in a series which would illustrate the evolution of the old French colony into a modern state.[26] He hoped that Father Martin could help to gain entrance to the Hôtel Dieu in Quebec. At the conquest, the nuns in charge of it had not suffered from the English hostility to religious orders; a hospital was a necessity, and the sisters in charge of this one had not been disturbed. Viger surmised that this favored position might have led to the preservation of their early annals. In the fall of 1844, he took Father Martin down the river to call on the superioress, Sister Saint-Antoine. To his delight, she produced a bundle of manuscripts which had come from Fr. Jean-Joseph Casot, the last remaining Jesuit at the close of the French regime in Canada. Dying in the nuns' hospital, he left with them these papers from the college of his Order. They were handwritten originals covering: the Canadian mission's annual reports between 1673 and 1679; a separate manuscript concerned with the life and work of Father Marquette, accompanied by a holograph map of the Mississippi Valley; and a holograph journal of the missionary's second trip to the Illinois Indians, whom he had contacted first on his trip with Jolliet. The superioress turned this material over to Father Martin and, by letter of November 25, 1844,

25. Paul Desjardins, *Le Collège Sainte-Marie de Montréal* (Montreal, 1940–45), I, 17–19, 44.

26. Archives du Séminaire des Missions Étrangères, Quebec, Jacques Viger, "Ma Saberdache Rouge," 26 vols. about New France; "Ma Saberdache Bleue," 14 vols. about English Canada, ending with Viger's death, 1858. The volumes are indexed in Ferdinand Ouellet, ed., "Inventaire de la *Saberdache* de Jacques Viger," *RAPQ, 1955–1956 and 1956–1957*, pp. 31–76.

formally conveyed these papers to the new college in Montreal.[27]

Viger was permitted to copy the manuscripts which he had been instrumental in obtaining. In volume "F" of "Ma Saberdache Rouge," as he called the work he was editing, he included the items which tell about Father Marquette. He introduced them with the story of how the originals had been recovered, signing the account "Montreal, 20 Decembre 1844, I.V." The biographical data he entitled "Recit des Voyages et des Découvertes du P. Iacques Marquette. . . ." The holograph journal of the second trip he presented as "Fragment du Iournal du P. Marquette." Speaking of the latter, he says, "c'est une precieuse Relique . . . par le seul fait *qu'il est tout entire de la main de ce Père* [this one is a precious Relic by the fact alone, *that it is completely in the hand of this Father*]." [28]

When Father Martin returned to Montreal, he likewise publicized the good fortune which had come to the Collège Sainte-Marie in *Lettres des Nouvelles Missions,* a little magazine aimed at gaining goodwill for his school. The article was intended for general reading; it accentuated the virtues of the men whose writings had been found rather than the amount of history which was contained in the find. But on the second blank page within the binding which guards the Marquette manuscripts, Martin wrote out in French script his own endorsement for them. The one dealing with Marquette's life work, he entitled: "Recital of the Voyages and Discoveries of

27. Desjardins, *Le Collège Sainte-Marie,* I, 216–17. For Fr. Jean-Joseph Casot, see Auguste Carayon, *Documents Inédits Concernant la Compagnie de Jésus* (Potiers, 1863–86), XIV, 27.

28. Archives du Séminaire des Missions Étrangères, Quebec, "Ma Saberdache Rouge," F, 19–23 (emphasis in original). The initials "I. V." stand for Jacques Viger, wherever he endorses a statement. The letters "J" and "I" were frequently interchanged in French of the nineteenth and earlier centuries. Viger's pronouncement concerning the authenticity of the unfinished holograph journal of Father Marquette ends with the same "I. V.," ibid., F, 120.

Rev. Fr. Jacques Marquette of the Company of Jesus in the year 1673 and following, his death, his virtues and the continuation of his voyages by the Rev. Fr. Allouez." The other he called "The autograph journal of Rev. Fr. Jac. Marquette in 1674 and 1675." To this, he added, there is "the map of his voyage drawn by his hand." He told how these documents were saved by the nuns and handed over to him in 1844; at the end of his testimony, Fr. A. C. Jones, his pupil and later his successor as archivist, witnessed the statement as being in the script of Fr. Felix Martin.[29]

It was six years after the Collège Sainte-Marie received these documents before their whereabouts were made known to the world of scholarship. The occasion presented itself when, in 1847, Edmund J. O'Callaghan gave an address before the New York Historical Society which found its way into print. At the time, he was doing for New York what Benjamin French had done for Louisiana and Florida. O'Callaghan's eleven-volume *Documents Relative to the Colonial History of the State of New York* is still a source apt to be mentioned in any history of early America; in addition to preparing these materials for others, he employed them in his own writing. It was while he was working on a *History of New Netherlands* that his research led him to contact the Jesuit Relations about which he spoke in his address to his fellow historians.[30]

29. ACSM, 296, is the volume at the Collège Sainte-Marie in Montreal on which Martin wrote his deposition. Item ACSM, 687, is Marquette's autograph map.

30. Edmund B. O'Callaghan, *Jesuit Relations of Discoveries and Other Occurrences in Canada and the Northern and Western States of the Union, 1632–1672, from the Proceedings of the New York Historical Society* (New York, 1747 [should be 1847]), is the reprint of his address; and his other works, mentioned in the text, are, *The History of New Netherlands; or New York under the Dutch* (New York, 1846–48); O'Callaghan, ed., *Documents Relative to the Colonial History of the State of New York, Procured in Holland, England, and France by John Romeyn Brodhead* (Albany, 1853–61). For a

When Cardinal Richelieu, minister plenipotentiary for King Louis XIII, turned the entire mission field of New France over to the Jesuits, in 1632, Fr. Paul Le Jeune, who received the trust, had commenced a periodical by writing a Relation of his trip to Canada and what followed during the year. Le Jeune continued to publish the Relations because by them he accomplished a double purpose. He supplied benefactors, actual and possible, with interesting news, and he fulfilled the requirement of the annual letter.

From 1632 to 1672 Canadian superiors sent a like Relation to the French provincial in Paris, with the understanding that, after he had noted the work of the missionaries, this account would be passed on, in periodical form, for the perusal of a mission-minded public.[31] During all those years, the publication was produced by the Parisian press of Sébastien Cramoisy, which issued it regularly with a title containing the words "Relation de Ce Qui S'Est Passé en la Nouvelle France," followed by the date of the narratives it recorded. As the missions increased, not all the events of the previous year could be included in the modest dimensions of the volumes; hence, the title reflected this fact by inserting the limiting clause, "de Plus Remarquable aux Missions des Pères de la Compagnie de Iésus," between "Passé" and "en la Nouvelle France." Only a few libraries have assembled the full run of the seventeenth-century Relations.[32]

---

bibliography of more than thirty other publications by him, see Francis S. Guy, *Edmund Bailey O'Callaghan, a Study in American Historiography, 1797–1880* (Washington, 1934), pp. 86–87.

31. Leon Pouliot, *Etude sur les Relations des Jésuites de la Nouvelle-France (1632–1672)* (Montreal, 1940), pp. 4–9, 16–18, traces the evolution of the periodical.

32. For a list of such depositories, James C. McCoy, *Jesuit Relations of Canada, a Bibliography* (Paris, 1937), "Synoptic Table," unn. pp. at the end of the book. The set at the University of Minnesota is described in Frank K. Walter and Virginia Doneghy, *Jesuit*

In O'Callaghan's 1847 address, its author deplored his inability to trace certain volumes of the Jesuit Relations anywhere in America, adding that it was only by combining what he found in the collections of several contemporary bibliophiles that he had been able to consult most of the copies. It was 1850 when Father Martin came into possession of the O'Callaghan reprint; in making a French translation of it, he took the opportunity to advertise the manuscripts he had received from the Hôtel Dieu in 1844:

Il y [dans la collection] existe deux Relations completes fesant suite à celle de 1672, et destinées comme les autres à voir le jour. L'une est Relation de 1673; l'autre comprend une periode de six annees, depuis 1673 jusqu'en 1679. Elles ont heureusement échappés au pillage des archives du Collège des Jésuites à Québec. Le R. P. Casot, dernier Jésuite mort à Québec en 1800, les avoit confiées avec d'autres manuscrits à des mains pieuses [Les Religieuses de l'Hôtel Dieu de Québec] qui les ont conservées longtemps comme un dépôt sacré, et qui les ont rémises entre les mains des Jésuites, revenus en Canada en 1842. . . . Ils portent de nombreuses corrections, des notes et même des pages entières de la main du R. P. Dablon . . . .[33]

Relations and Other Americana in the Library of James F. Bell (Minneapolis, 1950), pp. 3–194. The forty original volumes have been reprinted in *Relations des Jésuites Contenant Ce Qui S'Est Passé de Plus Remarquable dans les Missions des Pères de la Compagnie de Jésus dans la Nouvelle-France. Ouvrage Publié sous les Auspices du Gouvernement Canadien,* 3 vols. (Quebec, 1858). Thwaites, *JR,* already cited, offers another reproduction of the seventeenth-century Relations, with their French text on the left page and the English translations opposite. Thwaites' first edition appeared between 1896 and 1901. In 1959 Pageant Press reprinted it with each two volumes bound in one cover. In the text of the present book, only Thwaites' original reprint will be cited. Appendix II directs to the same passages in the Quebec edition.

33. [Felix Martin], *Relations des Jésuites sur les Découvertes et les Autres Évènements Arrivés en Canada, et au Nord et à l'Ouest des*

[There are extant (in this collection) two complete Relations following in order after the one of 1672, and having been intended like the others to be brought out in print. The one is the Relation for 1673; the other comprises a period of six years, from 1673 to 1679. Happily, these escaped the pillage of the archives of the Jesuit college in Quebec. The Rev. Fr. Casot, last Jesuit deceased at Quebec in 1800, had confided them with other manuscripts to pious hands (The Religious of the Hôtel Dieu of Quebec) who protected them through the years as a sacred deposit and which they have returned to the possession of the Jesuits, who came back to Canada in 1842. . . . They show numerous corrections, notes and even pages in the hand of Rev. Father Dablon.]

Father Claude Dablon spent more than forty years in New France, and the charge of all the Jesuit missionaries working there twice fell upon him.[34] The first term as superior extended from 1671 to 1680; the second included the years 1686 to 1693. During Dablon's first administration, he was responsible for the volumes of the Jesuit Relations which were printed in 1672 and 1673, and for the unprinted manuscripts prepared from 1674 to 1678 and sent to the French provincial after the Relations ceased publication. Because Dablon's handwriting was very hard to read, a secretary transcribed these narratives. Father Martin had good grounds for saying that they were corrected by Dablon's hand, since known examples of his script are not hard to find.

Etats-Unis (1611–1672) par le Dr. E. B. O'Callaghan, Membre Correspondent de la Société Historique du Connecticut. Traduit de l'Anglais avec Quelques Notes, Corrections et Additions (Montreal, 1850), p. 62.

34. Born at Dieppe on January 21 in 1618 or 1619, Dablon entered the Province of France of the Society of Jesus, August 27, 1639. Sixteen years later, ordained priest and with some experience as a teacher in Europe, he set out for Canada, where he spent the rest of his life in a very active apostolate. He died at Quebec on September 27, 1697.

Father Martin goes on to say, in his translation of O'Callaghan's reprint, that in the packet he received from the nuns
of Quebec was "Voyage et mort du P. Marquette," which
he describes as the text which must have been used by Thevenot
in his *Recueil de Voyages*. However, he insists that the manuscript which was given him by the sisters is much fuller than
the printed book, in which the Maître of the Bibliothèque du
Roi had evidently synopsized. At last Father Martin states:

> Nous avons même eu le bonheur de trouver deux autres monu-
> ments tres-precieux qui interessent sa [Marquette's] mémoire, et
> qui complettent cette richesse historique, 1° le journal autographe
> de son dernier voyage des 25 octobre 1674, jusqu'à le 6 avril
> 1675, un mois environ avant sa mort; et 2° la carte autographe
> de la découverte du Mississipi dressée par le même missionaire.
> Elle ne descend que jusqu'aux Akansea, terme de son voyage.[35]

> [We have also had the good fortune to find two other very
> precious memorials which concern his (Marquette's) memory
> and which complete this historical treasure, 1st, the autograph
> journal of his last voyage from October 25, 1674, to April 6,
> 1675, about a month before his death; and 2nd, the autograph
> map of the discovery of the Mississippi drawn by the same mis-
> sionary. It goes no further than the Akansea, the end of his
> voyage.]

Martin won an honorary membership in the New York State
Historical Society for his translation of O'Callaghan's reprint,
and his work furnished the occasion for another of the Society's
members, John Gilmary Shea, to become the editor for the first
publication of the Canadian Marquette documents.[36]

35. Martin, *Relations des Jésuites*, pp. 65–66.
36. Born in 1824, John G. Shea began writing while only a boy.
Though he passed the New York State bar exam in 1846, he preferred
a literary career and supported himself by editing such periodicals as
Frank Leslie's *Popular Monthly, Chimney Corner,* and *Sunday Magazine,* while he wrote his many monographs about Catholic church
history.

In 1848 Shea joined the Jesuits. After his novitiate, his New York superior sent him to Montreal, where he might have access to the archives of the Collège Sainte-Marie. O'Callaghan had become a friend of Shea, and kept in touch with him during this move; so it is probable that Shea was the channel through which Father Martin came into possession of the New York State Historical Society address dealing with the Relations, since he translated it a few months after Shea joined the community.[37] When Father Martin's pamphlet acquainted Benjamin French with the manuscripts so pertinent to his own work, he asked Shea to translate the Marquette narrative for his *Historical Collections*. Shea put aside the history of the missions of the United States on which he had been working and began to edit.[38] In 1852, assisted by some of the best historians of the era, he published the Marquette docu-

37. Shea, through his interest in early American history, became a close friend of Edmund O'Callaghan. Indeed, it has been said that this was the "one real friendship" in his life. See Peter Guilday, *John Gilmary Shea, Father of American Catholic History, 1824–1892* (New York, 1926), pp. 14–16, 21–26. Correspondence between O'Callaghan and Shea is described in Henry P. Beers, *The French in North America, a Bibliographical Guide to French Archives, Reproductions, and Research Missions* (Baton Rouge, La., 1957), p. 28, n. 54.

38. John G. Shea, *History of the Catholic Missions among the Indians of the United States 1529–1854* (New York, 1855), p. 16, announces it as "the result of ten years collection and research." Therefore, he began his study for it in 1845. French's request for a translation of the Marquette documents appears in John G. Shea, *Discovery and Exploration of the Mississippi Valley: with the Original Narratives of Marquette, Allouez, Membré, Hennepin and Anastase Douay* (New York, 1852), pp. lxxvii–lxxviii. This edition was small; in 1853 Shea published a second edition without mention of French's *Historical Collections*. In the first 145 pages of the 1852 edition, some footnotes signed "F" evince cooperation by French. Shea's own notes quote from 10 documents, 10 volumes of the scarce Jesuit Relations, and 37 other primary or secondary printed sources.

ments.[39] In that same year Shea secured a dispensation from his vows and left the Jesuits.[40]

In 1855 in New York, with an acknowledgement for "This precious manuscript, which we have through the kindness of Reverend Father Felix Martin, present Rector of the College Saint Marie in Montreal," Shea cooperated with the local book lover, James Lenox, in editing the Marquette papers from the Canadian Jesuit archives. The documents were transcribed in old French form. Special type, with the long "s" and other characteristics of the seventeenth century, was employed. The Lenox-Shea product was praised as being almost indistinguishable from the real volumes which had come from the Cramoisy press in Paris between 1632 and 1672.[41] Shea spent the rest of his life producing an almost incredible flow of historical literature.[42]

39. The 1852 edition was dedicated to "Jared Sparks LL.D. . . . as a mark of personal regard" for the president of Harvard College who had been the first to translate Thevenot into English. In the Bancroft Collection of the New York Public Library is found a first edition of the book, with a holograph letter from Shea pasted in. The letter thanks Bancroft for his encouragement and for "the use of your valuable library."

40. Guilday, *John Gilmary Shea*, p. 29.

41. [James Lenox and John G. Shea, eds.], *Recit des Voyages et des Decouvertes de R. Père Jacques Marquette de la Compagnie de Jesus, en l'Année 1673 et aux Suivantes; La Continuation de Ses Voyages Par le R. P. Claude Alloüez, et Le Journal Autographe du P. Marquette en 1674 & 1675. Avec la Carte de Son Voyage Tracée de Sa Main. Imprimé d'après le Manuscrit Original Restant au Collège Ste. Marie à Montreal* (Albany, N.Y., 1855).

42. Edward Spillane, "Bibliography of John Gilmary Shea," *Historical Records and Studies*, VI, pt. 2 (1912), 249–72, catalogs 247 titles. About 24 of these were printings of manuscripts by Canadian Jesuits. These books are known as Shea's Cramoisy Series, because he published them privately at what he chose to call "la presse Cramoisy de Jean-Marie Shea." They are often cited as "Cramoisy No. 1" through to "Cramoisy No. 24," and must not be confused with the

Shea's *History of the Catholic Church in the United States,*
which was finished just before his death, contains a final tribute
to the manuscripts "gathered by . . . Felix Martin, S. J." as
supplying groundwork for his narratives of the seventeenth
century. Further, Shea bases the beginnings of the Conception
Mission in Illinois on Marquette's autograph journal which
was recovered from the Hôtel Dieu.[43]

Seventeenth-century Jesuit Relations which are also spoken of as
"Cramoisys" from the name of their Parisian printer.

The nature of his work clearly reveals his preference for research
in the primary sources. For a critique of his methodology see Henry
W. Bowden, "John Gilmary Shea: A Study of Method and Goals in
Historiography," *Catholic Historical Review,* LIV (1968), 235–60.

Shea's preference for primary sources may have led to an unjust
criticism of [Pierre F.-X.] de Charlevoix, *Histoire et Description
Generale de la Nouvelle France avec le Journal Historique d'Un
Voyage Fait par Ordre de Roi dans l'Amerique Septentrionale* (Paris,
1744). Shea deplored the lack of research in the "manuscripts at the
[Jesuit] college at Quebec in preparation for this work." See [Pierre
F.-X. de Charlevoix], *History and General Description of New
France by the Rev. P. F. X. de Charlevoix, S. J.,* tr. and ed., John G.
Shea (New York, 1866–72), III, 182. In 1720–22 when Charlevoix
was in America, he had no intention of compiling a history of New
France; that idea took shape in his mind about a dozen years after his
return to Europe. See "Projet d'un corps d'histoire de nouveau monde,"
Mémoires de Trévoux [1735], pp. 161–72, in Carlos Sommervogel,
ed., *Bibliothèque de la Compagnie de Jésus, Première Partie: Bibliographie par les Pères Augustin et Aloys Backer, Seconde Partie: Histoire
par le Père August Carayon* (Bruxelles, 1890–1932), II, col. 1075. By
1735, research in Quebec was out of the question. Moreover, since in
his 6-volume history he allotted only 78 lines to the discovery of the
Mississippi, he probably considered his reference to Thevenot as an
ample authority. See Charlevoix, *Histoire et Description Generale de
la Nouvelle France,* II, 248–50. Charlevoix accounts for his dependence
on secondary sources, ibid., VI, 297–301.

43. John G. Shea, *The History of the Catholic Church in the United
States* (New York, 1886–92), I, iii, mentions Father Martin. Shea
speaks of the beginning of Christianity in Illinois, ibid., pp. 317, 319,
citing as his authority, his *Discovery and Explanation of the Missis-*

While such scholarly monographs were completing the image of Father Marquette, the Canadian government sent Father Martin to Europe in 1857 seeking documents of its colonial era. This led to another edition of the papers from the Collège Sainte-Marie, plus several unprinted Relations of New France which Martin had come upon in the "Fonds Brotier" at the headquarters of his Order in Rome. This collection, containing 199 volumes of manuscripts, was so named because at the expulsion of the French Jesuits by Louis XV, in 1762, their librarian, Fr. Gabriel Brotier, managed to save these documents by transferring them from Paris to Rome. In the middle of the nineteenth century, after Martin's visit, the Fonds Brotier were returned to the Jesuit Collège Saint-Geneviève in the French capital. When the Third Republic expelled the Society again, these papers traveled to Canterbury, England, then to a seminary on the Island of Jersey. Finally, after World War II, they became part of the archives at the Society's house of studies at Chantilly, France.[44] During his European researches, Father Martin stopped in Paris. When he told his fellow Jesuits about the material dealing with the old Canadian missions, Fr. Fortuné M. de Montézon, of the faculty of the Collège Sainte-Geneviève, became especially interested. He was at work on a series of reprints which was coming from the Parisian press of Charles Douniol, under the general title *Voyages et Travaux des Missionnaires de la Com-*

---

sippi Valley, pp. 258–64. These pages contain his transcription of Marquette's holograph journal of his second trip to the Illinois Indians, 1674–75.

44. Jean Delanglez, "The 'Recit des voyages et des decouvertes du Pere Jacques Marquette,'" *M-A,* XXVIII (1946), 175–78, tells of the contents and travels of Fonds Brotier. AMU, N. Amer., Fr. Reg., 8, "Dehergne Correspondence," supplies the date of their return to France. Since vols. 155–76 are about New France, they are cited as "Canada–1 to 22." Henri Cordier, *Mélanges Américains* (Paris, 1913), pp. 62–65, summarizes their contents.

pagnie de Jesus. From Martin, he obtained permission to include the Canadian findings in the series. They were printed in 1861 with the individual title *Relations Inédites de la Nouvelle-France.*[45]

In 1902, Thwaites wrote the first book-length biography of Marquette. The next year, a French author, Alfred Hamy, published a study of Marquette and Jolliet with a transcription of the documentary account of their trip, taken from the Fonds Brotier.[46] Both works were devoted primarily to the exploration of the Mississippi. The attitude of the authors was eulogistic. Americans commonly held the missionary-explorer in esteem. In 1896, Wisconsin chose him as one of its citizens to be commemorated in the Statuary Hall of the National Capitol in Washington. Other monuments to him were erected in places as widely separated as Laon, France; McGregor, Iowa; Mackinac Island, Michigan; and Helena, Arkansas.[47]

45. Desjardins, *Le Collège Sainte-Marie,* I, 242, 247–48. The full title of the nineteenth-century Parisian work is [Fortuné M. De Montézon, ed.], *Mission du Canada, Relations Inédites de la Nouvelle-France, 1672–1679, pour Faire Suite aux Anciennes Relations, 1615–1672* in *Voyages et Travaux des Missionnaires de la Compagnie de Jésus Publiés par les Pères de la Même Compagnie pour Servir de Complément aux Lettres Édifiantes,* Charles Douniol, publisher, vol. III in 2 pts. (Paris, 1861) [cited hereafter as De Montézon, *Rel. Inédites*]. Thwaites prints the same "unpublished Relations" in *JR,* LVII–LX. For the corresponding accounts in these two editions, see Appendix II.

46. Reuben G. Thwaites, *Father Marquette* (New York, 1902) and Alfred Hamy, *Au Mississippi la Première Exploration, 1673, le Père Jacques Marquette de Laon Prêtre de la Compagnie de Jésus, 1637–1675, et Louis Jolliet, d'après M. Ernest Gagnon* (Paris, 1903).

47. Henry S. Spalding, "The History of the Marquette Statue Presented to Statuary Hall in the Capitol, by the State of Wisconsin," *Historical Records and Studies,* III (1904), 409–18; Société Académique de Laon, *Jacques Marquette et l'Inauguration de Son Monument à Laon le 13 Juin 1937* (Laon, 1937). Mary C. Arth, "Marquette Memorials," *M-A,* XIII (1930–31), 291–303, expands this topic.

In 1923, the 250th anniversary of the Jolliet-Marquette discovery was observed in many places along the route traveled by them in 1673. Such celebrations were hardly forgotten when a priest-historian, Francis B. Steck, published a doctorial dissertation in which he took a stand at odds with the traditional attitude toward Father Marquette. He argued that all previous writings about Marquette had missed the proper historical setting and that the whole exploration had "been generally misinterpreted and misrepresented." [48] The author found fault with the use of the word "discovery" as applied to what Jolliet and Marquette had done, because "the Spaniards must be credited with the discovery of the Mississippi." He felt Marquette "himself would be the first to disclaim as wholly unreasonable and unhistorical" the credit accorded him for contributing to the success of the expedition. Steck believed the praise given the missionary had been "entirely out of proportion with the part he actually played." Finally, he brought together evidence which he advanced as lending "great probability" to an opinion favoring Jolliet as the only journalist of the exploration. The manuscript narrative of it which Father Martin had found was suggested to be "Jolliet's journal recast and amplified by Dablon." [49] A professor of American history

48. Francis B. Steck, *The Jolliet-Marquette Expedition of 1637, Revised and Enriched with Maps and Documents* (Quincy, Ill., 1928), p. vii. Steck was born in St. Louis in 1884. He entered the Franciscan Order in 1904 and was ordained in 1911. His life was devoted to the study and teaching of history. In 1927 he received his Ph.D. at Catholic University after writing a dissertation with the title of the above book. In 1933 he became a staff member of the Catholic University of America, teaching Latin-American history. From his retirement in 1947 to his death on July 5, 1962, he resided at Quincy, Illinois.

49. Ibid., pp. 224, 260, 310. From time to time, Steck continued to write about Father Marquette. Ultimately, he persuaded himself that Father Dablon had faked the narrative of the exploration and that Father Martin had forged the papers which he pretended to have received from the nuns in Quebec. Francis B. Steck, *Marquette*

at Saint Louis University, Fr. Gilbert J. Garraghan, reviewed
Steck's book. He was critical of portions. The author responded.[50] Shortly thereafter, Agnes Repplier wrote a popular
life of Father Marquette in which she chided Steck for trying
to detract from her hero. He answered her.[51] Things might
have stopped there had not Jean Delanglez joined the Institute
of Jesuit History at Loyola University, Chicago, in 1936.

The Institute of Jesuit History had its origin in 1935, when
Loyola University took over the publication of the *Illinois
Catholic Historical Review* and brought to its campus several
members of the Order, interested in early missionary history
of America, to form a core of researchers and writers who
could edit the periodical. These men began gathering photocopies of those original documents which were pertinent to
their work. From such material, Delanglez set out to investigate the manuscript reprint collection compiled by Pierre
Margry, nineteenth-century librarian of the Bibliothèque Nationale, Paris. Francis Parkman had depended very heavily on
him, while producing his classic series, *France and England in
North America.* Delanglez was aware that Margry had taken
liberties in copying his documents and thought that from the
photocopies at the Institute he might propose certain revisions
in the story written by Parkman.[52] From this beginning until

---

Legends, ed. August Reyling (New York, 1960), pp. v–vi, lists all of
Steck's publications and contains the accusation against Dablon ibid.,
pp. 86–87 and n. 217; and against Martin ibid., pp. 175–78, 243–44.

50. Gilbert J. Garraghan, "The Jolliet Marquette Expedition of
1673," *Thought,* IV (1929), 32–71, and Francis B. Steck, "Father
Garraghan and the Jolliet-Marquette Expedition, 1673," *Fortnightly
Review,* XXXVI (1929); XXXVII (1930).

51. Agnes Repplier, *Père Marquette, Priest, Pioneer and Adventurer*
(Garden City, N.Y., 1929), and Francis B. Steck, "Miss Repplier's
Père Marquette," *Fortnightly Review,* XXXVI (1929).

52. The collection referred to is in Margry, *Découv. et Étab.* When
Francis Parkman discovered no directive to the provenance of the
manuscripts in Margry's first two volumes, he demanded a remedy,

his premature death in 1949, about thirty articles and seven books dealing with the era of French discovery and exploration came from Delanglez' pen.[53] All of these were revisionary in character. Some of them treated the entry into the Mississippi Valley in a way which reopened the discussion about Père Marquette.

Delanglez proved to be an indefatigable researcher in his compilation of evidence about the priest-explorer. In this regard, he unearthed much which had been overlooked by others. What he did not do was to apply the criteria of historical criticism to the documents themselves to prove them genuine; thus it is possible to question the value of the information, since statements are only to be trusted if their source is trustworthy. The present study, which will make a detailed inquiry into the credence deserved by these original manuscripts, is believed to be the first one to undertake such a rudimentary consideration of their intrinsic truth.[54]

John S. Bassett, ed., "Letters of Francis Parkman to Pierre Margry," *Smith College Studies in History,* VIII (1923), 172–73; [Francis Parkman], *The Letters of Francis Parkman,* ed. Wilbur R. Jacobs (Norman, Okla., 1960), II, 96–97. Margry remedied this defect in Vol. III and thereafter. Jean Delanglez, "La Salle, 1669–1673," *M-A,* XIX (1937), 197–216 and 237–53, adds other criticisms.

53. Jerome V. Jacobsen, "Jean Delanglez—In Memoriam," *M-A,* XXXI (1949), 208–12; Guy Frégault, "Jean Delanglez, S.J., 1896–1949," *Revue d'Histoire de l'Amérique Française,* III (1949), 165–71; Beers, *The French in North America,* pp. 133–34.

54. Joseph P. Donnelly, *Jacques Marquette, S.J., 1637–1675* (Chicago, 1968), adds facts about the missionary omitted by Delanglez, but, like him, accepted the authenticity of the documents without comment.

CHAPTER 3

Some Problems
of Provenance

Two handwritten narratives, almost identical in contents, are the leading sources for the particulars of the first French expedition to the Mississippi River and for the adventures of the French discoverers. The narrative unfolded by them begins with events immediately preceding the departure of Jolliet and Father Marquette, in company with five boatmen, from the mission of St. Ignace in 1673, and tells how they made the trip to the lower channel of the Mississippi and back to Green Bay. Next, Marquette's activities in the year 1674 and 1675 are told, up to the night of his death and last burial. Finally, the story in both manuscripts is brought to an end by a short declaration regarding Father Allouez' labors in continuing the work at Old Kaskaskia, where Marquette had preached to the Illinois Indians just before he died. In what pertains to the 1673 trip, the style indicates direct dependence on Marquette's journal, borrowing his wording to outline his experiences. Once his exploration is narrated, the subsequent events of his life are recounted after the manner of a biography.

The first of these two documents has the title "Recit Des Voyages et Des Découuertes Du P. Iacques Marquette De la Compagnie de Jesvs En l'annee 1673. Et aux Suiuantes [Recital of the Voyages and Discoveries of Fr. Jacques Marquette of the Company of Jesus in the Year 1673 and Those Following]." It is the one in the archives of the Collège Sainte-Marie at Montreal, which Father Martin obtained from the Hôtel Dieu of Quebec and publicized in his translation of O'Callaghan's reprint. The other is in the Jesuit house of studies at Chantilly, France, where the Fonds Brotier came to rest in the late 1940's. It is in volume 159 of the series. Inside the cover, the first handwritten title is "Relation . . . les Années 1677–1678," but after a dozen pages, "Recit Des voyages et Descouuertes du Pere Jacques Marquette de la Compagnie de Jesus en 1673 et autres," is inscribed, prefacing the document itself.[1]

The first thing which strikes the researcher examining these two Marquette documents is the presence in them of three distinct chapters with proper titles, and the division of each chapter into sections with subtitles stressing the sequence of adventures. In the manuscript at the Collège Sainte-Marie, under "Chapitre j.er Du premier Voyage qu'a fait Le P. Marquette Vers le nouveau Mexique et Comment s'en est formé

1. ACSM, 296, 1–62, is the Montreal manuscript. The Chantilly manuscript is bound together with an account of what went on in the missions during 1677–78. This account covers the first twelve sheets of paper in the volume. Pages in this volume are numbered on both recto and verso at the top, but only on the recto at the bottom of the page. Citations in the present work will be made to the latter numbers, APF, Fonds Brotier 159 (Canada–5), 13–34. Attention is called to the use of quotation marks in citing the titles of these manuscripts. This practice will be the rule with all titles of handwritten documents. Titles of printed sources will be italicized.

le dessin [Chapter One. Concerning the first voyage which **Fr.**
Marquette made toward New Mexico and how the plan took
shape]," the whole exploration with Jolliet is told in ten sections.[2] In the other manuscript in France, everything is identical
except for some capitalization and spelling.[3]

"Chapitre Second Recit du second voyage que le Pere
Jacques Marquette a fait aux Jlinois pr. y porte la foy, et la
glorieuse mort du mesme Pere dans les trauaux de cette Mission
[Chapter Two. Recital of the second voyage which Father
Jacques Marquette made to the Illinois to carry the faith
thither, and the glorious death of the same Father midst the
works of this mission]" is the second division of the Montreal
manuscript. Here are brought together in three sections the
details of Marquette's subsequent career from the autumn of
1674 until his bones found their final resting place in the
chapel at St. Ignace.[4] The corresponding portion of the Chantilly manuscript tells the same story, with practically the same
wording.[5]

Finally, the Canadian Récit has "Chapitre 3em Recit d'un
3e. Voyage fait aux Jlinois Par le Pere Claude Allouez [Chap-
ter Three. Recital of a third voyage made to the Illinois by
Father Claude Allouez]," with two sections.[6] The French document adds to this heading a short paragraph not found in
the one at Montreal. Put there as a lead for what is to come,
it tells how Marquette's successor is equipped to carry on the
work he had begun.[7] In its turn, the model at Montreal ends
with a passage telling how, in 1678, Allouez had commenced
his second year among the Illinois Indians; this is not in the
Chantilly version.[8]

2. ACSM, 296, 1–37.
3. APF, Fonds Brotier 159 (Canada–5), 13–26v.
4. ACSM, 296, 37–51.
5. APF, Fonds Brotier 159 (Canada–5), 26v–31.
6. ACSM, 296, 52–60.
7. APF, Fonds Brotier 159 (Canada–5), 31–34.
8. ACSM, 296, 60. The Chantilly manuscript must have been

The differences between these manuscripts are truly slight. They are mentioned explicitly to make clear how paragraph structure, sentence structure, and even word order are otherwise identical. Indeed, with the two documents side by side, a description may be begun in one and finished from the other without confusion. In the present book the one word Récit will stand as a short title for either of the two complete manuscripts. When necessary, modifiers will indicate which one is being considered.[9]

In Montreal, the last two chapters of the Récit are present in another bound manuscript which the nuns returned to Father Martin, in 1844. His description of it was the "Relation . . . [qui] comprend une periode de six annees depuis 1673 jusqu'en 1679 [Relation . . . which describes a period of six years from 1673 to 1679]." In the Fonds Brotier are four similar remnants of what may have been rewrites of either the archetype in Montreal or Chantilly. Of them, three lack some of the beginning pages, three have lost a number of the final folios, and the one which begins correctly comes to an end so quickly that it is the shortest of them all. The mutilations of the individual manuscripts are such that a third example of the Marquette document cannot be fashioned from any combination of them. Any surmises on how they assumed their present dissociated condition are purely hypothetical.

---

mailed before Allouez' departure, see Jean Delanglez, "The 'Recit des voyages et des decouvertes du Pere Jacques Marquette,'" *M-A*, **XXVIII** (1946), 210–11.

9. Alfred Hamy, *Au Mississippi la Première Exploration, 1673 . . .* (Paris, 1903), pp. 222–23, thought there was a third complete manuscript of the Récit in Rome and a fourth at Harvard College. His mistake about Rome is exposed in a letter, AMU, N. Amer., Fr. Reg., 7, Burrus to Hamilton, May 30, 1956. John G. Shea, *Discovery and Exploration of the Mississippi Valley* (New York, 1852), p. xxxiv, n., explains that Sparks wrote about Marquette from [M. Thevenot], *Recueil de Voyages* (Paris, 1681), and had no manuscript at Harvard.

They are bound together in volume 158 of the series.[10]

Before studying these manuscripts, a word of warning about the printed editions of them is necessary. In the *Discovery and Exploration of the Mississippi Valley*, 1852, Shea did the entire three chapters of the Montreal Récit into English and in the appendix transcribed the original French version of its first chapter only. He took some unimportant stylistic liberties in the transcription and, by a footnote near the end of Section VI, admits that from this point to the first few lines of Section VII the narrative was supplied by him from Thevenot.[11] Shea's reason for doing this is explained by consulting the manuscript Récit at the Collège Sainte-Marie. At the end of Section VI, the original page which should have been "23" on the recto and "24" on the verso is missing and two newer sheets, numbered "23–23²" and "24–24²," written in a clear modern hand fill the gap. Evidently Shea was behind this emendation because, on these sheets, the writer portrays an Indian calumet dance, using the same words which, according to the note in *Discovery and Exploration,* are borrowed from Thevenot. Furthermore, in 1855, when Shea cooperated with James Lenox in editing all the chapters of the Montreal Récit in French, he commented in the *Avant-propos* on his finding, in Thevenot's *Recueil de Voyages,* the material which he recognized as probably having been on the missing folio 23–24 of the original Montreal Récit, and assumes credit for employing it to fill the lacuna. Two years later, in 1857, when Father Martin's research in Rome uncovered the unmutilated Chantilly Récit, its first chapter, from the end of Section VI to the beginning of Section VII, was found to describe an

10. ACSM, 314, "1673–1679 Relation, Original," is the Canadian fragment. Delanglez, "Recit des voyages," pp. 178–79, compares the Chantilly Récit with the fragments in the Fonds Brotier.

11. Shea, *Discovery and Exploration of the Mississippi Valley,* pp. 247–49. Shea's transcriptions usually corrected spelling and added capitalization to suit modern style.

Indian calumet dance in language identical with that which Shea had taken from Thevenot, and thus the substitution made in the Montreal Récit was proven correct as far as it went. It lacks a graph, appearing in the Chantilly Récit, which pictures a musical staff with the notes for the melody to which the Indians danced. This was not transcribed by Thevenot and hence not copied by Shea.[12]

De Montézon, in his 1861 *Relations Inédites,* was less careful in transcribing the Marquette documents. In places, his copy transposed the order, dropped sentences and added misleading comment. A glaring instance of the latter is his adoption of the *Avant-propos* from the Lenox and Shea *Récit* to preface his own book. Lenox and Shea had mentioned that their interpolation from Thevenot, to make up for the missing folio 23–24 in the Montreal Récit, would be found on pages 55–63 in their edition. In de Montézon the interpolation does not come until the second volume, pages 262–74, but his *Avant-propos* tells his readers to expect it on pages 55–63.[13]

The Marquette material became only a small fraction of the *Jesuit Relations and Allied Documents* which Thwaites reproduced at the beginning of the twentieth century. Commencing with the forty printed volumes of the Relations, which he considered the best contemporary authorities, he bolstered their narratives with additional data uncovered by his research. The

12. James Lenox and John G. Shea, eds., *Recit des Voyages et des Decouvertes de R. Père Jacques Marquette* (Albany, N.Y., 1855), pp. 55–63, carry the story of the calumet dance. It is in Thevenot, *Recueil de Voyages,* pp. 23–27. Thevenot copies the exact words of the Chantilly Récit, Fonds Brotier 159 (Canada–5), 19–22. It has been suggested that, long ago, someone interested in music was tempted to appropriate the missing page of the Montreal Récit. The author furnished a replica of the notes to Dr. Roy Harris, who composed the Père Marquette symphony for the Tercentennary of Père Marquette's coming to America, 1968–73. For correspondence about his interest in the Indian melody, see AMU, D-2, 8.

13. De Montézon, *Rel. Inédites,* II, 240, has the bungling preface.

Jesuit periodical was a mission magazine, not a chronicle of all that went on in Canada, and even in telling of the Order's activity, the rule allowed a superior the same freedom in sorting the field notes from his missionaires as a newspaper re-write-editor employs with the stories from his reporters. Thus, the superior could add facts where details of importance had been glossed over; and he had the privilege of cutting out what he thought to be lacking in interest to the prospective readers. It would seem that Canadian superiors indulged this privilege frequently by omitting incidents from the printed Relations, which may once have been in letters from missionaries, but this cannot be said with certainty since, after revisions were made for the press, the originals were usually destroyed.[14]

The additional data, which Thwaites inserts in his series, he scatters among the reprints of the Relations and calls "allied documents" because they are at least contemporaneous with them. In undertaking this method of expansion, he encountered editorial problems, which he did not always solve in the best way. For the sake of order, he determined on a chronological presentation. Certain annals, which included more than twelve months in their coverage, were divided into parts according to the year they dealt with and printed as separate units. When Thwaites found the same events recited in two papers, he sometimes fused the best part of each into a continuous treatment and, in the narrative thus created, dropped matter which became repetitious in the process. This makes it necessary to consult his "Bibliographical Data," placed at the end of each

14. *Institutum Societatis Iesu* (Florentiae, 1892–93), III, 43–44, "Formula scribendi," no. 30 and no. 27. The rule binds superiors to historical accuracy, but it leaves them free to write, "rejectis vel additis iis, quae videbuntur [omitting or expanding those points which they (the superiors) may wish]." Thwaites, *JR*, I, 38–39, assesses the truth of the Jesuit Relations.

volume, to determine how much of the text has been juggled.[15]

In handling the Montreal Récit, which narrates events that took place from 1673 to 1677, Thwaites' method of editing is responsible for having confused many who have written about Marquette after the publication of his *Jesuit Relations and Allied Documents*. The first chapter of the Récit, which describes the exploration of 1673, is found there among transcriptions of documents for this year. After an interruption of twenty pages, the second chapter is placed among reprints of material originating in 1674, because this was the year Marquette commenced his return to Old Kaskaskia. Finally, chapter three, which recounts Allouez' work among the Illinois, is relegated to the place where events of 1676–77 are enumerated, and this happens to be in an entirely different volume of Thwaites' series from the one containing his reprint of the Récit's first two chapters. Thus, the illusion is created that Thwaites has printed three separate manuscripts about Father Marquette rather than parts of a unified narrative.[16]

15. *Ibid.*, LXI, 265, tells what he did to the unfinished manuscript, ACSM, 314, "1673–1679 Relation, Original," reprinted in John G. Shea and Felix Martin, *Cramoisy No. 12, Relation de Ce Qui S'Est Passé de Plus Remarquable aux Missions des Pères de la Compagnie de Jesus en la Nouvelle France les Années 1673 à 1679 par R. P. Claude Dablon Recteur du Collège de Quebec & Superieur des Missions de la Compagnie de Jesus en la Nouvelle France* (New York, 1860). Thwaites admits dissecting this and transferring parts of it "to their proper [chronological] places." Likewise, he says he patched up other narratives by grafting parts of this document on to their story. *Ibid.*, LIX, 300–301.

16. *Ibid.*, pp. 86–163, reprints ch. 1, then ch. 2 turns up, *ibid.*, pp. 184–211, and ch. 3 is found *ibid.*, LX, 148–67. Thwaites increases the confusion by reproducing ch. 2 and ch. 3, not from the original, ACSM, 296, 37–60, but from the printed Shea and Martin, *Cramoisy No. 12, Relation . . . les Années 1673 à 1679*, pp. 99–134, where these chapters are transcribed from ACSM, 314, 44–65. For the way this has led scholars to misinterpret the contents of the Récit, see Louise

It is also disappointing to find Thwaites admitting dependence on de Montézon's printed books instead of on the originals when he reproduces his Marquette documents.[17] In his
"Bibliographical Data" about the Récit he says he has seen
"the original MSS., now resting in the archives of St. Mary's
College, Montreal."[18] But, strangely enough, he asserts that
this one "lacks pp. 55–63, a lacuna which we have supplied
from the 1681 edition of Thevenot's Recueil."[19] He must
have been looking at de Montézon's or at Lenox and Shea's
printed editions of the Récit when he repeats this mistake in
regard to the missing pages 23 and 24 of the Montreal document.

Father Donnelly's *Jacques Marquette, S.J., 1637–1675,* published in the fall of 1968, has a passing remark about the
missing folio in the Montreal Récit which supplies the occasion for a brief comment about this biography, notable as
the first to dwell at some length on Marquette's youth. In
1967, Donnelly published *Thwaites' Jesuit Relations, Errata
and Addenda,* with an introduction explaining that the "errata"
which were corrected were translations of phrases so peculiar
to Catholic ecclesiastical usage that more than a literal rendering of them was needed to convey their true sense. The "ad-

---

P. Kellogg, *Early Narratives of the Northwest, 1634–1699* (New
York, 1917), pp. 223–57, and Edna Kenton, *The Jesuit Relations and
Allied Documents, Travels and Explorations of Jesuit Missionaries in
North America 1610–1791, Selected and Edited* (Toronto, 1925),
pp. 333–66 and 376–87. Both reprint Thwaites' English translation of
the Récit but miss ch. 3. This discussion will show how Steck, Delanglez, and Donnelly were also misled by Thwaites' arrangement.

17. Thwaites, *JR,* LVIII, 291, concedes recourse to Douniol, publisher for de Montézon.

18. Ibid., LIX, 293. However, Thwaites published from longhand
transcripts sent by the college archivist, Father Jones, see Archives of
the State Historical Society of Wisconsin, U.S., "les Relations des
Jesuites."

19. Thwaites, *JR,* LIX, 294.

denda" were English translations of Latin Biblical quotations and the inclusion of titles for articles and books needed to bring Thwaites' bibliography up to date.[20] From the research this involved, Donnelly acquired a deep knowledge of Thwaites' series and an acquaintance with many fine modern monographs relevant to the French regime in North America. This gave him such an advantage over Marquette's previous biographers that in writing his *Jacques Marquette* he did not need to make a detailed exploration of the seventeenth-century documents, and did not often turn to this kind of source material. For example, in telling what may be found in the Chantilly Récit, his assertion that the narrative of the Mississippi discovery immediately precedes a copy of Marquette's journal of his voyage to the Illinois in 1674–75 fits the sequence in Thwaites' fifty-ninth volume, but is not the order in the manuscript which has been considered in the present chapter.[21] The same arrangement from Thwaites is said to be in the original Montreal Récit and Donnelly says of it, "pages one to thirty-seven contain the *Récit* except for pages four and five, which are missing, and have been replaced by copying, in modern script and ink, the portion from Thevenot's published edition." Such a description does not accord with the original, but is in agreement with the elements of a commentary on the Récit written by Delanglez in 1946.[22] Because

20. Joseph P. Donnelly, *Thwaites' Jesuit Relations, Errata and Addenda* (Chicago, 1967), p. 24.

21. Joseph P. Donnelly, *Jacques Marquette, S.J. 1637–1675* (Chicago, 1968), pp. 283–84, describes the order of Marquette documents found in Thwaites, *JR*, LIX, 86–183, as identical with that in the manuscript Récits.

22. Donnelly, *Jacques Marquette*, p. 284, n. 19, repeats what may be found in Delanglez, "Recit des voyages," pp. 173–94 and 211–58, where the title Récit is limited to what is in reality only its first chapter. Delanglez, in this article, in a confusing manner, applies "4" and "5" to indicate certain of the fragmentary copies of the Récit at Chantilly which may have led to the substitution by Donnelly of

of such confusion, often encountered in secondary sources, this book will go directly to the original manuscripts whenever there is question about the Marquette documents.

There is a shorter account of Marquette's part in the exploration of the Mississippi among the papers of the Fonds Brotier. It proves to be hardly less interesting and revealing than the first chapter of the Récit itself. It is entitled, "Relation de la decouverte de la Mer du Sud faite par les Riuieres de la nouvelle france Enouyée de Quebec par le Pere Dablon superieur general des missions dela Compagnie de Iesus le 1ᵉʳ. Iour d'Aoust 1674 [Relation of the discovery of the Sea of the South made by the rivers of New France. Sent from Quebec by Father Dablon superior general of the missions of the Company of Jesus the first day of August, 1674]." [23] In it Dablon announces the very recent return to Quebec of Jolliet, bringing the first news of the Mississippi discovery. The priest goes on to say that the young man could only recite his adventures orally because his canoe had upset in the St. Louis rapids close to Montreal and, in sinking, took with it everything aboard, including the journal he had kept. Dablon felt obliged to write down this dictation and sent it to the friends in Europe rather than make them wait longer for news of the expedition which he had announced as imminent in the *Relation . . . les Années 1671–1672*. A duplicate of this verbal summary of the discovery, with the address in a hand characteristic of Dablon, "A Mon R. Pere Clud le Moisne de la Comp[agnie] de Jesus. A Reims [To my Rev. Father Claude le Moisne of the Company of Jesus. At Reims]," is catalogued in the Bibliothèque Nationale, Paris, as "Envoye de quebec par le Pere d'ablon [Sent from Quebec by Father Dablon]." The Séminaire de Sainte-

---

these numbers in designating the pages 23–24, which are missing from the Montreal Récit.

23. APF, Fonds Brotier 155 (Canada–1), 10–13. The dictation introduces "Relation . . . les Années 1672–1673."

Sulpice, also in Paris, has an example of the same story, but in a different handwriting.[24]

There are three other manuscripts in the Fonds Brotier which are primarily concerned with the announcement of Father Marquette's death in 1675. A free translation into Latin of the "Letter circulaire du P. Jacques Marquette" is in the Fonds Brotier, where it is entitled "Mors p. Iacobi marquette"; and in the same Fonds is a "Lettre du P. Cholenec au P. Fontenay (10 octobre, 1675)," which originated at La Prairie de la Madeleine, near Montreal, from the pen of a Jesuit missionary there who tells a friend in France what he had heard about Marquette's demise from two Frenchmen who were with him at the end. A synopsis of this is found in the "Relation . . . les Années 1674–1675."[25] Each one of these longhand documents repeats incidents common to either the Récit or the Jolliet dictation, but adds other things not found elsewhere. The same may be said of the holograph map of the Mississippi and the holograph journal of Marquette's second trip to the Illinois Indians which Viger and Father Martin attributed to him and which are in the archives of the Collège Sainte-Marie.[26]

There are several documents attributed to Jolliet which are pertinent to the present study. A collection of his reports about various services performed for the Court is kept in the National Archives of France. Here is found a "Relation de La descouverte de plusieurs pays Scituës au midy de La Nouuelle france faitte A 1673 [Relation of the discovery of several countries situated to the south of New France made A.D. 1673],"

24. BN, Moreau, 842, 31–32v; and Archives du Séminaire de Saint-Sulpice, Paris, Doc. pour Servir a l'Histoire de l'Eglise du Canada, I, pt. 1, 1–12.

25. APF, Fonds Brotier 155 (Canada–1), 38–45, is the "Mors p. Iacobi marquette"; APF, Fonds Brotier 166 (Canada–12), no. 4, 26v, is the Cholenec letter; APF, Fonds Brotier 162 (Canada–8), no. 3, is the "Relation." The "Lettre Circulaire" was mentioned in Ch. 1.

26. ACSM, 687, is the map; and ACSM, 296, 63–70, is the holograph journal.

which is identical in contents with what he dictated to Dablon, except for one paragraph which is out of place. Jolliet's upset in the St. Louis rapids is not mentioned by the Jesuit superior until toward the middle of the dictation he took down from the explorer on August 1, 1674. The "Relation de La des-couverte," among Jolliet's documents, details the tragedy prom-inently on the first page. The Bibliothèque Nationale, Paris, possesses a copy of Jolliet's dictation, with the accident on the first page. It is among the papers of Eusèbe Renaudot, the editor of the seventeenth-century Paris newspaper, *Gazette de France*.[27]

Other documents about the Mississippi, which are assigned to Jolliet, include three maps, each one carrying the same short dedicatory letter about his adventure. Two of these have titles, identical except for a single word, which read, "Carte de la decouuerte du Sr Jolliet ou l'on voit la communication du Fleuue St Laurens auec les Lacs Frontenac, Érié de quel on entre dans celuy des Hurons, et par une mesme Nauigation a celuy des Ilinois au bout duquel on va joindre la Riuiere diuine par un portage de Mille pas qui [cette riuiere] tombe dans la Riuiere Colbert et se descharge dans le sein Mexique [Map of the Discovery of Sr. Jolliet where one Sees the Communication of the St. Laurence River with the Lakes Frontenac (Ontario), Erie from Which One Enters into the One of the Hurons, and by a Similar Navigation to the One of the Illinois (Michigan) at the Bottom of Which One Goes to Meet the River Divine (Ohio) by a Portage of a Thousand Paces, which (River) Falls into the River Colbert (Mississippi) and Empties into the Gulf of Mexico]." The last "qui" on the larger map, in the service of clarity, becomes "cette riuiere" on the smaller one. The terrain outlined is so much the same on both as to leave no doubt of one having been used as a model for the other, but the larger one is distinct in having the arms of Louis de

27. ASH, 5, no. 16, 2; and BN, Mss. fr., n.a., 7491, 351–55.

Buade, Comte de Frontenac in its upper left-hand corner. At present, they belong to the library of the Service Hydrographique in Paris. The third map, presenting quite a different picture of the same geographical region, has a scroll across the top in which is written, "Nouuelle Decouuerte de Plusieurs Nations dans la Nouuelle France, En L'annee 1673 et 1674." It is in the John Carter Brown Library, Providence, Rhode Island.[28]

None of the Marquette documents just enumerated, even those papers beginning with the word "Relation," ever appeared in the Jesuit mission magazine because the Cramoisy press ceased printing it with the 1671–1672 issue; hence, none of the published volumes contains news about the discovery of the Mississippi. The annual was discontinued because of an assumption of church power by Louis XIV, which historians call "Gallicanism." Announcing "Les Libertés de l'Église Gallicane" early in his career, the king had taken a stand similar to the Spanish "Patronato." By 1673, he had overcome most of the resistance of his own bishops. By 1682, he put himself almost on terms of equality with the pope.[29] How this affected the

28. Archives Nationales, Paris, Le Service Hydrographique, B 4044–37 and B 4044–49 are the first two of the group. Both are in the Karpinski reproductions in the Edward F. Ayer Collection of the Newberry Library, Chicago. The larger is sketched in Justin Winsor, *Narrative and Critical History of America* (Boston, 1884–89), IV, 212; the smaller in Gabriel Marcel, *Reproductions de Cartes & de Globes Relatifs à la Découverte de l'Amerique du XVIᵉ XVIIIᵉ Siècle* (Paris, 1893–94), pl. XXVII. Thwaites, *JR*, LIX, 86, has a facsimile of the third map.

29. Ludwig Freiherr von Pastor, *The History of the Popes from the Close of the Middle Ages, Drawn from Secret Archives of the Vatican and Other Original Sources* (London, 1891–1952), XXX, 5–6; W. Eugene Shiels, *King and Church* (Chicago, 1961); Jean Longnon, ed. *Mémoires de Louis XIV* (Paris, 1933), pp. 193–94, 197; Charles Gerin, *Recherches Historiques sur l'Assemblée du Clergé en France de 1682* (Paris, 1869), pp. 271–76.

Jesuit Relations is consequent upon a dispute which had its origin in the Orient.

China had been entered by Jesuits from Portugal toward the end of the sixteenth century. They found a definite non-European culture with an ethical code built largely on respect for the deceased. When they were convinced that there was no intention of worshipping the departed by the ceremonies practiced in their honor, permission was obtained from Rome in 1615 to allow the continuation of such practices among the converts to Christianity. The liturgy which ensued became known as the "Chinese Rite."[30] While the Jesuits were Christianizing the customs of their neophytes, Spain had gained control of the Portuguese throne. Spanish Franciscans and Dominicans joined the Catholic apostolate in China. Perhaps nationalism influenced their quick decision against the practices which had been allowed the Portuguese priests. At any rate, a controversy developed.[31] In the last third of the seventeenth century, Louis XIV became involved in the dispute by sending two vicars apostolic from the Parisian Society for the Foreign Missions to China to settle the squabble.[32] Neither Spanish nor Portuguese liked the French. Old wounds were torn open rather than bandaged up.[33]

30. Vincent Cronin, *The Wise Man from the West* (London, 1955); Pastor, *History of the Popes,* XXV, 353–54, 357.

31. Anastasius Van Den Wyngaert, ed., *Sinica Franciscana, Relationes et Epistolas Fratrum Minorum Saeculi XVI et XVII . . . Adnotavit* (Florence, 1933–54), II, 315–606 and *Collectanea S. Congregationis de Propaganda Fide, seu Decreta Instructiones, Rescripta pro Apostolicis Missionibus* (Rome, 1907), I, 30–35, no. 114, decree, S.C. de Prop., September 12, 1645, outline the Spanish stand. Alvarez Semedo and Martin Martini, *Histoire Vniverselle de la Chine* (Lyon, 1667), pp. 216–20 and *Collectanea Prop. Fide,* I, 36–39, no. 126, decree S.C.S. Officii, March 23, 1656, defend the Portuguese.

32. Henri Chapoulie, *Aux Origines d'Une Église, Rome et les Missions d'Indochine au XVIIe Siècle* (Paris, 1948), I, 103–4, 114–19. Pope Alexander VII approved these appointments.

33. [Fernandez Domingo De Navarrete], *The Travels and Con-*

To prevent scandal, the congregation of cardinals in Rome, which had been set up under the name *Propaganda Fide* to spread the faith in pagan lands, asked the pope to issue a decree which would bring the whole question under its control. On April 6, 1673, Clement X spoke officially in the papal brief *Creditae Nobis*. He addressed himself to all those any way occupied in missionary work "of whatever state, grade & condition even that of Religious of every Order, Congregation, Institute, & Society even [the Society] of JESUS." Neither the Franciscans, nor the Jesuits, nor anyone else was left out. All were told that the pope prohibited each one from printing, "books & writings, in which in any way there is discussion of missions or what pertains to missions, without the written permission of the Congregation of these same Cardinals [of *Propaganda Fide*], which [permission] must be printed in the beginning of the [published] work." The rest of *Creditae Nobis* invokes penalties on those who will not obtain this "imprimatur," as the permission to allow the printing of their work is called. The brief does not mention stopping any particular mission publications. It deals with all mission literature, and its concern is to safeguard this type of writing from becoming a cause of disedification.[34]

Had things been normal in France, the Jesuit Relations might have continued as usual. They were no way involved in the controversial area, tied up with Oriental custom. The annual volumes might have been submitted to *Propaganda Fide* with confidence of receiving its approval. But just a month before *Creditae Nobis* was issued, the French monarch had asserted his right over church property in France. Accord-

---

troversies of Friar Domingo Navarrete 1618–68, ed. J. S. Cummins (New York, 1962), I, lxxiii–lxxxiii, summarizes the situation.

34. *Bullarum, Priviligiorum ac Diplomatum Romanorum Pontificum Amplissima Collectio cui Accessere Pontificium Omnium Vitae, Notae et Indices Opportuni*, ed., Carolus Cocquelines (Romae, 1739–62), VII, pt. 21, 212–13.

ing to the "Libertés de l'Église Gallicane," no jurisdiction of
Roman cardinals could circumscribe the royal freedom. Therefore, Louis XIV's censors, who assigned the *Privilège du Roi*
to publish, were the only acceptable judges of books to be
printed in his realm. To the French provincial this presented
what appeared to be an insoluble dilemma. To continue the
Relations without the imprimatur of *Propaganda Fide* would
have been disobedience to the pope. To bring them out with
its approbation was impossible in his country. He apparently
decided that the data from America must be held up for the
present. For the first time in forty years, in the fall of 1673,
the Cramoisy press received no script for the periodical.[35] Had
this not been the case, had the Relations continued to be printed
and had the manuscripts enumerated in the present chapter appeared in printed issues of the seventeenth-century periodical,
such evidence would have established their antiquity. But, since
after 1672 there were no Relations for them to be published
in, their age can be determined only from new evidence.

To begin with, the Récit at the Collège Sainte-Marie was deposited by Father Casot at the Hôtel Dieu in 1800; hence, it
is immediately dated as extant before the Louisiana Purchase
generated American interest in Father Marquette. This Montreal Récit tells the same story, in the same paragraphing,
sentence structure, and language, as the Chantilly Récit which

35. Joseph Brucker, "[Review of] *Vie de Msgr. de Laval Premier
Évêque de Quebec et Apôtre du Canada (1622–1708),* par l'abbé
Auguste Gosselin, Quebec 1890," *Études Religieuses* (Paris), LII
(1891), 511–14, first proposed this dilemma (by a printer's error,
this volume carries "LIII" on the title page). Camille de Rochemonteix, *Les Jésuites et la Nouvelle-France au XVII⁰ Siècle, d'après Beaucoup de Documents Inédites* (Paris, 1895–96), I, xxvii–lxiv; William
R. Corrigan, "Propaganda and the Suppression of the Jesuit Relations," *M-A,* XII (1929–30), 306–310; and Léon Pouliot, *Étude sur
les Relations des Jésuites de la Nouvelle-France (1632–1672)* (Montreal, 1940), pp. 9–15, adopt Brucker's reasoning.

Father Brotier took to Rome in 1762; so, the story had taken its present shape before the existence of the United States. The presence of the Chantilly Récit combined with a handwritten "Relation . . . les Années 1677–1678," suggests the exact year in which this document was finished.[36] So much for what the two holograph Récits indicate themselves about the date of their composition. There is other evidence which testifies to their seventeenth-century origin. For example, the sheaf of papers, called by Father Martin "Relation . . . de six annees depuis 1673 jusqu'en 1679" in his enumeration of the manuscripts he received from the nuns in Quebec, supplies relevant data.

This document, touching on six years of Jesuit mission work, is bound and on the cover is inscribed "1673–1679 Relation." There follows a note asserting its handwriting to be from the pen of a priest who was at the college of Quebec while Father Dablon was superior. Finally, the title ends with the single word, "Original." Inside, the text begins immediately, "Chapitre premier Des Mission des Outaouacs." Thereafter, the chapters are arranged in a disorderly sequence. On the last leaf, in Dablon's script, there is written, "Relation de 1679 abrégé des précédentes." What he meant by stressing that here was the "Relation de 1679" with an epitome from similar writings of earlier years becomes clear by a comparison with the "Relation . . . les Années 1672–1673," which Father Martin also retrieved from the nuns in Quebec. Both this and the "Relation de 1679" have parts of previous Relations written verbatim and then scratched out to make way for short summaries of their contents. In both manuscripts such summaries lead into entirely new narration about more recent activities in the area with which they are concerned.[37]

The first of these rough copies, the "Relation . . . les Années

36. APF, Fonds Brotier 159 (Canada–5), 13–34, is the Chantilly Récit. The twelve folios preceding it make up the Relation.

37. ACSM, 314, 8–10, 19, 24, 27–30, etc., afford examples of corrections such as are found throughout the volume.

1672–1673," has a counterpart, with the same title, in the Fonds Brotier, but its text is clean, ready for the press, and shortened until it contains just the account remaining in the Montreal rough draft after the scratched parts are omitted and synopses inserted.[38] These different drafts of the same "Relation . . . les Années 1672–1673" demonstrate the method of composing a volume of the Jesuit Relations. First, a scribe brought together background texts from former years as a prelude to the new narratives. This enabled the superior to make digests of past performance in his presentations of subsequent developments of the Jesuit apostolate. If he did not wish to do so, he simply scratched out the whole passage. Ordinarily, such working copy would be discarded when the scribe had finished another clean narrative for the press. However, after 1672, it would be natural for the library of the college in Quebec to hold on to these originals, since there was no immediate expectation of a printed volume coming from the Cramoisy press to carry forward the history of the Canadian missions.

It seems quite safe to say the "Relation de 1679 abrégé des précédentes" in Montreal is a working model for the "Relation . . . les Années 1678–1679," but it is not quite ready for the press and there is no clean duplicate of a Relation for this year. The "Relation . . . les Années 1677–1678," which contains the Récit, is the last document with such a title in the Fonds Brotier. This is significant in establishing the year when the "Relation de 1679" was written.

By 1679, six years had passed in which, owing to *Creditae Nobis*, no Jesuit Relations had been printed in Paris. Many people in high places depended on this only regular annual from Canada for information helpful to colonial commerce. They became impatient when they no longer found the Jesuit Relations at their booksellers; they brought their complaints

38. Thwaites, *JR*, LVII, 34–305 and LVIII, 20–89, has printed this rough draft, using various kinds of type to indicate the material scratched and synopsized.

to King Louis XIV, and in 1679 his assistance was assured them.[39] There was a Jesuit at Versailles, Père François de La Chaise, who acted as preacher and confessor to the king. He had known for some time the grievances of those with Canadian interests, so he was prepared for the receipt in January, 1680, of a command in the name of the king to resume publication of the Relations.[40] It is not known how the crisis was resolved, but despite the order no new copies of the periodical were printed, and, taking Father de La Chaise's knowledge of what was to come together with the absence of the press copy for the "Relation . . . les Années 1678–1679" in the Fonds Brotier, it may be conjectured that in anticipation of the demand by the king, Father de La Chaise had asked the French provincial to tell the superior of the Canada missions to stop sending his press releases. This would enable the king's confessor to inform the monarch that no Relations were arriving from New France and to beg leniency on this account.

The year in which Dablon put away the "Relation de 1679," in its incomplete condition, has a direct bearing on the discussion about the antiquity of the Récit. Its second and third chapters are included in this rough draft being prepared for the "Relation . . . les Années 1678–1679." It may be assumed they are there, along with excerpts from other previous Relations, to freshen Dablon's memory and, perhaps, to be con-

39. Rochemonteix, *Les Jésuites et la Nouvelle-France,* I, li–lix; Pouliot, *Étude sur les Relations,* pp. 14–15.

40. Rochemonteix, *Les Jésuites et la Nouvelle-France,* I, lv, quotes, ARSJ, Epist. Gen., "P. de La Chaise au P. Oliva (Parisiis, 12 Jan. 1680)," "rex ad me misit illustrissimum Dnum archiepiscopum Parisiensem, qui mihi regio nomine juberet quaecumque gesta vel observata essent in . . . missionibus memoratu digna . . . colligere et in lucem dare quam primum fieri potest, . . . [the king sent me His Excellency the Lord Archbishop of Paris, who commanded me in the name of the king to collect from the missions whatever was worth knowing, both in work done and in observations made, and publish it as quickly as possible, . . .]."

densed as background for the activities at the Conception Mission of the Illinois, when the developments in 1678–79 were narrated. As things went, they were simply left unused, and their presence testifies to their having been completed prior to the date of the manuscript in which they are found.

Across the Atlantic in the Roman archives of the Society of Jesus, among letters sent in by members of the Order from all over the world, there is one from Father Dablon to Fr. Claude Boucher, dated 1678, which seems to demonstrate that the entire Récit was finished by this year. Dablon writes, "Jay remassé autant que Jay pû tous Les memoires du feu P. Marquette sur ses decouuertes, Je Les ay mis en ordre auec toutes Les raretez et Curiositez de ces Voyages, et L'establissement de La Mission des Jlinois; J'enuoye au P. Ragueneau ce petit ouurage, qui Le fera voire a V. Rᵉˢ. [I have gathered together, so far as I was able, all the memoirs of the deceased Fr. Marquette about his discoveries. I have arranged them in order, with all that is extraordinary in these voyages and the establishment of the Mission of the Illinois. This little work I am sending to Fr. Ragueneau, who will arrange to let Your Reverence see it]."[41]

To understand why Dablon was so sure that Fr. Paul Ragueneau would pass "this little work" on to Father Boucher requires a brief comment on the progress in administration of the Society from a small beginning in 1540 to the seventeenth century, when Jesuits had spread throughout the world. The general, residing in Rome, had a body of assistants called his curia and composed of men representing different language groups. In 1678, Father Boucher, who came to the curia from Paris, was the assistant representing all French-speaking Jesuits. Each European country had a number of Jesuit provinces; the more properous of these had missions attached to them where

41. ARSJ, Gal. 110, pt. 1, 62v, "Letters du P. Dablon au P. Boucher (Quebec 25 octobre 1678)."

some of their members worked among the infidels. At least one man in the mother province devoted full time to procuring the aid for their support; hence he was called a procurator. The superior of the missions sent him the annual letter. In 1678, Dablon was fulfilling this obligation through Father Ragueneau because he was the Canadian mission procurator and as such would publicize its contents to prospective patrons; then Ragueneau's further responsibility was to see that the Relation was sent to Rome where, with annual letters from all over the world, it would keep the curia current on the progress of the Order. Dablon knew that Father Boucher, the French assistant, would synopsize the news from French North America for presentation to the general, so Dablon could speak with assurance when he told Boucher that he would see what had been written about Father Marquette.

The importance of this letter, with regard to the age of the Récit, lies in this: when it went to Father Boucher in 1678, it enumerated the things included in Dablon's "little work" as not only the story of the exploration of the Mississippi River, but other voyages made by Marquette (the plural is used), and all the memoirs of the deceased missionary, and especially the establishment of the mission of the Illinois. These things are the topics developed in the second and third chapters of the Récit. This seems to warrant the conclusion that the Chantilly Récit, of which he spoke in 1678, was in the exact condition in which it is now. Furthermore, the identity of its contents with the Montreal Récit prevents any possibility of additions having been made to it since the seventeenth century. There is only one question which may come to mind before this discussion is finished. In 1681, Thevenot, in his *Recueil de Voyages,* only edited a synopsis of the first chapter of the Récit. Why did he stop there, if he had the other two chapters?

It is not known how Thevenot came into possession of the Récit. His avocation as editor of journals by French explorers and his membership in the Académie des Sciences made its

geographical tidings an ideal morsel for inclusion in his general
travel series, which he called *Relations des Divers Voyages,* but
the mission designs incorporated in the Récit did not have the
same interest for him. Perhaps for this reason, perhaps because
he knew how *Creditae Nobis* had influenced Jesuit publications,
he decided to omit the religious aspect when he edited the
Mississippi trip for his *Receuil de Voyages.* At any rate, in the
"Avis" to this book, Thevenot advertises only the geographic
value of what Marquette and Jolliet had done. He begins by
a reminder that his last volume was about Mexico. He then
says, "Cette Histoire des Ameriquains devoit estre suivie d'une
decouverte faite dans l'Amerique Septentrionale par le Pere
Marquette Jesuite, & le sieur Joliet [This History of the
Americans ought to be followed by a discovery made in North
America by Father Marquette a Jesuit and Sieur Jolliet]," who
made a long westward journey, found the Mississippi River and
embarked thereon. Their findings, he tells his readers, have led
him to believe that the Arctic Sea above New France does not
offer the only western route by which China may be reached,
"quan il y auroit un passage au bout de cette étendüe de terre
. . . [since there seems to be a crossing (of the continent) below
this part of the earth]."[42] At the end of the "Avis," he announces "Voyage & découverte du P. Marquette & Sr. Jolliet
dans l'Amerique Septentrionale [Voyage & Discovery of Fr.
Marquette & Sr. Jolliet in North America]." Then, with a
new series of page numbers and a new title, "Découverte de
quelques Pays et Nations de l'Amerique Septentrionale [Dis-
covery of Some Countries and Tribes of North America]," he
prints an abstract of the 1673 trip by employing the language
of the Récit but by making it fit into a secular, scientific pattern.
Its text is submitted to drastic surgery which apparently is
aimed at excising all mention of missions. Thus, the second
and third chapters, which are basically concerned with Mar-

42. Thevenot, *Recueil de Voyages,* "Avis," p. 7.

quette's religious work, are entirely eliminated. Likewise, the whole introduction and most of Section I of the first chapter, concerned with spiritual things, find no place in the *Recueil de Voyages*. Every other cut in its transcription omits a statement smacking of piety.[43] What remains is a travel story composed from the actual wording of the Récit but which emphasizes the water routes leading to the Mississippi and back and which offers Indian testimony in favor of a continental crossing to the Pacific by ascending the Pekitonoui (Missouri) River to its source and portaging to westward flowing streams which supposedly enter the sea. Considering Thevenot's purpose and the conditions existent when he wrote, this sort of synopsis affords no grounds for imagining that the three chapters of the complete Récit were not in the hands of the French provincial when the *Recueil de Voyages* was offered for sale in 1681. Before terminating a consideration of the age of the Récit manuscripts, a scrutiny of the watermarks found in the paper on which they are written will be worthwhile.[44] (See pp. 70–71.)

43. Compare Thevenot, *Recueil de Voyages*, "Découverte de quelques Pays . . .," 1–3, 4 and 20 with Thwaites, *JR*, LIX, 86–93, 96, 124–25.

44. Charles M. Briquet, *Les Filigranes, Dictionnaire Historique des Marques du Papier dès Leur Apparition vers 1282 jusqu'en 1600* (Leipzig, 1923), I, xiii, emphasizes the dependability of Renaissance watermarks for dating papers.

Two Canadian scholars, long associated with Marquette documents in Chantilly and Montreal, have made studies in this area and allowed their findings to be summarized here. One of them is Fr. Paul Desjardins, the archivist of the Collège Sainte-Marie in Montreal. The other is Fr. Lucien Campeau, the editor of the transcripts from the writings of the early Jesuits of New France, which are to have place in the series known as *Monumenta Historica Societatis Jesu*. Father Campeau's *Monumenta Novae Franciae*, volume 1, published by Laval University Press in 1967, brought the series to 96 volumes. AMU, N. Amer., Fr. Reg., 9, Desjardins to Hamilton, Montreal, December 5,

1

2

3

SAMPLES OF FRENCH WATERMARKS

INCIDENCE OF WATERMARKS ON MARQUETTE DOCUMENTS

"Relation . . . les Années 1673–1674"	—	2	—	4
"Relation . . . les Années 1674–1675"	1	—	3	—
"Relation . . . les Années 1676 and 1677"	—	—	—	4
"Mors p. Iacobi Marquette"	1	—	3	4
Holograph Journal	1	2	3	—
Chantilly Récit	1	—	3	—
Montreal Récit	—	—	—	4

The watermark on some pages of the Chantilly Récit is a heart with a superimposed cross; within the heart are the letters "IHS," which are employed in the Jesuit seal. Others have a quadrilateral enclosing a heart with "B" to the left and "C" to the right. Both these devices are found in the holograph journal of Marquette's second trip to the Illinois Indians, which Father Martin retrieved from the Hôtel Dieu in Quebec. They are also on the Latin notice of Marquette's death, "Mors p. Iacobi marquette," and the "Relation . . . les Années 1674–1675," both of which are in the Fonds Brotier at Chantilly.[45] Another watermark found in the holograph journal is a large circle enclosing six smaller ones. A lily within and a lily above this emblem create a sort of apex from which elaborate scroll-work descends to right and to left. This circular shield with its decorations occurs on the paper of the "Relation . . . les Années 1673–1674," in the Fonds Brotier. In this Relation, also, is found a watermark which Father Campeau describes as, "large, very characteristic and complicated, . . . a sort of escutcheon with three *fleurs de lys* supported on either side by a winged figure." This is present on some pages of "Mors p. Iacobi marquette" and the "Relation . . . les Années 1676 & 1677," both in the Fonds Brotier. The same device is found on pages of the Récit in the archives of the Collège Sainte-

---

1954, and Campeau to Hamilton, Montreal, October 23, 1961, afford full details on these watermarks.

45. APF, Fonds Brotier 159 (Canada–5), 13–34, "Recit des voyages . . ."; ACSM 296, 63–71, holograph journal; APF, Fonds Brotier 155 (Canada–1), 38–45, "Mors p. Iacobi marquette"; APF, Fonds Brotier 162 (Canada–8), no. 3, "Relation . . . les Années 1674–1675," which has a title different from the ordinary. It is "Etat présent des missions des Pères de la Compagnie de Iesus en la Nouvelle-France 1675." Its pages are unnumbered, see A. Léon Leymaire, *Analyse des Documents Exposés par la Compagnie de Jésus et sur les Jésuites . . . Paris avril-juin, 1929* (Paris, 1929), p. 70.

Marie.[46] William A. Churchill's treatise on watermarks traces
the escutcheon with winged figures to a French papermaker
and dates it as of 1674.[47] Thus, the seventeenth-century watermark on the pages of the Montreal Récit becomes witness to its
antiquity and the antiquity of the "Mors p. Iacobi marquette"
and, since the latter shares common watermarks with the Chantilly Récit, the genesis of all three documents may be accepted
as contemporaneous.

Since the holograph journal of Marquette's second trip to the
Illinois Indians has the watermarks built round the monograms
with the hearts, and since these are common to the "Mors p.
Iacobi marquette," and have a place in the Chantilly Récit
and in the "Relation . . . les Années 1674–1675"; and since
the "Relation . . . les Années 1676 & 1677" has the winged
figure watermarks, which are in the "Mors p. Iacobi marquette," there can be little doubt that the paper on which all
these documents are written belongs to the seventeenth century. All the announcements of Father Marquette's death,
mentioned at the beginning of the present chapter, are included
in this group of manuscripts, except for the one in the Archivum Romanum Societatis Jesu beginning "Lettre circulaire du
P. Jacques Marquette." However, this one is bound in the
volume containing obituaries of French Jesuits whose deaths
were made known to the superior general in 1675, and the letter reciting the incidents of Marquette's departure from life is

46. APF, Fond Brotier 157 (Canada–3) pt. 2, 1–97, "Relation . . .
les Années 1673–1674"; APF, Fonds Brotier 155 (Canada–1), 38–45,
"Mors p. Iacobi marquette"; APF, Fonds Brotier 160 (Canada–6),
1–31, "Relation . . . les Années 1676 & 1677, Des Missions iroquoises
l'année 1676"; ACSM, 296, 1–62, "Recit des voyages . . . .

47. William A. Churchill, *Watermarks in Paper in Holland, England, France, etc., in XVII and XVIII Centuries and Their Interconnection* (Amsterdam, 1935), p. 83, no. 393, with reproduction pl.
CCXC; also, p. 83, no. 402, with reproduction pl. CCXCVII, is a
1677 watermark with the Jesuit "IHS" and cross, which is very
similar to the one in the Récit at Chantilly.

clearly dated from Quebec, October 13, 1675; hence, its age need not be doubted.[48]

The present chapter, in its enumeration of the documents of the Mississippi discovery, included one more supposedly originating from Dablon. It is called "Relation de la decouverte de la Mer du Sud . . .," purports to tell what Jolliet dictated just after his return to Quebec, and is dated "le 1er Iour d'Aoust 1674." An endorsement for its age arises from a study of the "Relation de La descouverte de plusieurs pays Scituës au midy de La Nouuelle france faitte A 1673," which has identical contents and has been mentioned as being in the National Archives of France along with other manuscripts by Louis Jolliet. These are a summary of a trip he made to Hudson Bay in 1679 and a holograph journal of his exploration of Labrador in 1693. Accompanying the journal is a letter of transmittal to Jean Baptiste Lagny, intendant of commerce in charge of Canadian affairs, dated October 28, 1694.[49] These items came to their present resting place after a stop at the Archives of the Service Hydrographique, which had received them from the old Archives of the Marine and Colonies set up in 1669 by Jean Baptiste Colbert, Louis XIV's minister of the colonies.[50] The "Relation de La descouverte," because of the company it keeps, seems to be the selfsame report promised by Frontenac to Colbert, in a letter dated November 14, 1674, which says the minister will receive "la carte qu'il [Jolliet] en faite et les remarques dont il s'est pu souvenir . . . de cette decouverte, dont il s'est tres bien acquitté [the map which he

48. ARSJ, Gal. 110, pt. 2, 195–196v.

49. ASH, 5, no. 16, 2, is with ASH, 5, no. 4, 16–23, translated in Jean Delanglez, "The Voyage of Louis Jolliet to Hudson Bay in 1679," *M-A*, XXVI (1944), 245–50 and the holographs ASH, 5, no. 15, 8a and 9a, edited by Jean Delanglez, "Journal de Louis Jolliet Allant à la Descouverte de Labrador 1694," *RAPQ, 1943–1944*, pp. 161–206.

50. Joseph E. Roy, *Rapport sur les Archives de France Relatives à l'Histoire du Canada* (Ottawa, 1911), p. 158 and AMU, N. Amer., Fr. Reg., 21, Dehergne to Hamilton, Paris, 29 mai, 1956.

(Jolliet) made of it and the observations which he was able to recall . . . about this discovery, which he carried out very well]," as soon as it can be carried to France by Jacques Barrois, who was the Canadian governor's secretary. This supposition is strengthened by the document, similar to the "Relation de La descouverte," found in the papers of Eusèbe Renaudot.[51]

Renaudot's copy of Jolliet's report is in the Bibliothèque Nationale in a volume which includes a synopsis of the Mississippi discovery with a heading, "Relation de la Nouvelle france 1673." [52] The latter is prosaic in style, incorporates a few quotations from the longer account, treats the exploration with considerable sarcasm, and completely omits Father Marquette's name. From its title, this piece seems to have been made ready by the publisher of the *Gazette de France* to be run in his newspaper, when the "Relation . . . les Années 1672–1673" would come out, but because of *Creditae Nobis* no Relation was printed this year or thereafter, and no article about the Mississippi exploration found its way into the *Gazette*.[53]

The social milieu in which Renaudot moved will explain

51. *RAPQ, 1926–1927*, p. 77, "Lettre du Gouverneur . . . au Ministre (14 novembre 1674)." For Renaudot's copy, see BN, Mss. fr., n.a., 7491, 351–55.

52. BN, Mss.fr., n.a., 7485, 176–177v; printed in Ernest Gagnon, *Louis Jolliet Découvreur de Mississipi et du Pays des Illinois, Premier Seigneur de l'Ile d'Anticosti* (2nd ed., Montreal, 1913), Appendix C, pp. 316–26; Margry, *Découv. et Étab.*, I, 259–62. Jean Delanglez, "The 1674 Account of the Discovery of the Mississippi," *M-A*, XXVI (1944), 308, thought this synopsis originated in Canada, but corrected himself in "The Discovery of the Mississippi, Secondary Sources," ibid., XXVIII (1946), 4–5.

53. The *Gazette de France* between December 8, 1674 and December 28, 1675, BN, Lc²1, 674, 1183–1242, has been consulted. It says nothing about the discovery, and de Granges de Surgères, *Repértoire Historique et Bibliographique de la Gazette de France depuis l'Origine jusq'à la Revolution, 1631–1790* (Paris, 1902–6), does not mention Marquette, Jolliet, or the Mississippi River.

why he would omit Father Marquette's name in an article about
the discovery of the Mississippi River, although it quotes from
Jolliet's report which credits the Jesuit with being a partner to
the discovery. Certain affiliations of the editor also suggest
why such a timely article never was printed in the *Gazette de
France*. Renaudot was a Jansenist who, in collaboration with
Antoine Arnauld, was popularizing the doctrine of *The Augustinus,* the religious tractate which the lately deceased Cornelius
Jansenius had left his disciples.[54] The third volume of this
work, running well over a thousand pages, is divided into
treatises on "De Gratia Christi Salvatoris" and "Erroris Mas-
silensium et Opinionis Qvorvndam Parallelum et Statera," in
which the outstanding Jesuit theologians—Bellarmine, Lessius,
Suárez, and Molina—are accused of rational materialism and
of having fallen into the heresy of the Massilians, who had
been denounced by St. Augustine and condemned by the
church; hence, their followers, in the Society of Jesus, are to
be opposed by Jansenists.[55] Renaudot would find in this sufficient reason for withholding any praise from the Jesuit Marquette, and such an attitude would keep him from going to the

54. Cornelii Iansenii Episcopi Iprensis, *Avgvstinvs* (Lovanii, 1640;
facsimile reprint, Frankfurt/Main, 1964), is the Latin work from
which Arnauld and Renaudot were translating and expanding for
French readers. Jean Delanglez, *Some La Salle Journeys* (Chicago,
1938), pp. 10–14, discusses Renaudot's Jansenism.

55. Iansenii, *Avgvstinvs,* III, 79–1071, "De Gratia Christi Salvatoris" and III, 1072–1143, "Erroris Massiliensium et Opinionis Qvorvndam [Parallelvm] et Statera. In Qua Discrimen Utriusque Sen-
tentiae [Parallele] Indagatur, & Compluribus Notis Perspicue
Ostenditur [Of the Errors of the Massilians and the Belief of Their
Imitators and the Value of the Same, in Which the Distinction
between the Teaching of the Two Groups is Traced by Comparison
& Clearly Shown with Many Notes]. The Jansenistic opposition to
the Jesuits is developed in René Rapin, *Histoire du Jansénisme, depuis
Son Origine jusqu'en 1644,* ed., l'abbé Domenech (Paris, n.d. [1861]),
pp. 479–82 and 144–45. See also, Jean Orcibal, *Les Origines du
Jansénisme* (Paris, 1947–48), for later findings.

Jesuits for news of the discovery, if he could find it elsewhere. He did have access to the Court because his father had acted as royal physician and because his own knowledge of English had been helpful to the king in dealing with the Stuart cousins who had recently returned to the English throne. Renaudot would not be embarrassed by turning this way. That he did so, and found what he wanted, can be surmised from the position of the paragraph about the shipwreck, which is on page one of his copy, but at about the center of the material dictated to Dablon.[56]

If Jolliet's report was in Colbert's possession in 1674, it is almost certain that Dablon's "Relation de la decouverte de la Mer du Sud . . . Enuoyée de Quebec . . . le 1ᵉʳ Iour d'Aoust 1674" was in the hands of the French provincial this same year. To begin with, both documents tell the same story in the same words. Then, Dablon's is bound in one of the volumes of treasured manuscripts which Fr. Gabriel Brotier took to Rome in 1762. There is no logical hypothesis for supposing it was fabricated between 1674 and 1762. If an examination of the manuscript itself is made, its seventeenth-century origin becomes quite evident. The "Relation de la decouverte de la Mer du Sud . . ." is not a separate letter, as its title might suggest and as it has been called by several historians who have quoted it. Instead, it holds the position of a preface to the "Relation . . . les Années 1672–1673." Its last three lines are written on the top of the page whereon the first chapter of this annual narrative begins.[57] The linking together of the two communications on the same piece of paper leaves scant possibility for separating the time when they were written. However, before

56. BN, Mss.fr., n.a., 7491, 351–55. Grace L. Nute, *Caesars of the Wilderness, Médard Chouart Des Groseilliers and Pierre Esprit Radisson, 1618–1710* (New York, 1943), pp. 156–57 and 270, treats of Renaudot's friends at Court.

57. APF, Fonds Brotier 155 (Canada–1), 13. Thwaites, *JR*, LVIII, 90–109, prints this material as if it were a separate letter.

asserting that the two are contemporaneous, a word needs to be said which will make clear why the news item of 1674 is placed ahead of the "Relation . . . les Années 1672–1673."

It was in 1673 that, owing to *Creditae Nobis,* the contract between the Cramoisy press and the French provincial was discontinued, and the printing of the Jesuit Relations ceased. This relieved Dablon from the necessity of preparing data for a publication deadline. Enjoying his freedom, he may well have postponed, from day to day, the chore of editing the annual letter, until not enough days were left for its completion prior to the departure of the French fleet in the autumn. Once these ships were gone, about the end of October, there was no chance to send mail to Europe until the next year.[58] Jolliet had returned to Quebec by the summer of 1674 and the news value of his dictation took precedence over other events which were to go into the tardy "Relation . . . les Années 1672–1673," so the scribe was instructed to place it first. This conjecture is made stronger by a letter to the French provincial which Dablon sent on October 25, 1674. It recapitulates the activities of the previous twelve months, which would have been tautological had the "Relation . . . les Années 1673–1674" been sent in the same mail.[59] Actually, the next three Relations seem to have suffered a year's lag in the time of their completion, judging from the "Relation . . . les Années 1676 & 1677." It tells events beginning with the autumn of 1675, continuing through all of 1676 and ending with what hap-

58. [Pierre F.-X. de Charlevoix], *Journal of a Voyage to North America . . .* (London, 1761), I, 144, October 28, 1720, terminates his letter with haste because "the King's ship is just going to set sail, and the merchantmen are making ready to follow her, so that perhaps in three days time, there will not be so much as a single vessel of any sort in the road."

59. APF, Fonds Brotier 157 (Canada–3), pt. 1, 2–5v, Le P. Dablon a Mon R. P. (de Quebec 25 octobre 1674), is the letter and the "Relation . . . les Années 1673–1674" is in APF, Fonds Brotier 157 (Canada–3), pt. 2, 1–97.

pened in the spring of 1677. To include two years in one volume would not have been necessary unless the editor had fallen behind with previous issues, and, in 1677, employed this method of bringing his work up to date.[60] This leaves little fear in asserting that the "Relation de la decouverte de la Mer du Sud" was written on August 1, 1674, exactly according to the date it bears.

The dedicatory letter, with the signature "Joliet," which is inscribed on the three maps depicting details of his 1673 trip is undoubtedly of seventeenth-century origin. Jean Delanglez has established Jean-Baptiste Franquelin as draftsman for the map with the arms of Frontenac. He made a careful analysis of its penmanship in comparison with a twenty-five page "Memoir concerning the voyages which Franquelin, hydrographer of the king in Canada, has made both to Quebec and to Paris." All the mapmaker's peculiarities in writing show up in the memoir. They are also to be found in six other narratives by Franquelin and an autograph letter, now in the Bibliothèque Nationale, Paris, and used by Delanglez.[61]

The writing on the smaller map, with the same title as the one by Franquelin, has been compared, for the present study, with the calligraphy of de La Salle's European agent, abbé Claude Bernou, with the result that characteristics of his script were found to match the idiosyncracies in the descriptive wording of the chart. It was presumably made by him.[62] The map of the Mississippi Valley in the John Carter Brown Library is probably not quite so old as the other two and most certainly

60. "Relation . . . les Années 1676 & 1677 [*sic*]," APF, Fonds Brotier 160 (Canada–6).

61. Jean Delanglez, "Franquelin, Mapmaker," *M-A,* XXV (1943), 31, n. 8 and Jean Delanglez, "The Jolliet Lost Map of the Mississippi," *M-A,* XXVIII (1946), 91.

62. BN, Mss.fr., n.a., 7497, 9–325. The abbé calls de La Salle his employer, ibid., 7497, 108. See also, Jean Delanglez, "The Discovery of the Mississippi, Primary Sources," *M-A,* XXVII (1945), 226.

is not in Jolliet's script, which is available for comparison in his holograph journal of his trip to Labrador. However, this throws no doubt on the age of the original dedicatory letter which had already been written down by Franquelin and copied by Bernou, who were Jolliet's contemporaries.

CHAPTER 4

Chronicler
of the Discovery

THE antiquity of the Montreal and Chantilly Récits exclude
the possibility of their story having been the invention of a
modern author such as Father Martin. Father Dablon, who
was superior of the Canadian missions from 1671 to 1680,
would seem to have the natural right to authorship of the
Chantilly Récit because it is included in the yearly "Relation
. . . les Années 1677–1678," which he, as superior, had the
responsibility to edit. Then, the Montreal Récit, with identical
contents, could hardly be attributed to anyone else.[1] However
when Jolliet's canoe upset and spilled all the written accounts

1. See pp. 3–4 and 34 for a discussion of the superior's responsibility
in editing the Jesuit Relations. The pages devoted to the Récit begin on
the thirteenth page of the manuscript "Relation . . . les Années 1677–
1678." The first dozen pages are devoted to mission activities, see
APF, Fonds Brotier 159 (Canada–5), 13.

of the Mississippi exploration he was bringing to Quebec, a tantalizing question bubbled up from the wreck. If Dablon is chronicler of the discovery, who furnished him all the details he embodied in the first chapter of the Récit? Did he succeed in laying hands on a duplicate journal to edit, or did he depend on Jolliet's oral history, supplemented by his own missionary experience, in writing what he did? This is the next problem to be solved.

Thwaites pushes Dablon aside in his discussion of the authorship of "Chapitre j^{er}. Du premier Voyage qu'a fait Le P. Marquette Vers le nouveau Mexique et Comment s'en est forme le dessin. [Chapter One. Concerning the first voyage which Fr. Marquette made toward New Mexico and how the plan took shape.]." He was persuaded that the Montreal Récit told "the account of the first voyage (1673) in Marquette's handwriting." Therefore, the identical wording of the same story, which is found in the Chantilly Récit, would be a copy of the work of the missionary, rather than the narrative edited by his superior.[2] Thwaites presumes that Marquette had written a duplicate narrative of his adventures with Jolliet, and sent it to Dablon when he was apprised of the canoe accident. Thwaites was not unaware of the editorial procedure used in preparing copy for the annual Cramoisys, in which superiors of the Canadian missions were wont to select what they chose from their missionaries' letters and then to destroy the orignal material. Nevertheless, the importance of the discovery chronicled in the Récit and the presence in the same binding of Marquette's holograph journal of his second trip to the Illinois Indians supplied the occasion for Thwaites' thought that the

2. Thwaites, *JR*, LIX, 293, "Bibliographical Data." A comparison between Dablon's penmanship, see Thwaites, *JR*, XLVII, 268, and the script of the Récit makes clear that it was not written by his hand. Joseph P. Donnelly, *Jacques Marquette, S.J., 1637–1675* (Chicago, 1968), p. 281, agrees with Thwaites and defends Marquette as author of the Mississippi discovery, just as it is found in the Récit.

discoverer's personal account of the Mississippi might likewise have escaped destruction. Moreover, since Thwaites worked with longhand transcriptions of the Montreal documents, he did not make a study of their penmanship. Finally, his conclusion was probably influenced by the first notation on the title page. It says, "Marquette's Autograph Journal, 63 1673." On the original, the date 1673 seems to have been there before the other English words were added. Thumbing the pages of the manuscript itself makes clear that the person who wrote this caption intended to call attention to page 63, where begins Marquette's personal diary, written day-to-day as he returned south in 1674 to found the Conception mission. It was purely by chance that the directive was written so as to align with the figures 1673, which were already there. But to Thwaites, reading from the longhand transcription, the position of this "1673" seemed to be an integral part of a title. Since the pages which came after the date told of happenings within the year 1673, the preceding "63" might be viewed as a comment on the length of the journal devoted to the discovery of the Mississippi, so Thwaites saw nothing contradictory in his conclusion.[3] Had he been looking at the Montreal Récit itself, its calligraphy, which is identical for all three chapters, would have prevented his inference. The biographical part of the Récit tells of events which took place after Marquette's death. If his hand had written the narrative of his adventures with Jolliet, his fingers would have had to reach from the grave to complete the whole work. Thus from the original penmanship the decision must be that Marquette did not write any part of the Récit found in the Collège Sainte-Marie in Montreal.

The person who wrote "Marquette Autograph Journal 63" does not hint how he knew the journal of the second trip to the

3. Archives of the State Historical Society of Wisconsin, Madison, U.S., Mss. C., "R. G. Thwaites manuscripts," is the shelf reference for the longhand collection he gathered for his edition of *The Jesuit Relations and Allied Documents*.

Illinois Indians was a holograph specimen of the missionary's writing; probably he accepted Father Martin's evaluation, when in his translation of the O'Callaghan reprint he designated it "le journal autographe." Both may have recognized a striking difference in the script beginning with page 63. It was John G. Shea, when he printed the manuscript in his *Discovery and Exploration of the Mississippi Valley*, who first presented a basis for the truth of what Martin had said. Shea wrote that the Récit is in an unknown "very clear hand," while the map of the exploration is "in the handwriting of Father Marquette," as is the "letter begun but not ended by him . . . containing a journal of the voyage on which he died." [4] Then, he instanced a signed Marquette entry in the church annals of Boucherville as proof. The sacred character of such an ecclesiastical document and the care with which certifications of Indian baptisms had been guarded in Canada convinced him this could not be a forgery.[5] It is on the top of the first page of the church ledger, where one reads, "Je Jacques marquette de la compagnie de Iesus ay donné les ceremonies a marie fille de Victor Kiouentaoue et Antoinette de Miskouminich, & age de 2 mois et ondoyé a Saurel par monsieur morel prestre le parain Ignace Boucher et la marraine marie Boucher le 20 may 1668

4. John G. Shea, *Discovery and Exploration of the Mississippi Valley* (New York, 1852), p. lxxviii; or James Lenox and John G. Shea, eds., *Recit des Voyages et des Decouvertes de R. Père Marquette* (Albany, N.Y., 1855), *Avant-propos*, unn. p. Shea also expressed belief in the authenticity of the journal in his *The History of the Catholic Church in the United States* (New York, 1886–92), I, 317 and 319. He spoke of a "letter . . . containing a journal," because he was thinking of the annual letter missionaries had to send to the superior.

5. Extant annals in the venerable parishes along the St. Lawrence are listed in Ivanhöe Caron, "Inventaire des Documents concernant L'Eglise du Canada sous le régime Français," *RAPQ, 1939–1940*, pp. 155–353, and Henry P. Beers, *The French & British in the Old Northwest, a Bibliographical Guide to Archives and Manuscript Sources* (Detroit, 1964), pp. 55–59.

[I Jacques Marquette of the Company of Jesus have supplied the ceremonies for Marie daughter of Victor Kiouentaoue and Antoinette de Miskouminich, & 2 months old and privately baptized at Saurel (*sic*) by Monsieur Morel priest, the godfather Ignace Boucher and the Godmother Marie Boucher, the 20 May 1668]." [6] For a century, no one questioned Shea's evidence.

In 1951, the same Father Short who had offered difficulties about Marquette's ordination called attention to the nicety with which the discovery of the Boucherville register synchronized with the first publicity given Marquette's holograph journal of his second trip to the Illinois Indians and suggested that the register entry could have been forged to give authenticity to the latter.[7] He had visited Boucherville and thought he remembered that the ink of the missionary's writing looked "fresher" and was blue, while the rest of the ink had faded and turned brown from age. Furthermore, the title page bore the date "1669–1698." This meant to him that "Boucherville did not exist" when Marquette was supposed to have made his entry in 1668. Finally, because the same hand which made the notation seemed to have produced the script in the Marquette holograph journal, Short thought the latter was a fake. Since this holograph journal throws considerable light on the authorship of the Récit, these assertions must be discussed.

The village of Boucherville received its name from Pierre Boucher. He, like many another young Frenchman, had come to know Canada's great rivers, wide prairies, and deep forests

6. AMU, N. Amer., Fr. Reg., 19, "Livre des Registres," from Holy Family Church, Boucherville. The entry is printed in [Louis Lalande], *Une Vieille Seigneurie: Boucherville* (Montreal, 1890), p. 119, and Matthew A. Bernard, "La Signature du Pere Marquette," *Bulletin des Recherches Historiques,* Quebec, IV (1898), 286, with the error of substituting "l" wherever the original has long "s."

7. Joseph C. Short, *Reprint from the Sheboygan (Wis.) Press,* Thursday, February 15, 1951, AMU, N. Amer., Fr. Reg., 19. See Appendix I for Short's opinion of Marquette's ordination.

while traveling with Jesuits as a donné. Like few others of this sort he loved the new country and dreamed about its possibilities for becoming the site of peaceful farms where the poor of Europe might share in its bounty. By 1655, more than a decade after his first enthusiasm was aroused, Pierre had become governor of Three Rivers, but the fulfillment of his dream had not kept pace with his advancement. Actually, this was the period when the mother country was most neglectful of Canada. From south of Lake Ontario, the Iroquois Indians had come north, ruining the fur trade, the colony's most profitable export. Thereafter, France seemed to care little whether or not the Indian raids exterminated the colonists. In 1661, the desperate Canadians chose Pierre Boucher to lay their needs before Louis XIV and seek his aid. At Court, he spoke so eloquently of his homeland and placed such stress on its agricultural advantages that the monarch encouraged him to put his thoughts in writing. He did so and his *Histoire Veritable et Natvrelle . . . de la Novvelle France* had the desired effect. Soldiers were sent to quell the Indians; peasants came to farm the lands along the St. Lawrence.[8] In 1667, in the wake of the settlers, Boucher made his way westward. Having obtained a seigniory where the Sabrevoix River enters the St. Lawrence, in sight of Montreal, he built a palisade surrounding a manor house and opposite the latter, "he erected the first chapel of Boucherville." In the spring of 1668, he moved his family to the estate and began to translate his agricultural theory into practice.[9] The chapel he had built was not a parish church and

8. Seraphin Marion, *Un Pionnier Canadien: Pierre Boucher* (Quebec, 1927), pp. 80–82, eulogizes Boucher. Pierre's own book is Pierre Boucher, *Histoire Veritable et Natvrelle des Moevrs et Prodvctions du Pays de la Novvelle-France* (Paris, 1663; re-editée par G. Coffin, Montreal, 1882).

9. Lalande, *Boucherville*, p. 45. Archange Godbout, "Nos Ancêtres au XVII Siècle," *RAPQ, 1959–1960*, p. 300, cites Pierre-Georges Roy, ed., *Inventaire des Concessions en Fief Seigneurie Fois et Hommages et Aveux et Dénombrements Conservés aux Archives de la Province*

had no pastor until 1692.[10] This made Pierre Boucher responsible for maintaining a record of what went on within its walls.

On April 21, 1668, a band of Jesuits left Quebec to open the St. Xavier Mission at La Prairie just opposite Montreal. *Le Journal des Jésuites* records how in their company went, "Father Marquette, two men and a little lad to await there for the opportunity of going to the Ottawa country." [11] While Pierre Boucher was governor of the 153 people who lived in Three Rivers, Father Marquette had spent at least a year as his next-door neighbor.[12] Thus the occasion for making the

---

de Québec, 6 vols. (Beauceville, 1927–29), pp. 275 ff., for establishing 1667 as the year in which Boucher received his land grant. Cyprien Tanguay, *Dictionnaire Généalogique des Familles Canadiennes* (Montreal, 1871–90), I, 71, establishes the change of residence as completed on June 18, 1668, when Pierre's son, René Boucher, was baptized at Montreal.

10. Lalande, *Boucherville,* p. 45; Fr. Rodolphe Guybert de La Saudtays was the first pastor.

11. C. H. Laverdière and H. R. Casgrain, eds., *Le Journal des Jésuites Publié d'après le Manuscrit Original Conservé aux Archives du Séminaire de Québec* (Quebec, 1871), p. 360; Thwaites, *JR,* LI, 149. ARSJ, Franc. 23, 245, Catalogus Provinciae Franciae, 1668 Exeunte, lists Marquette's assignment: "Jn Mission. S. Spiritu Outaou P. Claudius Allouez Supr. P. Ludovicus Nicolas P. Jacobus Marquette Mission. Lud. Boesme omniu' offic. admin. [In the mission of the Holy Spirit for the Ottawa, Fr. Claude Allouez, Superior, Fr. Louis Nicolas, Fr. Jacques Marquette, Missionaries. Louis Boême has care of all offices]."

12. Grace L. Nute, *Caesars of the Wilderness* (New York, 1943), pp. 18 and 14, plan of Three Rivers and Cap de la Madeleine links Boucher's residences to those of the Jesuits. BN, collection Moreau, 842, 37v, "Le P. Marquette au P. Pupin (cap de la Magdelaine [*sic*], le 4 aoust, 1667)," Father Marquette addressed a letter to Father Pupin, which tells of his being there to study Indian language under Father Druillettes. The estimate of the population is in Benjamin Sulté, "Pierre Boucher et son livre," *Mémories de la Société Royale du Canada,* II (s. 2, 1896), 101.

first entry in the registry is accounted for. Next, the memoran-
dum is not of a baptism. It is of supplying "the ceremonies."
This technical expression signifies the fulfillment of a requirement in ecclesiastical law dealing with people who have been
hurriedly baptized in danger of death. If they outlive the
emergency, they are obliged to call on a priest and have him
supply those parts of the baptismal ritual which had been
omitted; hence, the years "1669–1698" may include all the
baptisms in the book, without casting doubt on Marquette's
visit to Boucherville in 1668 or what he did then. Moreover
after inspecting the "Livre des Registres," a member of the
Department of History from the Jesuit college in Montreal
reported: a single "N.B.," calling attention to some misplaced
entries and signed "PAL. ptre. vic." is "the only one on the
whole page written in blue ink." He adds, "I saw it and am
sure of the affirmation." Then, by consulting *Le Canada Ec-
clesiastique,* he was able to assert that the only priest ever at
Boucherville whose initials were "PAL" was Père Paul Aimé
Lafortune, who was vicar there from 1920 to 1924. This leaves
no mystery in finding his writing less faded than the rest.[13]
Finally, the identification of the godparents is notable. They
were two of Boucher's children, Ignace and Marie. The latter
was the wife of René Gaultier.[14] On the second page of the
Register, where her name appears again, one reads, "Marie
Ursule Boucher wife of Sr Rene Gaultier de Varrennes governor of Three Rivers." A forger would surely have copied
this formula. Father Marquette, who was writing his first certi-
fication in a blank book, simply gave her maiden name as he

13. AMU, N. Amer., Fr. Reg., 19, Giguere to Hamilton, December
4, 1954.
14. Archives du Séminaire des Missions Étrangères, Quebec,
Polygraphie VIII, no. 56, 26 septembre 1667 (with pages unnumbered
but marriages in chronological order); Tanguay, *Dictionnaire Généalogique,* I, 71.

had known it while living next door, "the godmother Marie Boucher." [15]

Since the days of Shea, additional proof has come to the surface which verifies his confidence in assigning the authorship of the Illinois journal to Marquette. In the Fonds Brotier, there is a seventeenth-century copy of a personal letter from Father Cholenec to Father de Fontenay "from the residence of St. Francis Xavier this 10th october 1675." [16] Cholenec spent his life at this mission. He was one of the old missionaries with whom Charlevoix conversed when he visited the place in 1721. Among his Indian neophytes was Katherine Tekakwitha, whose cause for canonization is being considered by the Congregation of Rites in Rome. He wrote a biography of her in 1695–96, which has been carefully scrutinized for evidence and has won the appreciation of scholars for its historical accuracy and objectivity.[17] His letter to Father de Fontenay tells of Father Marquette's death as it had been described by two donnés who were with the priest-explorer. It says they were bringing the news to Quebec from the Ottawa Mission where they returned the same summer, "I saw them,

15. J. B. A. Ferland, *Course d'Histoire du Canada* (Quebec, 1861–65), II, 7, renders intelligible the custom encouraging early marriages in seventeenth-century Canada. In 1668, Marie was only 12 years old.

16. APF, Fonds Brotier 166 (Canada–12), no. 4, 26–27v. This is reprinted in Camille de Rochemonteix, *Les Jésuites et la Nouvelle-France* (Paris, 1895–96), III, 606–612. ARSJ, Franc. 23, 323, Catalogus Provinciae Franciae, 1673 Exeunte, assigns Cholenec and Fontenay together as among the Jesuits ordained in 1673. Ibid., p. 337, Catalogus Provinciae Franciae, 1674 Exeunte, assigns Cholenec to the mission.

17. F. Antonelli, O.F.M., relator, *The POSITIO of the Historical Section of the Sacred Congregation of Rites on the Introduction of the Cause . . . of the Servant of God Katherine Tekakwitha . . .* (New York, 1940), Doc. XII, pp. 341–79. See above, ch. 2, n. 14–n. 15, for Charlevoix.

here, going and coming." [18] These companions of Marquette told Cholenec that while they wintered on the Chicago River, the missionary made a spiritual retreat, "the Exercises of St. Ignatius. After that he passed the rest of the time writing the memoirs of his voyages." [19] The holograph journal in the archives of the Collège Sainte-Marie, which Martin and Shea identified as being in the handwriting of Father Marquette, chronicles the events from the autumn of 1674 to the spring of 1675, which are the months when the donnés and the priest lived together. That this is the memoir which they watched him write finds proof from the recent uncovering of several letters to the general of the Society of Jesus, written by Marquette shortly before he came to America, and forgotten until they were found in the Roman archives more than eighty years after Father Martin publicized Marquette's holograph journal, which he had received from the nuns of the Hôtel Dieu.[20]

The ordinary method of tracing "handwriting back to its producer" is known as the science of bibliotics. In determining the identity of the hand which wrote several manuscripts, it pays attention to: (1) margins; (2) slant of lines; (3) grouping of letters in individual words, i.e., which letters are always joined, which are separated from those before and after; (4) the employment or omission of initial upstrokes and the terminal tails on words; (5) characteristic letters, e.g., the width and length of loops in "l," "h," "g"; (6) the dot over "i" and the cross on "t," which are apt to be omitted or employed with habitual similarity.[21] Every writer acquires a style with regard

18. APF, Fonds Brotier 166 (Canada–12), no. 4, 26.

19. Ibid., no. 4, 26v.

20. Gilbert J. Garraghan, "Some Newly Discovered Marquette and La Salle Letters," *Archivum Historicum Societatis Jesu,* Rome, IV (1935), 268–69, tells how he found these letters in 1935, and on 284–86 reproduces them from Fondo Gesuitico Societatis Jesu, Rome, Indipetae, Busta 26 [changed recently to "Indipetae 757"], no. 126 and no. 156.

21. Gilbert J. Garraghan, *A Guide to Historical Method* (New

to these things. Therefore, sick though Marquette was and in primitively furnished winter quarters when he wrote the journal, there was need only for a pen, some paper, and a surface to write on and the characteristic traits of his handwriting would be revealed.

In the Marquette letters penned before he came to America, his margins on the left side of the page are retained with remarkable evenness. He extends his script close to the right edge of the paper. His lines are well spaced and slant neither up nor down. The tails of final letters point along in the direction of the writing. Certain unvarying peculiarities appear in characteristic letters. His final "t" lacks a tail; it is crossed and his "i" is dotted with exceptional but consistent precision. His letters "p," "q," "r," and "s" take shapes which set them apart from the ordinary. All these things are identical in the hand which wrote the holograph journal.

Steck, in his *Marquette Legends,* said that graphologists had told him that the identity of ink and the scratches produced by the pressure of the pen on the paper were important in proving the absence of forgery in manuscripts with similar calligraphy; hence, he objected to a decision about authorship depending alone on collated idiosyncrasies in handwriting.[22] In the present instance, this objection is invalid because the Marquette letters to the general of the Society of Jesus were not accessible to a nineteenth-century forger and yet the sum of bibliotical likenesses in them and in the holograph journal is too great to be attributed to chance alone. The same may be said of the map of the Mississippi River which Father Martin received from the nuns of the Hôtel Dieu and described as coming from Father Marquette's pen. To the present, no other

---

York, 1948), p. 180, enumerates these six points of bibliotics as the most commonly used by historical researchers.

22. Francis B. Steck, *Marquette Legends,* ed. August Reyling (New York, 1960), pp. 166–67.

document in his script and concerned with the missionary's Canadian experiences has been found.

Thwaites dismissed Dablon as chronicler of the Mississippi exploration only because he believed the first chapter of the Montreal Récit to be in Marquette's hand. When Steck criticized the Marquette documents, he dismissed Marquette and chose Jolliet as the chronicler for two reasons. In the dedicatory letter, inscribed on the three maps of the Mississippi which the present work has traced to Franquelin, Bernou, and a nameless cartographer of more recent date, Jolliet uses the singular, "mon journal," when speaking of the narrative he lost in his wreck. Steck believes this makes Jolliet the sole person to have kept a diary of the trip. Then, Steck calls attention to Frontenac's letter to Colbert, dated November 14, 1674, which announces to the minister that a short account of the discovery is being brought to him by Barrois. This letter goes on to promise that a duplicate of Jolliet's longer account will be forthcoming later, as soon as it can be obtained from the Jesuits at the Sault in whose care Jolliet had left it. Of course there was ample time for Jolliet's duplicate to arrive in Quebec before the Récit was finished, in 1678, and so Steck thinks it became the narrative of the Mississippi exploration found in the original document.

Before investigating Steck's conjecture, it must be made clear that despite what historians have said in the past, it can now be shown that there is no holograph journal or any other holograph narrative of Jolliet's Mississippi adventure coming from his pen known to exist in the depositories of Canada or of any other country.

A letter dated "Quebec le 10 octobre 1674," addressed to a nameless "Monseigneur" and signed "Joliet," which is in the archives of Saint-Sulpice, Paris, has been advanced as being in his handwriting.[23] Undoubtedly, the original was sent to

23. Archives du Séminaire de Saint-Sulpice, Paris, Doc. pour Servir a l'Histoire de l'Eglise du Canada, I, pt. 1, 12.

Bishop François de Laval-Montigni, who was in the French capital that year.[24] Jolliet, who as a boy had studied in Quebec for the priesthood, knew the bishop well. After some years as a seminarian, he decided the clerical state was not his calling. His friend, the prelate, approved his decision and followed his lay career with interest and financial aid. While in Quebec in the summer of 1671, Jolliet made his way to the episcopal chancery to repay a loan.[25] He found the bishop anxious over an incident which had occurred at Sault Sainte-Marie. His majesty's administration, with its Gallican tinge, had sent a representative there to take possession of the West. It was not clear just what might happen to ecclesiastical jurisdiction if the secular authority became more active on the frontier. Because of his uncertainty, Laval had decided to go to Europe to secure a more precise definition of his status in respect to the king and the pope. Knowing how Court business dragged on, he may well have asked Jolliet to send him a note if the discovery took place during his absence.[26] When, in the summer of 1674, Jolliet did bring the good news to Quebec, and found Laval still in Paris, it is probable that the original letter of October 10 was sent to him. Étienne Faillon and Henry Harrisse think this is the manuscript now in the Sulpician ar-

24. Étienne M. Faillon, *Histoire de la Colonie Française en Canada* (Montreal, 1865–66), III, 314, suggested that the Monseigneur to whom the letter is written was Frontenac, but *Jugements et Deliberations du Conseil Souverain de la Nouvelle France, 1663–1704 et du Conseil Superieur, 1705–1716* (Quebec, 1885–91), I, 816, prove there was no need for Jolliet to write Frontenac since both men were in Quebec on October 10, 1674.

25. Amedée Gosselin, "Jean Jolliet et ses enfants," *Proceedings and Transactions of the Royal Society of Canada,* XIV (s. 3, sec. 1, 1921), 71, verifies this visit from Jolliet, citing vouchers receipted by Laval to him, on September 12, 1671.

26. August H. Gosselin, *Vie de Mgr. De Laval Premier Évêque de Québec et Apôtre du Canada, 1622–1708* (Quebec, 1890), I, 642–48.

chives.[27] Nothing but a very superficial scrutiny of the paper could admit of such a conclusion. The letter lacks all similarity to the known Jolliet holographs. It has its initial lines midway on a page which it shares with the last sentences of a reproduction of the young explorer's dictation about his discovery, which he made to Dablon on August 1, 1674. The sender's name is spelled with a single "l" contrary to Louis' practice. A copyist's mark "./." ends each paragraph.[28]

The events of the year 1684, when M. Louis Tronson was superior of Saint-Sulpice, offer a cause sufficient for occasioning him to acquire reproductions of the Jolliet notices of his discovery, which were in Paris. M. de La Salle had contacted the Sulpicians in 1684 with a request for chaplains to sail on a return trip to Louisiana via the Gulf of Mexico.[29] Tronson was not satisfied with de La Salle's rehearsal of details connected with his former explorations. In a letter to abbé François de Belmont, he observed, "That which the two men who accompanied him have reported of it to you does not agree with that which he himself told me about the same."[30] In

27. Faillon, *Histoire du Canada,* III, 314 and Henry Harrisse, *Notes pour Servir à l'Histoire, à la Bibliographie et à la Cartographie de la Nouvelle-France et des Pays Adjacents, 1545–1700* (Paris, 1872), p. 323.

28. Archives du Séminaire de Saint-Sulpice, Paris, Doc. pour l'Hist. du Canada, I, pt. 1, 1–12. Ernest Gagnon, " 'Jolliet' ou 'Joliet'?" *Bulletin des Recherches Historiques,* Quebec, XII (1906), 309–310, proves the spelling. Examples of Jolliet signatures are listed in "Calendar of Manuscripts in Archives of the Chicago Historical Society," *Report Concerning the Canadian Archives, 1905* (Ottawa, 1906), pp. xxxii–xlvii. For his handwriting see ASH, 5, no. 15, 9ª.

29. [Chrestien Le Clercq], *First Establishment of the Faith in New France by Father Christian Le Clercq, Recollect Missionary, Now First Translated with Notes,* ed. and tr., John G. Shea (New York, 1881), II, 203. De La Salle arrived at La Rochelle on December 23, 1683; hence, he could hardly have been in Paris before 1684.

30. Margry, *Découv. et Étab.,* II, 355, "Extrait d'une lettre de l'abbé Tronson à l'abbé Belmont (Paris, n.d.)," also Jean Delanglez, *Some La Salle Journeys* (Chicago, 1938), p. 93.

search for better knowledge of the Mississippi Valley, he had the option of seeking it from the Jesuit provincial, who received the annual letters from Canada, or from Fr. Jean Dudouyt, who was the Parisian agent for the metropolitan of Quebec, Bishop Laval.[31] The presence, in the archives of Saint-Sulpice of a copy of Jolliet's dictation made to Dablon on August 1, 1674, and of the letter to "Monseigneur," from "Quebec le 10 octobre 1674," is an indication that Tronson availed himself of both opportunities. Both were easy to take advantage of in the seventeenth century, but the whereabouts of the Laval letter is no longer known.

It was Francis Parkman who thought that the dedicatory letter on the two maps in the library of the Service Hydrographique, Paris, which depict Jolliet's discovery and call attention to it by the long title beginning "Carte de la decouuerte du Sʳ Jolliet . . .," were holographs by him.[32] The same synopsis of the discovery, on the chart in the John Carter Brown library, was proposed as a Jolliet autograph by Gabriel Gravier when he found it in the possession of a Paris book dealer in 1880.[33] His belief was approved by Thwaites, Ernest Gagnon, Nellis Crouse, and, most recently, by Sara Tucker.[34] These historians arrived at their conclusion before the art of photocopying had facilitated the bibliotic comparison of what is on the maps and what Jolliet's penmanship looked like. The dissimilarities in

31. *Report Concerning the Canadian Archives, 1885* (Ottawa, 1886), p. cxx, a letter of Father Dudouyt identified him as Laval's Agent.

32. Francis Parkman, *La Salle and the Discovery of the Great West* (Boston, 1898), pp. 480–81, 479–80, n. 7.

33. Gabriel Gravier, *Etude sur Une Carte Inconnue, la Première Dressée par Louis Joliet en 1674, après Son Exploration du Mississippi avec le P. Jacques Marquette en 1673* (Paris, 1880), frontispiece.

34. Thwaites, *JR*, LIX, 89; Ernest Gagnon, *Louis Jolliet* (2nd ed., Montreal, 1913), p. 74; Nellis Crouse, *Contributions of the Canadian Jesuits to the Geographical Knowledge of New France, 1632–1675* (Ithaca, N.Y., 1924), p. 114; and Sara J. Tucker, *Indian Villages of the Illinois Country, pt. 1, Atlas* (Springfield, Ill., 1942), pl. IV.

the original handwritings are striking enough to prove that
Jolliet did not pen what is on the maps.[35] If the original dedicatory letter exists, it has evaded the search of scholars.[36] The one
other seventeenth-century narrative of the Mississippi exploration which might be a Jolliet holograph is "Relation de La
descouverte . . ." in the Archives Nationales, Paris, but it fails
the bibliotic test.[37]

In brief, Steck's conjecture about the chronicler of the
Mississippi exploration is this: Dablon wrote the first chapter
of the Récit from Jolliet's duplicate journal, editing it "in such
a way as to create the impression that Marquette had written
it," and it may be presumed that, thereupon, he destroyed the
Jolliet copy without ever showing it to Frontenac.[38] To evaluate this hypothesis, three things must be considered: (1) the
contingency by which Jolliet's journal might have come into
Dablon's hands; (2) the likelihood of his using it dishonestly;
and (3) the odds for and against his destruction of property
belonging to the governor.

In the autumn of 1674, when Frontenac told Colbert why
Barrois would only bring him Jolliet's digest of the events of
the 1673 expedition, the exact words of his letter were: "je
vous envoye par mon sécretaire la carte qu'il [Jolliet] en a faite
et les remarques dont il s'est pu souvenir, ayant perdu tous ses
mémoires et ses journaux dans la naufrage qu'il fit à la vue de
Montreál [By my secretary (Barrois), I am sending the map
which he (Jolliet) made of it and the observations which he
was able to recall, since he lost all his memoirs and his journals
when he was shipwrecked and almost drowned in sight of

35. See above, ch. 3, n. 61–n. 62.
36. Jean Delanglez, "The Jolliet Lost Map of the Mississippi,"
M-A, XXVII (1946), 67–144, made the investigation which justifies
this conclusion.
37. ASH, 5, no. 16, 2.
38. Steck, *Marquette Legends*, pp. 86 and 99. The attitude of
Jesuit editors toward original letters was mentioned above, ch. 3, n. 14.

Montreal]."[39] Then the governor's letter goes on to say, "il avait laissé dan le lac Supérieur, au Sault Ste-Marie, chez les pères, des copies de ses journaux [he left with the (Jesuit) fathers of Sault Ste. Marie on Lake Superior copies of his journals]," and the digest itself promises full details "d'une descouuert sy considerable [of a very considerable discovery]," as soon as the duplicate of the lost "relation dont Le pere Marquette garde une Copie [of which Father Marquette retains a copy]" can be secured.[40] In like manner, the Relation sent by Dablon this year tells of Jolliet's mishap, without too much sorrow, because of the expectation of having before long, "vne pleine relation, Lepere Marquette ayant gardé vne Copie de celle qui a esté perdue [full relation, Father Marquette having kept a copy of the one which was lost]."[41] This mutual dependence on Father Marquette for the complete story of the exploration, plus the identical wording in what is found in Dablon's "Relation . . . les Années 1672–1673" and in Frontenac's short report, "Relation de La descouverte . . . ," have confused scholars in their study of the first chapter of the Récit.[42] The signs of cooperation have been assumed to bespeak teamwork between the governor and the superior in their efforts to bring all incidents of the discovery to their European audience. This supposition is what underlies Steck's conjecture. If the two men were sharing their knowledge, it would be plausible for the priest to request the desired Jolliet duplicate from his Jesuit confrères. Once it was in his hands, he might have practiced the deceit imputed to him. In reality there was no partnership between the superior and governor as they set

39. *RAPQ, 1926–1927,* p. 77, "Lettre du Gouverneur . . . au ministre (14 novembre 1674)."
40. ASH, 5, no. 16, 2.
41. APF, Fonds Brotier 155 (Canada–1), 12.
42. Jean Delanglez, "The 1674 Account of the Discovery of the Mississippi," *M-A,* XXVI (1944), 317–24, prints the Frontenac and Dablon version of these manuscripts for comparison.

out, in the late summer of 1674, to repair the loss of what
Frontenac called Jolliet's "memoirs" and "journals."

It was not just the frigid winter of 1674–75 which im-
mobilized communications between the master of the château
Saint-Louis and the rector of the Collège des Jésuites. The
temperature had begun to fall some years before, when the
Gallican breeze began to ruffle the fathers' cassocks. Dedicated
to the defence of papal authority, they did not like the ecclesiastical pretensions of those who represented the French Court.[43]
Sensing resistance to his dominion over church affairs, Louis
XIV took subtle action for maintaining his control. In 1670,
Recollect missionaries, belonging to a branch of the Order
founded by St. Francis of Assisi and noted for their strict poverty, were returned to Canada. They had been there while
Samuel de Champlain was still living, but had been excluded
by Richelieu owing to his desire to eliminate from the annual
budget the alms necessary for their support.[44] In 1672, when
Frontenac first became governor, he was instructed to promote
the Franciscans in the hope of neutralizing the anti-Gallican
position of the Jesuits.[45]

The new master of the Château, who was at least a Jan-

43. Thomas Chapais, *Jean Talon Intendant de la Nouvelle France,
1665–1672* (Quebec, 1904), pp. 297–300.

44. Jean Delanglez, *Frontenac and the Jesuits* (Chicago, 1939),
pp. 35–65, 104–5.

45. *RAPQ, 1926–1927*, pp. 1–6, has Frontenac's instructions.
Francis Parkman, *Count Frontenac and New France under Louis XIV*
(Boston, 1898), pp. 450–52, being aware of the "Chinese Rites"
quarrel, imagined King Louis was eager to transplant the feud to
Canada. François de Belmont, *Histoire du Canada (Collection de
Mémoires et Relations sur l'Histoire Ancienne du Canada d'après des
Manuscrits Recemment Obtenus des Archives et Bureaux Publics en
France Publiée sous la Direction de la Société Litteraire et Historique
de Québec* (Quebec, 1840), p. 13, reprints the opinion of the Sulpician
who was superior at Montreal from 1713–24. He lived close to the
event and assigns reasons similar to those in the present study for the
return of the Franciscans.

senist fellow traveler, was pleased to interpret his orders as an encouragement to adopt the style of *The Augustinus* in what he had to say of the inmates of the Collège.[46] To Jansenius' devotees, whatever a Jesuit did was motivated either by the quest for wealth or the pursuit of power. Their contemporary leader, Arnauld, was to write a half dozen volumes under the general title *Morale Pratique des Jesuites,* which exploit this theme. When he dwells on the successful missions of the Order in Paraguay, he says, "if the Jesuits have such magnificent temples in these remote lands, although they have neither gold nor silver nor other metal there, and no other commerce is carried on except in the herb, which is known as coming from Paraguay [Ilex paraguayensis, commonly called mate or Paraguay tea], I do not see how these so magnificent churches can be built." His friend Renaudot, who had said nothing about the Mississippi discovery in his newspaper, *Gazette de France,* has left in his personal papers the opinion that the Canadian Jesuits had gained such control over the bishop of Quebec as to render him *leur créature.*[47] Frontenac had just arrived in Canada, when he wrote a memorial to Colbert containing standard, Jansenist accusations. The Jesuits "think more of converting the beaver, than of souls, because most of their missions are a pure farce." In 1673, he tells the

46. Ludwig F. von Pastor, *History of the Popes* (London, 1891–1952), XXX, 219, says Jansenism was, just then, a fad in the French salons, where Frontenac's wife was most popular. His devotion to her can explain the effect produced, W. J. Eccles, *Frontenac, the Courtier Governor* (Toronto, 1959), pp. 29, 71, n. 89; Ernest Maynard, "M. et Madame de Frontenac," *Bulletin des Recherches Historiques,* Quebec, VIII (1902), 97–110, 129–36.

47. Antoine Arnauld, *Morale Pratique des Jesuites,* 8 vols. (Cologne, 1669–95), V, 190. These are the date and place of publication for the first edition; the volume used lacked the title page, but seemed to conform to the description of this edition. Renaudot's evaluation is among his papers, Archives Nationales, Paris, K. 1232, no. 1, 1–98.

Minister, "it is said . . . that Msgr. the Bishop of Pétrée [Laval was only vicar of Quebec with title "Bishop of Pétrée" at this time] . . . having taken the same vows to the general of the Jesuits, they are all together the same except some of them wear the Roman collar and others do not do so [seventeenth-century Jesuits wore a collar open in front]."[48] It is unrealistic to imagine the man who wrote so disapprovingly of the missionaries was at the same time cooperating with their superior in friendly confidence.[49] So too, it is fanciful to imagine a governor like Frontenac turning to Father Dablon as if in need of his help. It is not to be presumed that the man who required the Sovereign Council to address him as *"hault et puissant Seigneur"* ("high and mighty lord") and who made the Sunday congregation wait outside until he arrived and led it into the cathedral, would yield his prerogative to anyone, when it came to demanding Jolliet's official copy from "the fathers of Sault Sainte-Marie on Lake Superior."[50] A final proof of no rapport between himself and Dablon arises from his very presumption that Father Marquette was at the mission of Sault Sainte-Marie. Only because he kept aloof from the Collège, was he ignorant of what its rector knew: Father Marquette had

48. *RAPQ, 1926–1927*, p. 20, "Lettre du Gouverneur . . . au Ministre (2 novembre 1672)" and ibid., p. 31, "Lettre du Gouverneur . . . au Ministre (13 novembre 1673)." The charge of illicit trade by the Jesuits has been refuted repeatedly, see Rochemonteix, *Les Jésuites et la Nouvelle-France*, I, 340–62; Patrick J. Lomasney, "The Canadian Jesuits and the Fur Trade," *M-A*, XV (1933), 139–50 and Jean Delanglez, *Frontenac and the Jesuits* (Chicago, 1939), pp. 133–65.

49. Frontenac died unreconciled to the Jesuits and suspected of Jansenism, Archives du Séminaire des Étrangères, Quebec, Viger, *Ma Saberdache Rouge*, F, 197–247, "Oraison Funèbre du Comte de Frontenac 1698, MS. suivie de Remarques critiques par un anonyme &c."

50. *Jugements du Conseil Souverain*, I, 689, and for the attitude toward the Sunday congregation, *RAPQ, 1926–1927*, pp. 113–16.

stopped at Green Bay, in the summer of 1673, and was still there.[51]

Dablon, on his part, was too sensible to intrude himself into official business of the Château without an invitation. Even Frontenac called him "fort sage et prudent." In 1670, François Le Mercier, suggesting him to General Paul Oliva for superior of the missions, chose the same quality as worthy of special attention; and Bishop Jean Baptiste de St. Vallier, Laval's successor in the see of Quebec, spoke of this Jesuit with particular esteem, in his 1688 *Etat Present de l'Église . . . dans la Nouvelle France*.[52] Such a man, aware of the governor's hostility, certainly would not chase after trouble by conniving with the fathers out on Lake Superior to divert Jolliet's duplicate in his direction instead of letting it return to Quebec through the proper channel. With his missionaries under criticism, it was his duty to avoid any tampering which could turn the false charges into fact. With the lack of collaboration substantiated, the similarity between the short report to Colbert and the intro-

51. APF, Fonds Brotier 157 (Canada–3), pt. 1, 3, "Mon R. P. de Quebec le 25 octob 1674." "Nous auons chez les Ontavuak . . . 3 maisons fixes . . . l'une est dans la baye des puants qui est la mission de St francois Xauier ou sont le P Alloues ce St et veritable missionnaire, le P Marquette dont ie uiens de de [*sic*] parler, le P Louis André qui fait de grands fruicts . . . [Among the Ottawa we have . . . 3 permanent residences . . . one is in the Bay of the Stinkers (Green Bay), which is the site of the Mission of St. Francis Xavier, where are stationed that holy and true missionary Fr. Allouez, Fr. Marquette of whom I was just speaking, Fr. Louis André who is making a vast harvest of souls . . .]."

52. *RAPQ, 1926–1927*, p. 73, "Lettre du Gouverneur . . . au Ministre (14 novembre 1674)"; ARSJ, Gal. 110, pt. 1, 54v, "Lettre du P. Le Mercier . . . au P. Oliva (Quebec, 1670)." [Jean Baptiste St. Vallier], M. l'Évêque de Québec, *Estat Present de l'Église et de la Colonie Françoise dans la Nouvelle France* (Paris, 1688), p. 16. Proof that Dablon was above criticism is offered by Jean Delanglez, "Claude Dablon, S.J., 1619–1697," *M-A*, XXVI (1944), 91–110.

duction to the "Relation . . . les Années 1672–1673," remains to be accounted for.

In the fall of 1674, the primary purpose for Frontenac's memorial to Colbert was not the description of new discoveries. He was refuting, as adroitly as possible, charges of ineptitude in office leveled against him by the minister. His defense covered many pages. A few lines sufficed to tell of Jolliet. They come at the very end of this missive which is dated November 14, so they must have been written just when the St. Lawrence was likely to freeze tight. Because the king's ships had to be at sea before this happened, there was little time left for new interviews with the discoverer.[53] On the other hand, Frontenac could be quite sure that there was a chapter about the discovery in the Relation which Dablon had intrusted to the mail. No one could stop the governor if he made up his mind to see what was said there. And his having taken a look at it is not a groundless supposition. King Louis, in his April 1675, answer to Frontenac's report, expressed his suspicion that the governor was taking advantage of his official position to censor the Jesuits' mail. He wrote, "it is said . . . that you have meddled with their [the clergymen's] letters."[54] Such a charge renders plausible the conjecture that under pressure such as he experienced in November, 1674, Frontenac had resorted to the expedient of having a copy made of the introduction to the "Relation . . . les Années 1672–1673" and sending it to the Court for his own report, under the title "Relation de La descouverte des plusieurs pays . . . 1673."

53. *RAPQ, 1926–1927,* pp. 55–60, "Lettre du Ministre . . . au Gouverneur (17 mai 1674)," censured the governor's bungling, who replied, ibid., pp. 65–78, "Lettre du Gouverneur . . . au Ministre (14 novembre 1674)." This year the St. Lawrence seems to have remained open until the first week in December, see *Jugements du Conseil Souverain,* I, 884. Such uncertain weather could not delay the departure of the ships.

54. *RAPQ, 1926–1927,* p. 82, "Lettre du Roi au Gouverneur . . . (22 avril 1675)."

Although in the fall of 1674, Father Marquette was not at Sault Sainte-Marie where Frontenac had thought him to be, there is every reason to believe that Jolliet's duplicate journal had been left at this mission. To begin with, the Sault had been his home, with only one break, for the five years preceding this date. In 1668, Louis Jolliet, after trying the seminary and taking a trip to Europe, decided on the career of a fur trader.[55] This same year, Jean Baptiste Talon, intendant of New France, commissioned Adrien Jolliet, Louis' brother, and Jean Péré "to go and find out whether the copper mine which is beyond Lake Ontario . . . is rich and easy to exploit and whether the ore can be brought here [to Quebec] with facility."[56] Next spring M. René de Galinée and M. François Dollier, Sulpician missionaries undertaking the exploration of the country below Lake Ontario, saw Adrien's company take off for the West. The journal of the religious expedition has come down to the present. On September 24, 1669, it says, their group arrived at an Indian village called "Tinaoütoüa," which was in the vicinity of Niagara Falls. Here, close to the site of present-day Westover, Ontario, they found a Frenchman. The diarist continues, this man, "who had arrived the day before, was the one named Jolliet who left Montreal a little before us with a fleet of 4 canoes loaded with goods for the Ottawa." This is the first announcement of Adrien's success in fulfilling his part of Talon's commission to investigate an easier way than the Ottawa River for the journey to and from the West. He is the first white man known to have traveled the Great Lakes route from Sault Sainte-Marie.[57] When he said good-bye to

55. Amedée Gosselin, "Jean Jolliet et ses enfants," *Proceedings and Transactions of the Royal Society of Canada,* XIV (S.3, sec. 1), 70.

56. Margry, *Découv. et Étab.,* I, 81, "Lettre du M. Patoulet [writing for Talon, who went to France in November, 1668] . . . au Ministre (11 novembre, 1669)."

57. BN, Mss.fr., n.a., 7485, 15, "Ce qui s'est passé de plus remarquable dans le voyage de Mrs. D'Ollier [*sic*] et Galinée"; transcribed [de Bérhant de Galinée], *Exploration of the Great Lakes,*

Galinée and Dollier and pushed his canoe over the horizon, he might as well have fallen off the world on the other side. He never again beached his boat where civilized men recorded his arrival. On the first day of the following spring, Jeanne Dodier, Adrien's wife, was officially recognized as a widow.[58]

In 1674, when Louis Jolliet returned to lower Canada after the exploration of the Mississippi, Jeanne had married Maturin Normandin dit Beau Soleil and was living in Montreal. That same year, when Jolliet visited Jeanne shortly after his wreck in the nearby St. Louis Rapids, Beau Soleil opened a friendly legal process to make certain his wife would receive the late Adrien's share of the profits derived from "The Old Association and Corporation composed of the said Sieur Adrien Jolliet deceased, & the said Sieur Louis Jolliet and Associates."[59] The only "Old Association" which could have included Adrien and Louis was the one which Galinée saw putting out for the West in 1669. Before then, Louis was not

---

1669–1670 *by Dollier de Casson and de Bréhant de Galinée, Galinée's Narrative and Map with an English Version, Including All the Map Legends,* ed. and tr., James H. Coyne, *Ontario Historical Society Papers and Records,* IV, pt. I (1903), 15 and 45. Jean Delanglez, "Louis Jolliet, Early Years, 1645," *M-A,* XXVII (1945), 9–15, upholds Adrien's discovery of a Great Lakes route. Louise P. Kellogg, *Early Narratives of the Northwest, 1634–1699* (New York, 1917), pp. 167–209, reprints Coyne.

58. Jean Delanglez, *Life and Voyages of Louis Jolliet, 1645–1700* (Chicago, 1948), pp. 11–12, n. 50 and n. 52, quotes Archives judiciaires, Three Rivers, where a registry by Jean Cusson, March 22, 1670, calls Jeanne Dodier "la veuve de feu Sr. Adrien Jolliet."

59. Archives of the Chicago Historical Society, Schmidt Collection, I, 53, "Pretantions que le Sieur Beau Soleil a Contre Monsieur Ioliet tant pour luy que p^r La Vefue de feu Sieur Ioliet [Adrien] a present son Espouse." Delanglez, "Louis Jolliet, Early Years," p. 19, n. 73, speaks of this summons, which he prints in full, ibid., pp. 28–29, as in the "Gunther Collection" of the Chicago Historical Society. Both the Schmidt and the Gunther collections are in the Society's vault, but the Beau Soleil lawsuit is among the papers Schmidt collected.

available; after that, Adrien was missing. Hence, Louis must have been plying one of the paddles in the flotilla of "four canoes loaded with goods for the Ottawa" which Galinée saw. The lawsuit also advances the testimony for Jolliet's residence having been at Sault Sainte-Marie during most of these years. As the trial proceeded, an appeal was made to Louis' duplicate account book of the Old Association because the original one was among the things "which he says he lost in his recent shipwreck." Jolliet could not immediately produce the ledger because it was out West. This places the headquarters of his business in the fur trading country up above Montreal.[60]

The memoirs of Nicolas Perrot and a document in the Fonds Brotier in Chantilly name Sault Sainte-Marie as Jolliet's western home. In 1671, Louis XIV sent Simon François Daumont Sieur de St. Lusson to this spot to make formal proclamation that all America beyond the Great Lakes was being added to the royal domain of France. His majesty's envoy traveled to the Sault to carry out the commission and had the Europeans present sign a document in proof of his having completed the task. Nicolas Perrot was his interpreter and listed the signers in his memoirs. After his own signature and those of the missionaries came those of "the Frenchmen who were found trading at the place." Louis Jolliet's autograph is affixed to the paper among the rest.[61] After the ceremony, he went to Quebec and remained there until 1672 when he was sent to search for the Mississippi. Beau Soleil's lawsuit leaves little room for doubt that this was the one time Jolliet came down from the Sault, after going there in 1669, because his departure in 1672

60. Archives of the Chicago Historical Society, Schmidt Collection, I, 53, *Pretantions.*

61. [Nicolas Perrot], *Memoire sur les Moeurs, Coustumes et Religion des Sauvages de l'Amerique Septentrionale par Nicolas Perrot,* ed., J[ules] Tailhan (Leipzig, 1864), p. 128. A copy of the St. Lusson document with Jolliet's signature is in APF, Fonds Brotier 155 (Canada–1), 48.

was spoken of at the trial as the second time he went to the
"Outaoaks." After this, until 1674, Jolliet's activity was all in
the West. Probably, with the exception of the Mississippi exploration, he did not leave his headquarters.

In 1672, Louis Jolliet brought his younger brother, Zacherie,
to Sault Sainte-Marie as a new partner under a freshly obtained
contract. The younger man was needed to hold the business
together while his older brother was off seeking the Mississippi.[62] As soon as the discovery was successfully accomplished,
the latter would naturally feel anxious to get right back to the
Sault. He needed to be there during the winter of 1673–74 to
bring to a profitable issue the fur trading venture which had
been left in Zacherie's inexperienced hands. The supposition
that the two spent these months working together at their
headquarters is bolstered by the description of the route Louis
followed to Quebec as he told it to Father Dablon, when he
arrived there, in the summer of 1674. He spoke of encounter-
ing forty rapids, which is the number found on the usual
canoe passage from the Sault via the Ottawa River.[63] If Jolliet
had wintered with Father Marquette at Green Bay, it would
have been more sensible for him to employ the Great Lakes
route, which is free from portages and furnishes the natural
waterway from Lake Michigan to the Lower St. Lawrence.
These things all point to the Sault as Jolliet's home for the five
years before he announced to Frontenac and Dablon his success
as an explorer.

Jolliet's eagerness to deliver his *cassette* ("strong box")
full of papers to the authorities as quickly as possible accounts

62. Delanglez, "Louis Jolliet, Early Years," p. 22, n. 78, prints the
contract for the new company with the names of the partners and
hired trappers.

63. ASH, 5, n. 16, 2. Galinée-Coyne, *Galinée's Narrative,* frontispiece, marks 26 rapids on the Ottawa. Faillon, *Histoire de Canada,*
III, 304–5, says this number represents portages where canoes were
unloaded; and Galinée's text enumerates close to 40 chutes in all,
BN, Mss.fr., n.a., 7485, 24v.

for his leaving Zacherie to wind up the business and bring down their harvest of beaver. If a second draft of what had been written about the 1673 trip was held back anywhere, it seems safe to conclude it was deposited where his brother would have supervision over it.[64] Though the younger Jolliet might supervise Louis' duplicate, he, along with the other French traders at the Sault, lived in a cluster of primitive cabins next to the Algonquin village. The only safe place to store valuables was in the Jesuit house or in their church because these were enclosed inside " a square stockade of cedar posts 12 feet high . . . so they, now, experience complete independence from the savages in every way." [65] That the white men took advantage of the safety afforded by this securely protected mission compound, is demonstrated in a letter of de La Salle after he had visited the place in 1680. He came to ask whether certain pelts had been left with the Jesuits by some men who had deserted his outfit. The fathers gave him permission to look for them in the attic of the church, which he found well packed with goods belonging to the neighboring traders.[66] Since the Jesuits supplied a sort of safety deposit vault in the wilderness, it becomes clear that Frontenac was quoting Jolliet

64. Amedée Gosselin, "Jolliet," pp. 79–80, makes certain Zacherie was not with Louis on this trip to Quebec. The letter on the "Map of the Arms of Frontenac" tells of Jolliet having his "papers" in a "strong box," Archives Nationales, Paris, Le Service Hydrographique, B 4044–37; Karpinski reproductions in the Edward F. Ayer Collection of the Newberry Library, Chicago.

65. BN, Mss.fr., n.a., 7485, 23–23v; Galinée-Coyne, *Galinée's Narrative*, p. 69. After Galinée's visit, building replacements were made in a style "qui surpasse de beaucoup la primiere [which surpasses the first in many respects]," Thwaites, *JR*, LV, 130–31.

66. Margry, *Découv. et Étab.*, II, 116, de La Salle, "22 aout, 1680–1681." The church at Green Bay was used by Perrot for keeping his furs, Claude C. de Bacqueville de La Potherie, *Voyage de l'Amerique, Contenant Ce qui S'Est Passé de Plus Remarquable dans l'Amerique Septentrionale depuis 1534 jusqu'à Present* (Amsterdam, 1723), II, 209. See above ch. 4, n. 48, for Jesuits and the fur trade.

correctly when he spoke of his papers as entrusted to "the fathers of Sault Sainte-Marie on Lake Superior." Contrarily, it was the governor's own misinterpretation when he jumped to the conclusion that Father Marquette was among these fathers in 1674, and could be asked to send Jolliet's duplicate journal to him from there.[67] Events at the Sault in this year disclose why, despite the careful precautions taken, no account by Jolliet of the 1673 expedition is in the Paris archives which hold his other manuscripts. The catastrophe which overtook it is narrated in the unpublished "Relation . . . les Années 1673–1674."

Ten Sioux came to the mission proposing negotiations of peace with the savages in the neighborhood. Most of the dwellers at the mission were happy about the embassy. There were some few who were not. The meeting was encouraged by the Jesuits and took place in their residence within the stockade. All who came were supposed to have surrendered their weapons. Some of the malcontents managed to smuggle in knives. Trouble began when one of these first threatened, then stabbed an unarmed Sioux. His fellow warriors sprang to the fray. The mission Indians, as well as the treacherous neighbors, were set upon. The Sioux gained possession of the house. Having found some guns and ammunition, they began shooting from the windows. The brawl had suddenly turned into a deadly fight. The Indians outside now managed to pile straw against the building and set it on fire. The defenders fled from the flames to a cabin and continued to fight until their powder gave out. Theerupon, they fell before the force of numbers. The narrative concludes, "during all this disorder and massacre, the fire which the savages had set to the house of the missionaries spread faster and faster and, despite every effort, since the edifice was a wooden one, it was completely consumed by the blaze." Dablon mourned the carnage and,

67. *RAPQ, 1926–1927,* p. 78, "Lettre du Gouverneur . . . au Ministre (14 novembre 1674)"; and ASH, 5, no. 16, 2.

addressing his provincial, he added a bit of information not found in other narratives of the disaster. He said: "on ne pust rien sauuer de tout ce qui estoit dedans et particulieremᵗ. une partie des memoires de ce qui s'estoit passe de plus remarquable cette année dans ces missions fure brulez [Nothing within (the residence) was saved and, specifically, a part of the memoirs of the more remarkable things which had taken place in these missions that year, was burned with it]." [68]

When a Canadian Jesuit spoke of a narrative as containing "the more remarkable things which had taken place in these missions," it is logical to suppose that the Relations were in his mind. This is a technical expression common to the title of the periodical. Thus, Fr. Louis André was excusing himself for failing to send his notes for it, when he wrote of a different fire which had struck Green Bay in 1673. "Le feu s'estans pris a ma Cabane, dans le mois de Decembre, et l'ayant reduite toute en cindres, mon journal n'a pas pû echaper les flammes, c'est ce qui m'a ôte le moyen d'ecrire auec exactitude ce qui s'est passé de plus remarquable touchant le christianisme de la bay St francois Xauier [In the month of December, fire having been set to my cabin and having reduced everything to ashes, not even my journal escaped the flames. Thus it is that I am without the means of writing in detail about the more remarkable things concerning the Christianizing of the Bay St. Francis Xavier]." [69]

Though Dablon's lament was primarily for the data needed to compose his annual letter, nevertheless, considering the simple arrangement of a Jesuit dormitory, it probably did not

68. APF, Fonds Brotier 157 (Canada–3), pt. 2, 65v. Thwaites, *JR,* LVIII, 256–63, lacks the detail about the burning of the papers because he copied from John G. Shea and Felix Martin, *Cramoisy No. 12, Relation . . . les Années 1673 à 1679* (New York, 1860), pp. 4–10, where it is not mentioned. See, Thwaites, *JR,* LVIII, 297, n. 23–n. 24.

69. APF, Fonds Brotier 155 (Canada–1), 28v; ACSM, Relation . . . les Années 1672–1673, transcribed in Thwaites, *JR,* LVII, 265.

boast more than one cupboard where literary materials were stored. If any papers were burned in this fire at the Sault, it seems likely that the whole collection went up in smoke. This conclusion is not affected by Dablon's expression, "a part of the memoirs . . . was burned." Here, he means that the total number of letters sent from the several missions in the Ottawa country was incomplete because of what befell the memoir at the Sault. The "Relation . . . les Années 1673–1674" makes this clear by telling of the activities in the other places except this one mission.[70] The fate of Jolliet's diary is confirmed in the introduction to the Récit. In 1678, when Dablon wrote it, he deplored the failure to deliver a narrative of the discovery as constituting the one thing to be desired in the young Canadian's conduct of the 1673 exploration. If Frontenac had been unable to obtain the duplicate journal by then, it must have perished in the fire.[71] The governor's correspondence with the French Court for the period 1674–78 is missing from the archives.[72] There is evidence that it contained allusions unfavorable to Jolliet, who had asked permission to begin a settlement on the Illinois River.[73] If these letters should ever come to light, his failure to obtain the written narrative from Jolliet may well be found enumerated among the things which oc-

70. APF, Fonds Brotier 157 (Canada–3), pt. 2, 69.

71. APF, Fonds Brotier 159 (Canada–5), 13v, reprinted in Thwaites, *JR*, LIX, 88–89.

72. *RAPQ*, 1926–1927, pp. 79–97.

73. *Report Concerning the Canadian Archives, 1885*, n. C, p. cxvii, Lettre du P. Dudouyt au Msgr. Laval, announces Jolliet's request. *Collection de Manuscrits Contenant Lettres, Mémoires et Autres Documents Historiques Relatifs a la Nouvelle France Recueilles aux Archives de la Province de Québec, ou Copiés a l'Étranger* (Quebec, 1883–85), I, 262, Lettre du Ministre au Sr. Duchesneau (Paris, 28 avril 1677), "Sa Majeste ne veut accorder au Sieur Jolliet la permission qu'il demande de s'aller establir avec vingt hommes dans le pais des Illinois [His Majesty is not at all willing to grant Sieur Jolliet the permission he has asked, to go with twenty men to establish himself in the Illinois country]."

casioned Frontenac's opposition to the Illinois River project.

Steck's conjecture that it was Jesuit plagiarism of Jolliet's journal which supplied Thevenot with the data for his *Receuil de Voyages,* required the presumption that a "permanent estrangement [existed] between Jolliet and the Jesuits after 1682." This date was chosen because he believed that by then the young fur trader had read Thevenot's book and recognized the theft.[74] Of course, no such plagiarism was possible from journals which had perished. Furthermore, Jolliet's subsequent activities bespeak continual close relationship with the men of the Order. His oldest son, Louis, Jr., spent his entire college career, normally at least seven years, in the classes of the Jesuit college of Quebec, graduating in 1694.[75] The professor of mathematics during these years was Father André, who had been a missionary to the Ottawa while Jolliet was at the Sault. When the priest came to Quebec in the summer of 1684, he and Jolliet spent the warm months together at the new trading headquarters Jolliet had acquired on Anticosti Island. In 1695, André was placed in charge of the Christian Indians from Tadoussac to the Gulf of St. Lawrence. Jolliet's island fell within these boundaries, which must have led to further visits during the five years which remained before the explorer's death.[76]

The purpose of the present chapter is to discover, if possible, the original chronicler of the Mississippi exploration of 1673 as set down in the first chapter of the Récits in Montreal and Chantilly. Father Dablon, the superior of the Canadian mis-

74. Steck, *Marquette Legends,* p. 216, n. 188. Below pp. 116–17, uncovers Jolliet's own admission that he was not the sole chronicler of the discovery.

75. Amedée Gosselin, "Jolliet," p. 71.

76. Archives du Séminaire des Étrangères, Quebec, *Registre des Baptêmes et Sépultures des Sauvages du Lac St. Jean Chicoutimie et Tadoussac de 1669 à 1692,* LV, col. 1, in Jean Delanglez, "The 'Recit des voyages et des decouvertes du Pere Jacques Marquette,'" *M-A,* XXVIII (1946), 183–84, n. 25–n. 26.

sions, was proposed as the man who would ordinarily edit such a report because his was the responsibility of sending a yearly Relation to his provincial. However, before seeking evidence to establish his accomplishment of this duty, it was necessary to discuss others who had been suggested as chroniclers. At the end of the discussion these individuals have been eliminated. Now, the source of Dablon's information must be considered.

When Dablon learned that Jolliet had lost everything in the watery disaster near Montreal, he was consoled by the news that Marquette had a duplicate narrative of the exploration which could be obtained. Here is where the emphasis on the lack of teamwork between Frontenac and Dablon in their endeavors to replace the papers which had sunk in the St. Louis rapids simplifies the present study, because even after the governor became aware that both Jolliet's original and duplicate journals were lost, the probability remains that the Jesuit superior was not thinking of Frontenac's effort to obtain Jolliet's duplicate, but of something different, written personally for the Relations by Marquette, when he began his own attempt to secure the duplicate which the missionary was said to have had.

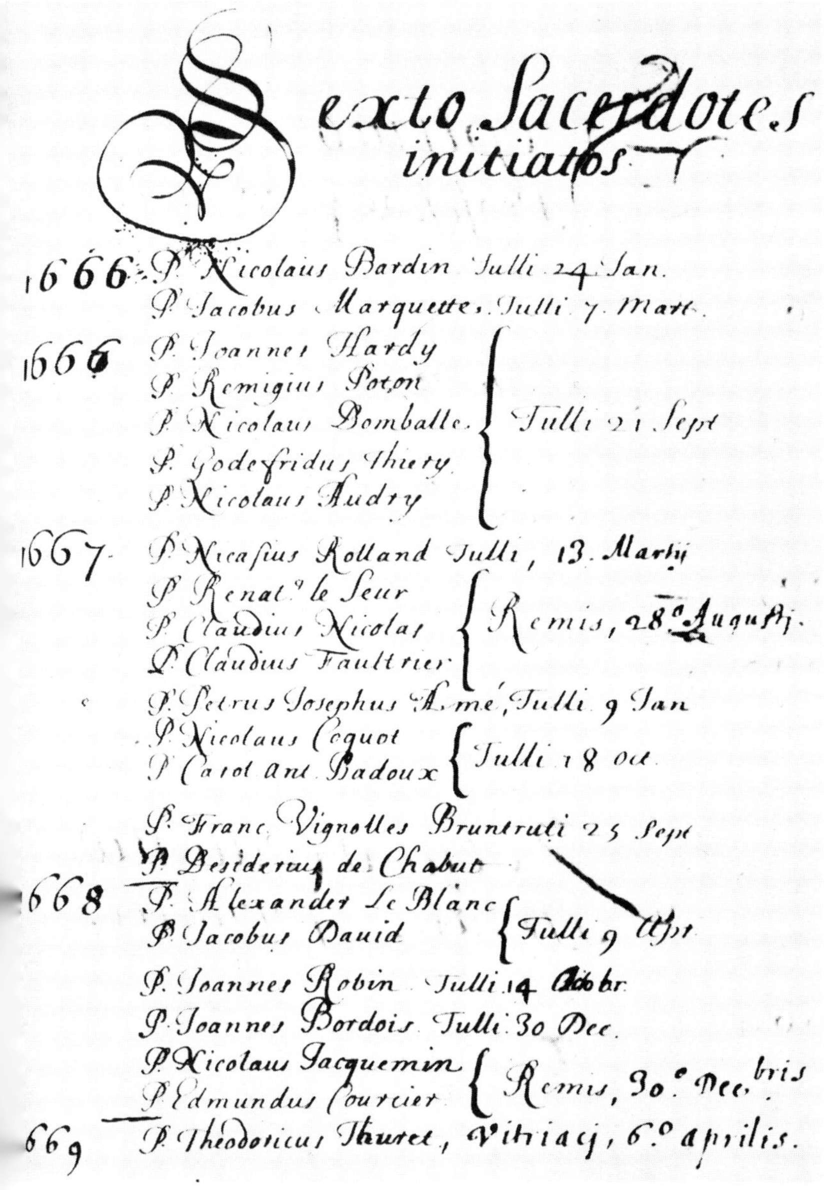

Sexto Sacerdotes initiatos

1666 — P. Nicolaus Bardin Julii 24 Jan.
P. Jacobus Marquette. Julii 7 Mart.

1666 — P. Joannes Hardy
P. Remigius Poton
P. Nicolaus Domballe. } Julii 21 Sept
P. Godefridus Thiery
P. Nicolaus Audry

1667 — P. Nicasius Rolland Julii, 13 Martij
P. Renal. le Seur
P. Claudius Nicolas } Remis, 28.° Augustij.
P. Claudius Faulttrier

P. Petrus Josephus Aimé, Julii 9 Jan
P. Nicolaus Coquot
P. Carol ant. Badoux } Julii 18 Oct.

P. Franc. Vignolles Bruntruti 25 Sept
P. Desiderius de Chabut
1668 — P. Alexander Le Blanc
P. Jacobus Dauid } Julli 9 Xbr.

P. Joannes Robin Julli 14 Octobr.
P. Joannes Bordois Julli 30 Dec.
P. Nicolaus Jacquemin
P. Edmundus Courcier } Remis, 30.° Dec.bris
1669 — P. Theodoricus Thuret, Vitriacij, 6.° aprilis.

PLATE 1 The sixth part of the Supplement from the triennial catalog for 1669. This is the official record of Father Marquette's ordination from the Roman Archives of the Society of Jesus. ARSJ, Camp. 11, 282. Courtesy Fr. Joseph Teschitel, Archivist, Jesuit headquarters, Rome.

1663

P. Theodoric Boschetes
P. Martinus de Lienecourt
P. Joannes Michael
P. Guilielmus ——
P. Ger. ans Modo

Tulli 15 augusti 1661
—— 28 7bris 1662
Tulli 18 Septemb. 1663

1664

P. Gabriel de la Bassée
P. Renatus Hannuel
P. Joannes Basile
B. Nicolaus de Tournay
P. Joannes de ..manville
P. Henricus Braux
P. Joan. Pierron
P. Nicol. franc. Merigno
P. Nicol. la Viruille —

Tulli 29 aprilis 1663 mortuus 29 aprilis 1663
Tulli mense Junio 1664
volontaire ad Illustrissimo suffragano 28 7bris 1684

Tulli 10 Octob. 1664

1666

P. Nicol. Bardon —
P. Jacobus ...grathes
P. Joannes Flatty
P. Remigius Petor
P. Nicolaus Dembaulle
P. Godofridus Tissery
P. Nicolaus Audoy
P. Petrus Josephus Corret

Tulli 24 Januarii 1666
Tulli ... Martii 1688
(P. Nicasius Rollan) Tulli Junio 1667 13.° martii
Tulli 25° septembris 1688

1667

Tulli 9 Januarii 1667

PLATE 2 (*facing page*) Official catalog of the Champagne ordinations, 1655–67. The misplaced entry, "P. Nicasius Rolland 13 Martii 1667" apparently led the person transcribing the names for the Supplement to write 1667 in its margin before he realized that 1666 was the year of ordination for "P. Ioannes Hardy" and several others still to come. The error was corrected by superimposing a "6" on the "7." BPN, 560 (138), 20. Courtesy Mme. M. A. Geoffrey, Conservateur de la Bibliothèque Publique de Nancy, France.

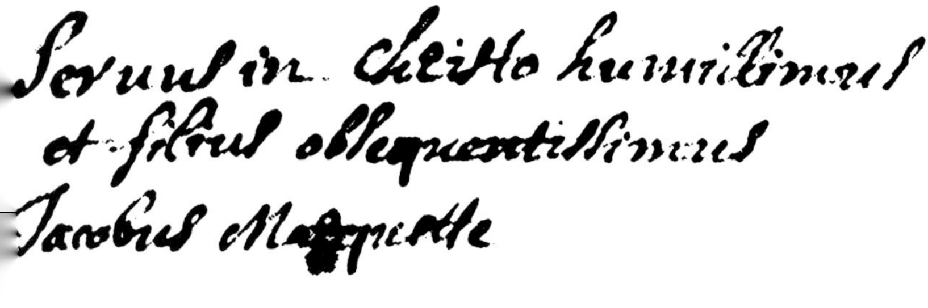
Servus in Christo humillimus
et filius obsequentissimus
Iacobus Marquette

PLATE 3 Enlarged signature from Marquette's holograph letter (Plate 4) establishing some peculiarities of his handwriting.

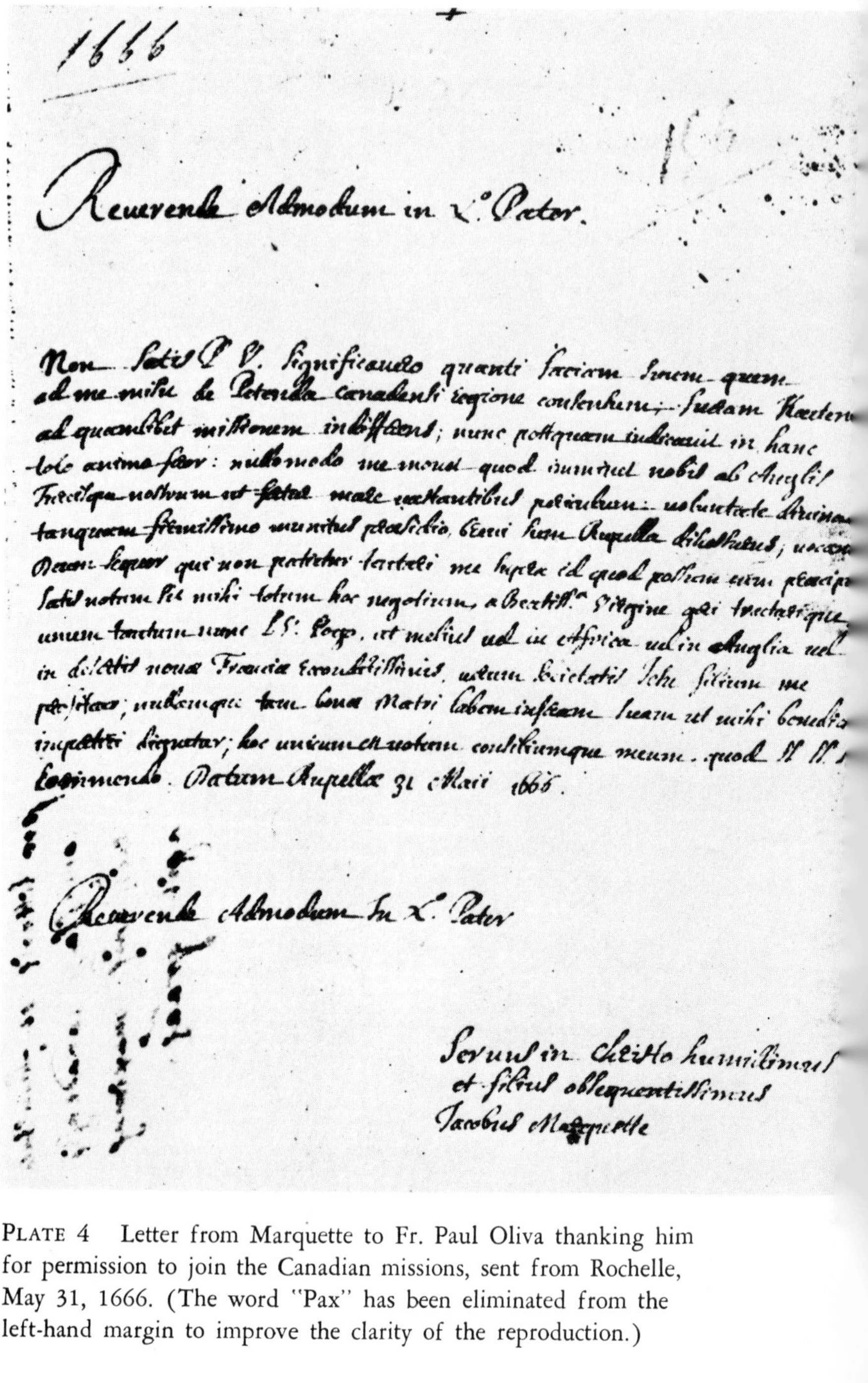

1666

Reverende Admodum in Xº Pater.

Datum Rupellae 31 Maii 1666.

Reverende Admodum In Xº Pater

Servus in Christo humillimus
et filius obsequentissimus
Jacobus Marquette

PLATE 4 Letter from Marquette to Fr. Paul Oliva thanking him for permission to join the Canadian missions, sent from Rochelle, May 31, 1666. (The word "Pax" has been eliminated from the left-hand margin to improve the clarity of the reproduction.)

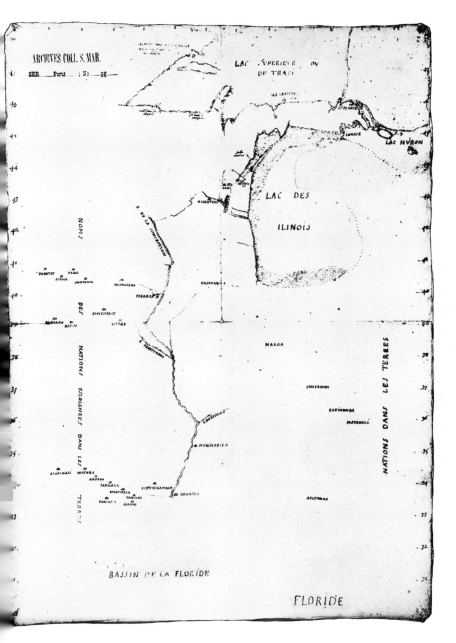

PLATE 5   Holograph map by Marquette; actual size 13½″ by 18″.
ACSM, 687. Courtesy P. Paul Desjardins, Archivist, Collège
Sainte-Marie, Montreal.

QUEBEC

A. Le Fort
B. les Recollets
C. La plate forme
D. Les Jesuites
E. La Cathedralle
F. Le Seminaire
G. L'Hostel Dieu
H. L'evêché
I. La Redoute
... Le magazin a poudre

PLATE 6
A sketch made for
De La Potherie's
Voyage de
l'Amérique (1722)

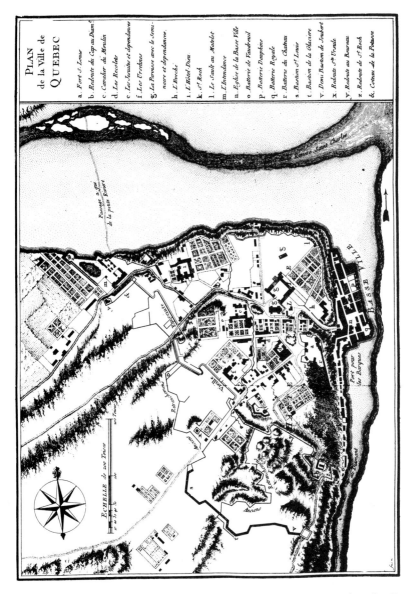

PLAN
de la Ville de
QUEBEC

a. Fort S.t Louis
b. Redoute du Cap au Diam.s
c. Cavalier du Moulin
d. Les Recolets
e. Les Jesuites et dependance
f. Les Urselines
g. La Paroisse avec le seminaire et dependance.
h. L'Evesché
i. L'Hôtel Dieu
k. S.t Roch
l. Le Sault au Matelot
m. L'Intendance
n. Eglise de la Basse Ville
o. Batterie de Vaudreuil
p. Batterie Dauphine
q. Batterie Royale
r. Batterie du Chateau
s. Bastion S.t Louis
t. Bastion de la Glacière
v. Demi Bastion de Joubert
x. Redoute S.te Ursule
y. Redoute au Bourreau
z. Redoute de S.t Roch
&. Coteau de la Potance

PLATE 7
A plan engraved
for Provost,
Histoire Général
des Voyages (1757)

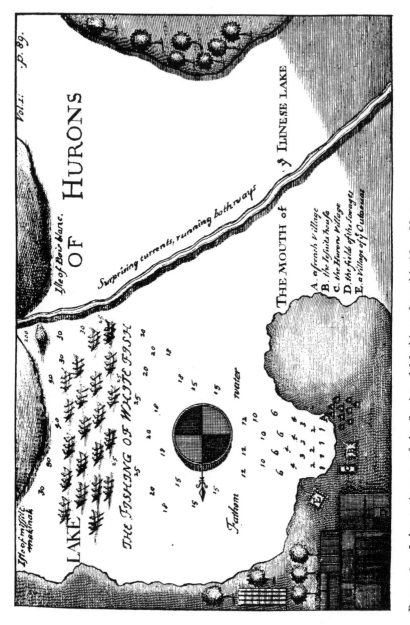

PLATE 8   Lahontan's map of the Straits of Mackinac from his *New Voyages*
(1703). Here may be found "the Jesuits house," where Marquette

CHAPTER 5

Dablon Gathers
His Data

THERE was sense in Dablon's belief that Marquette would write a journal of his 1673 trip. From one summer to the next, the keeping of a daybook in which a missionary to New France jotted down the more remarkable things which took place among his Indians was a routine chore. He knew his portrayal of their customs, wilderness experiences, and Christian progress was needed to make the Relations attractive reading for the folk back home in France. Marquette's appreciation of this duty is manifest from his own words about it as well as from a careful performance of it during the years of his active career.[1] He wrote of his founding the church at Sault Sainte-

1. In 1670 when Marquette finished his first year at Chequamegon Bay, he began his letter to Father Le Mercier, "Ie fuis obligé de rendre compte à V. R. de l'état de la mission . . . selon l'ordre que j'en receu . . . [I am under obligation to give an account to Your Reverence of

Marie in the *Relation . . . les Années 1668–1669*.[2] His work
at the mission of the Holy Spirit, at the far end of Lake Superior, found a place in the volume for the next year.[3] In the
Relation . . . les Années 1670–1671, he narrated his migration
with his Huron Indians to Michilimackinac.[4] The winter of
1671–72, when he was overburdened with those activities
consequent upon the establishment of St. Ignace, his superior
noted for the first time, "Father Jacques Marquette, who followed [the Hurons] from the point of the Holy Spirit, continued to have charge of them, . . . he has not furnished any
special memoirs of the occurrences at this mission."[5] These
words are in the last printed Relation, but just before setting
out for the Mississippi, Marquette dispatched to Quebec an
account of his activities during the twelve months prior to the
spring of 1673.[6] Such fidelity in recounting the ordinary would
favor the presumption of his having kept a day-by-day journal
of what happened to him as he made the extraordinary trip
with Jolliet. However, as he set out, a change in circumstances
was in progress which might have led him to dispense himself
from writing such a narrative.

The year 1673 was disastrous for the Jesuit Relations. During its twelve months, Pope Clement X promulgated *Creditae
Nobis* and the Paris provincial brought to an end the contract
with the Cramoisy press for the publication of the magazine.
To keep a diary up to date, Marquette had to steal a portion
of the time allowed for sleep; after his day's work, this was
no easy thing. Therefore, if he had known of the demise of
the Relations, he might readily have excused himself from an

the state of the mission . . . following the order received]." Thwaites,
JR, LIV, 168–69.
   2. Ibid., LII, 212–13.
   3. Ibid., LIV, 168–95.
   4. Ibid., LV, 170–71.
   5. Ibid., LVI, 116–17.
   6. Ibid., LVII, 248–63.

unnecessary burden. A chronological review of the days leading up to the one on which he broke contact with civilization makes sure he did not have that knowledge. Such a survey would begin with October, 1672, when after being commissioned to find the Mississippi, Jolliet bade adieu to Quebec. This was before the French provincial had made his decision.[7] True, this was the fall in which the cardinals of *Propaganda Fide* were considering the necessity of placing an imprimatur on mission literature, but it was not until the spring of 1673, just a month before the Mississippi expedition left Michilimackinac, that the pope issued the brief approving their plan. The subsequent decision to discontinue the Relations could not have been known in Canada until a fresh contingent of missionaries arrived from France, late in the summer of the same year.[8] By then, Jolliet and Marquette were close to the end of their exploration. Therefore, as far as the latter knew, his superior was eagerly awaiting his story for inclusion in the Jesuit periodical and he was not released from his job of writing down the sequence of events as they occurred. A careful scrutiny of the manuscripts, other than the Récit, which have been under consideration in the present work evidences his good will in meeting such a responsibility.

Jolliet's letter, dated October 10, 1674, and sent to Bishop Laval in Paris, which is the one copied later by the superior of the Sulpicians, M. Tronson, contains an implication that Marquette's daybook was lost along with his own when the canoe capsized. He says the spill in the St. Lawrence did away with "tous les papiers et mon journal . . . sans le naufrage uostre grand' auroit Receu une relation assez [obliterated: 'complet'?] mais je ne m'est rien reste que la vie [all my papers and my

7. See above, ch. 3, n. 35.
8. In 1673, Fr. Martin-Samuel Bouvart and Fr. Antoine Silvy and two lay brothers, Bro. François-Guillaume Jetreau and Bro. Jean Vitry arrived in Canada, [Arthur Melançon], *Liste des Missionnaires Jésuites, Nouvelle France et Louisiane* (Montreal, 1929), p. 77.

journal . . . barring the shipwreck Your Excellency would have received a relation sufficiently (obliterated: 'full'?) but nothing was left me but my life]."[9] These words clearly point to the loss of other writings besides his own journal and in his telling Laval that, if the documents had not been lost, the bishop would have received a "relation" of the adventure, his use of the characteristic name of the Jesuit Relations could easily have meant that the prelate would be supplied with the "sufficiently full" details of the discovery in the current issue of this magazine. It is true that the printing of the Relations had ceased in 1673. However, it was only 1674 when Jolliet wrote and there is no reason to believe he was then aware of this happening. The Jesuits did not publicize the step they had taken in regard to the popular periodical. As late as 1679, Dablon was sending annual copy to Paris in case Louis XIV's Gallicanism should become reconciled to the papal demand for an imprimatur in mission writing.[10] The supposition that Jolliet was relying on Marquette's journal, when published, to be the account Laval would read gains force from his knowledge of the destiny awaiting his own journal, as soon as it reached Quebec. It would be delivered to Frontenac and, once the governor received it, the bishop would have small chance of seeing it.

Frontenac's letter to Colbert, November 14, 1674, telling of the accident which befell Jolliet, says the explorer's dousing in the river caused him to lose "tous ses memoires et ses journaux."[11] This supposes he was bringing other memoranda besides his personal diary of 1673. Adrien's widow had to wait for her share of the profits from the "Old Association" because when the canoe capsized the account book, the memoir

9. Archives du Seminaire de Saint Sulpice, Paris, Doc. pour servir a l'Histoire de l'Eglise du Canada, I, pt. 1, 12–13.

10. See above, ch. 3, n. 39–n. 40.

11. *RAPQ, 1926–1927,* p. 78, "Lettre du Gouverneur . . . au Ministre (14 novembre 1674)."

of the Jolliet brothers' trade, was lost.[12] If Louis had lost other notes of his business transactions, the governor had reason to change "memoir" into the plural. The plural of "journals" most naturally would mean the one Jolliet had written for Frontenac, and the one Marquette had written for Dablon. No one else on the expedition could be expected to have kept a daybook, because the companions of the explorers, simply called "5 men" in the contemporary sources, probably were, with the one exception mentioned below, the unlettered trappers of Jolliet's "New" association chartered in 1672.[13] The first of his partners, Zacherie, was not taken on the exploration because he had been brought to the Sault to carry on the business if Louis failed to return.[14] François de Chavigny, the other partner, was with Frontenac for the founding of his fort on the Cataraqui River from July 9 to August 1, 1673; hence, he could not have been on hand.[15] The personnel of the company was completed by four hired men, Pierre Moreau, Jean Plattier, Jean Tiberge, and Jacques Largillier.[16] The last mentioned is known to have gone with Jolliet. His presence on the expedition makes it almost certain that the other three participated in it.[17] There is contemporary evidence indicating that the fifth was an unnamed Canadian youth who was helping Father Marquette at St. Ignace. The catalog of Jesuit assignments for the year of the discovery, says, "P. Jacobus Marquette. mission.

12. See ch. 4, n. 59–60.

13. Pierre–Georges Roy, *Toutes Petites Choses du Régime Français Première Série* (Quebec, 1944), p. 201, first suggested this personnel.

14. Jean Delanglez, "Louis Jolliet, Early Years, 1645–1674," *M-A,* XXVII (1945), 22–23.

15. Richard A. Preston and Leopold Lamontagne, *Royal Fort Frontenac, Texts Selected and Translated from the French* (Toronto, 1958), p. 106.

16. See above, ch. 4, n. 62.

17. APF, Fonds Brotier 166 (Canada–12), no. 4, 26; Camille De Rochemonteix, *Les Jésuites et la Nouvelle-France* (Paris, 1895–96), III, 607.

Algonquinam S. Ignatii curat cum famulo. a verno tempore
suscepit iter versus mare pacificium seu sinense cum Gallis
comitibus et Algonquinis [Fr. Jacques Marquette takes care
of the Algonquin mission of St. Ignatius with a donné, he has
undertaken a journey this spring toward the Pacific or Chinese
Sea with French and Algonquin companions]."[18] Even if this
entry does not mean that the young man was sent, his dedica-
tion to helping the missionary favors him as the last of the
seven explorers. Many such men helped the Jesuits and none
was ever known to keep a journal. Thus, the whole group,
except for the leaders, was composed of the type of Canadian
who was more concerned with making history than writing
about it; so little chance is left for attributing either of "the
journals" to those who went with Marquette and Jolliet. Presumably, Frontenac used the plural of the word because he
knew the leaders had each written a narrative.

Frontenac's letter testifies further to his understanding that
Marquette wrote one of "the journals," which Jolliet lost. The
entire identity between the dictated account of the adventure,
which Jolliet gave to Dablon, and the governor's report of the
project's success has already been discussed.[19] This identity,
being such as it is, makes clear the governor must at least have
seen what Dablon had written. In his text, the latter had promised that he would send out West to Father Marquette for a
duplicate of the Mississippi narrative and forward the full

18. ARSJ, Franc. 23, 320, "Catalogus Provinciae Franciae, 1673
Exeunte." A literal translation, retaining the capitalization and punctuation of the original, is a bit confusing. The period after "mission" is
probably owing to its abbreviation for "missionem." There is no other
need for one. The period after "famulo" could indicate the end of a
sentence. "A verno tempore" should, then, begin with a capital letter.
If the small "a" means the dot after "famulo" calls only for such a
pause as a present-day comma requires, then, the sentence can be
taken to mean, Marquette made the journey with the donné.

19. ASH, 5, no. 16, 2 and see text above, ch. 4, n. 53.

account to the French Jesuits next year.[20] The governor was
ever on the alert for misdemeanors on the part of the fathers.
In this instance, he would have found cause for charging their
superior with circumventing proper procedure, if he knew that
there was only a single Jolliet journal to be sought out there.
In his accusations against the Order, Frontenac neglected to
capitalize on this opportunity, which leaves but one satisfactory
interpretation. Jolliet must have told him that there was another journal, written by the missionary and intended for
Dablon. Finally when, in 1674, Dablon put Jolliet's dictation
as an introduction to the Relation he sent this year, though he
said, "le Sr Joliet qui nous en apportoit la relation, avec vne
carte tres exacte de ces nouveaux pais, la perdue par naufrage,"
and that "l'année prochaine nous en donnerons vne pleine relation, La pere Marquette ayant garde vne Copie [The Sr.
Joliet who was bringing the relation, with a most exact map
of these new countries, lost it in a wreck, . . . next year we
will give a full relation of it (the discovery), Father Marquette
having kept a copy]," he did not mean the pronoun "we" to
include the petulant governor. The lack of cooperation between
the two precludes such a possibility. Dablon is employing the
editorial "we."[21]

The letter which Father Dablon sent to Paris on October 25,
1674, summarizing his missionaries' activities for the past
twelve months was considered when a reason was assigned for
Jolliet's dictation of this year appearing in the "Relation . . . les
Années 1672–1673." The digest of mission events which the
letter contained was primarily concerned with the superior's
attempt to make up for his neglect in not writing a full account of what had happened in the missions during the previ-

20. See above, ch. 4, n. 41.
21. APF, Fonds Brotier 155 (Canada–1), 12. Throughout this Relation, Dablon constantly substitutes "we" for "I" in making personal
comments.

ous twelve months. Hence he only mentions the discovery
of the Mississippi in passing; it is brought in, together with
an even earlier exploration by Fr. Charles Albanel, to impress
upon the provincial the eagerness of his men for spreading the
Faith in all quarters of the continent.[22] Yet, since what he says
of the 1673 trip apparently supplies a direct affirmation that
Jolliet, on his return, was to bring Marquette's journal with
him, the pertinent passage is quoted at length here from the
original. It seems necessary to give it so fully, because de
Montézon took damaging liberty in transcribing this letter and
Thwaites copied the text from the French priest's book.[23]

The first page of Father Dablon's letter is devoted to an
outline of what he intends to write about, plus the reference to
Father Albanel's journey to Hudson Bay in 1672. On the
verso, he continues:

> Apres la decouuerte de cette mer du nord que ce Pere fit Ily a
> deux ans, on attendoit de ns. la decouuerte de la mer du midy
> C'est ce qu'a fait cette année le Pere Marquette qui en est retourne
> heureusement le printemps passé   On pu dire que cette de-
> couuerte est la plus belle et plus hasardeuse de touttes celles qui
> ont esté faites jusque a present en ce pays. dans le mois de Iuin
> ib73 [1673] le pere ayant en fin trouué la fameuse riuière dont
> les sauuages ont tant parlé a plus de cent lieux des Ontavuak . . . .
> [Here, Dablon says a word about the country seen as Marquette
> descended to about the 33rd degree of latitude, where prudence
> dictated his return lest he fall into Spanish hands. He continues.]
> Le recit de ce voiage estoit plein de raretez et de curiositez tres
> considerables, mais ce luy qui ns. l'apportoit ay^t. fait noffrage
> proche montreal tous Les papiers ont este perdus, I'en attend

22. Father Albanel's journal of his trip to Hudson Bay had been
printed in the *Relation . . . les Années, 1671–1672*, Thwaites, *JR*, LVI,
148–217.

23. Ibid., LIX, 293, "Bibliographical Data." De Montézon, *Rel.
Inédites*, II, 13–15, prints the letter and Thwaites, *JR*, LVI, 64–83,
transcribes.

vne auᵗ. exemplaire l'an qui vient que iay demandé au P. marquette qui en a gardé copie.²⁴

[After making known the sea of the north which this Father
(Albanel) did two years ago, the making known the sea of the
south was expected of us. This is just what Father Marquette
did this year, who successfully returned news of it last spring.
In the month of June, 1673, the father, at last, found the famous
river of which the savages have had so much to say. One might
call this discovery, at a distance of more than a hundred leagues
beyond the Ottawa, the best and at the same time the most
hazardous of all those which have been made, up to now, in
this country . . . . The narrative of this voyage was full of things
quite unknown and curious, but he who was bringing it to us,
having had a shipwreck near Montreal, lost all the papers he
had. In the year which is coming up, I await a replica which I
have asked from Father Marquette, who retained a copy of it.]

The last sentence reasserts the presence of several papers ("Les
papiers") telling of the discovery ("Le recit de ce voiage")
and it drops the editorial "we" Dablon employed in his public
account. Here he says "I await a replica . . . which I have
asked for from Father Marquette." It is clear from this that he
is making a demand from Father Marquette in his own right.
He alone had a right to the Jesuit's journal. What seems to
be the direct affirmation that Jolliet had this with him when he
left Sault Sainte-Marie in the spring of 1674 occurs in the
first part of the present excerpt from the letter.

In interpreting what Dablon says about Marquette in his
letter, it must be remembered that Jolliet's dictated account
of the discovery, which formed the preface of the Relation
written by the mission superior in the fall of 1674, was sent
to France in the same mail; so in the letter, he only repeats the
salient news of Marquette's finding the Mississippi "dans le

24. APF, Fonds Brotier 157 (Canada–3), pt. 1, 2v, "Mon R. P. de
Quebec le 25 octob. 1674." Dablon's request to Marquette for this
copy is omitted in de Montézon, *Rel. Inédites*, II, 4–6.

mois de Iuin ib73 [1673] le pere ayant en fin trouué la fameuse riuière." The letter is a personal message to the provincial, written hurriedly, with confidence he would also read the account in the Relation, which had been carefully prepared for publication. Under these circumstances, Dablon would pay little heed to a scrutiny of his missive in search of vague expressions in it. Certainly, such writing was not intended to bring out new incidents of the exploration, especially if they would be contradictory to what he had composed for the public eye. This should be kept in mind during the discussion which follows.

What seems to be Dablon's direct reference to Marquette's journal occurs where he says, "After making known the sea of the north which this Father [Albanel] did two years ago [that is in 1672], the making known of the sea of the South was expected of us [.] This is just what Father Marquette did this year (cette année), who happily returned it (qui en est retourne) last spring." Had the writer been considering the publication of these words, he certainly would have been more specific in designating the dates related to Marquette's discovery. As things stand, "this year" may denote the year 1672, when Albanel returned from his trip. It would not be unnatural for Dablon, living in Quebec, to propose this chronology. In 1672, Jolliet left the city on his way to Marquette's mission to tell him he had been selected as partner for the exploration. However, the letter probably means that Father Marquette made known the sea of the South, in 1674, "this year" when Dablon was writing about it. This is why the next words seem relevant to Marquette's journal and not to himself. The French is "qui en est retourne heureussement la printemps passé," which translated literally becomes "who has happily returned it last spring." Since Jolliet's dictation announces the expedition's return from the discovery, at the end of September 1673, the pesky little "it," often so clear to the speaker but vague to the listener, must stand for a return from the discovery of something else than the men who made the trip because "it" was returned in the spring of 1674.[25] This being true, it seems that Dablon must have been thinking of Marquette's journal as "en." Hence, he would attribute the knowledge of the sea of the South to Marquette's journal which was happily returned last spring, but lost in Jolliet's accident, thus making a request for the duplicate necessary.

In the one hundred fifty-seventh volume of the Fonds Brotier, the French version of Dablon's letter of October 25, 1674, is in the clear hand of an unknown secretary. It is followed immediately by a Latin translation in the script of Father Ragueneau, who was the Paris Jesuit in charge of Canadian mission interests. Dablon's note had said many good things about his missionaries. Their Gallican and Jansenist assailants were saying the opposite. Ragueneau probably turned these commendations of his charges into the language of the Church against the need of seeking protection for them from the cardinals of *Propaganda Fide*.[26] Whatever his purpose was, he surely was in no way concerned with producing a painstaking reproduction of what is said about the discovery of the Mississippi. Therefore, his rendering this obscure passage into "qui inde feliciter reversus est verne hoc ultimo [who happily returned thence this last spring]," which brings Marquette home many months later than the date entered in Jolliet's dictation, need not be a cause for serious concern. This is particularly true when one considers how easily this mistake can be made by a translator who is not historically critical of the text. The past tense of "retourner," a verb of motion, is formed with *être* ("to be"), instead of *avoir* ("to have"). Turning the French

25. APF, Fonds Brotier 155 (Canada–1), 13, Jolliet's announcement is in the "Relation . . . les Années 1672–1673."

26. APF, Fonds Brotier 157 (Canada–3), pt. 1, 6–10, "Epistola Patris D'Ablon . . . Quebeci in Nova francia 25 octobrij 1674." De Montézon, *Rel. Inédites,* II, 4, n. 2, suggests the reason for Ragueneau's translation.

into Latin, "feliciter" stands for "heureusement" and "reversus est" for "est retourne." "Reversus est" is an intransitive, deponent verb which needs no object; hence, it comes naturally to add the temporal clause at once. With "verne hoc ultimo" taking the place of "le printemps passé," the combination of Latin words makes sense, "who happily came home last spring," but the "en" is overlooked. In this manner, Ragueneau must have missed its presence, and since this version was never sent to Rome, its author probably put it aside without ever making a more diligent comparison between his rough Latin copy and the French prototype.

In the letter of October 25, 1674, Dablon is definite in saying he had already asked for "a replica" of the lost narrative; hence an investigation of the results consequent upon this request is in order. Occurrences in the late summer of 1674 made it possible to contact Marquette shortly after Jolliet's call at the Collège. This came on August 1 and the friendly Ottawa who brought their furs down for trade could be depended on to launch their flotilla for their homeland about mid-August.[27] They were accustomed to offer escort to Jesuits going their way.[28] Brother Aegidius Mazier was assigned to Michilimackinac this summer.[29] Thus the messenger and the means of transportation were supplied. An announcement in the catalog telling where his men would be for the year 1674–75 signifies the seizure of this opportunity by Dablon. In speaking of Marquette, his work for this year is listed thus, "P. Iac. Marquette P. Ant. Silvy missionem nouam apparent versus mare merid. ubi nationes multae recens repertae [Fr. Jac. Marquette Fr.

27. Jean Delanglez, "The 'Recit des voyages et des decouvertes du Pere Jacques Marquette,'" *M-A,* XXVIII (1946), 188–89.

28. Thwaites, *JR,* XLVI, 74–75, tells of Fr. René Ménard going to Lake Superior with the Algonquin fleet. In 1665, Father Allouez' canoe was in their convoy, ibid., XLIX, 240–41.

29. ARSJ, Franc. 23, 327v, "Catalogus Provinciae Franciae, 1674 Exeunte," under "Missio apud Outaouacos."

Ant. Silvy are opening a new mission toward the central sea (the Gulf of Mexico) where recently many tribes were found]."[30] His superior could choose him for this venture only after Jolliet's visit because until then he did not know there was the possibility of opening such a mission; he could tell the provincial about choosing Marquette only after he had sent the message West. This almost demands that the appointment was made by means of the flotilla and lay-brother. If they supplied the agency of communication for this, they functioned similarly for the requisition of the duplicate Mississippi narrative. Happenings in the Ottawa country, eight weeks after these Indians started up the St. Lawrence from Quebec, vouch for the safe conduct of Dablon's message.

By the end of September, Fr. Henri Nouvel, rector at Sault Sainte-Marie, was sending ahead the order to Father Marquette for his new missionary operation. Father Cholenec's letter of October 10, 1675, quoting one of the young men who had been with the priest for his final apostolic journey says, "a week after Michaelmas two of our retainers who are donnés at our missions" were sent by Nouvel, "to pick [Marquette] up at [Green Bay] where he was, and whence he left, with them, at the beginning of November."[31] The feast of St. Michael falls on September 29. Nouvel's action during the first week thereafter means he must have received authorization to act by way of Brother Aegidius, who had plenty of time to get there by Michaelmas. A local superior could not have assumed the right to found a new mission on his own responsibility.

30. ARSJ, Franc. 23, 337, "Catalogus Provinciae Franciae, 1674 Exeunte."

31. APF, Fonds Brotier 166 (Canada–12), no. 4, 26. Delanglez, "Recit des voyages," pp. 188–89, asserts that the flotilla, leaving Quebec in mid-August, might have delayed up to ten days at Montreal, as often happened, and still have arrived at the Sault by the first week in October. For Marquette's wintering at Green Bay, see above, ch. 4, n. 51.

The introduction to the journal, which Marquette began as he started out on October 25, 1674, to fulfill the last task of his life, fixes Dablon as the source of his commission. The wording is:

Mon Reuerend Pere   Pax X^i Ayant este contraint de demeurer a St. François tout l'este, a cause de quelque incommodité, on ayant este guery dez le mois de Septembre I'y attendois l'arriuee de nos gens au retour de *la bas* [emphasis added] pour sçauoir ceque ie ferois pour mon hyuernement; les quels m'en apporterent les ordres pour mon voyage a la mission de la Conception des Ilinois [32]

[My Reverend Father, The Peace of Christ. Having been constrained to dwell at St. Francis (Green Bay) all summer, because of an indisposition, and having gained strength in the month of September, I was waiting there the coming of our people, at the return from down below, to find out what I would do this winter; they brought me the order for my voyage to the mission of the Conception of the Illinois.]

Canadians said "down below" (*la bas*), when they spoke of the Quebec area just as they called the neighborhood around Michilimackinac "up above" (*en haut*). Therefore the charge came from headquarters.[33] If one message arrived safely, the other, requesting a duplicate of the 1673 diary, must have. And the continuation of the paragraph just quoted affords an indication that Marquette fulfilled such a request before leaving Green Bay. It proceeds, "ayant satisfait aux Sentiments de V. R. pour les coppies de mon iournal touchant la Riuiere de Missisipi, Ie partie avec Pierre Porteret et Jacque . . . [Having discharged the duty which I owe to Your Reverence's wishes with regard to the copies of my journal dealing with

32. ACSM, 296, 63; photocopied in Thwaites, *JR*, LIX, 212, and translitterated in type, ibid., pp. 164–83.

33. Delanglez, "Recit des voyages," p. 189, overlooked the significance of "down below" and missed the source of Marquette's permission to return to the Illinois.

the River of the Mississippi, I left with Pierre Porteret and Jacques . . .]."[34] "To discharge a duty" (*acquitter ce qui est du*) is the first meaning assigned by French dictionaries to the intransitive verb "satisfaire" which opens the participial clause found in the quotation. This literal translation of the word clears up the peculiarity by which Marquette employs "copies of my journal," in the plural. Quite certainly, Dablon did not want several reproductions of the same thing. The "copies" which he put Marquette under obligation to send must have been of two different travelogs. Because in 1673 Marquette had met the Illinois as far west as the Mississippi, now in 1674, as he set out to establish a mission among them, he discharged a duty to Dablon for one "journal dealing with the River Mississipi" by commencing a daybook in which his future successes and failures in their haunts would be told. If Dablon had asked for the story of Marquette's exploration of 1673, he discharged a second duty to his superior with regard to another "journal dealing with the River Mississipi" by sending this duplicate to him. If this one failed to get through to Quebec as the original had, the word "copies" in the introduction to his new daybook could be hoped, at some future time, to let Dablon know how both obligations had been undertaken.[35]

A document which assuredly accompanied the duplicate narrative of the Marquette-Jolliet expedition when it began its journey to Quebec witnesses to its safe arrival there. This is a map of the discovery with handwritten captions containing enough bibliotic characteristics to establish Marquette as its

34. ACSM, 296, 63, "Jacque" is written in the manuscript, without a surname.

35. Thwaites, *JR*, LIX, 164–65, translates the words "ayant satifait aux Sentiments de V.R. pour les coppies," literally with no comment. It is believed that the explanation in the text of the present book is the first to clarify what must have been in Marquette's mind.

author.[36] The reason it was kept by a Jesuit superior, accustomed to destroy the field notes of his confrères, may be traced to his peculiar interest in the geography of Canada. Information about it was needed in guiding missionaries to new fields of labor. Dablon himself had collaborated with Father Allouez in delineating Lake Superior and its surrounding country for publication in the *Relation . . . les Années 1670–1671*.[37] When in 1674 Jolliet sketched the Mississippi from memory, so Frontenac might display its extent to Colbert, Dablon seems

36. ACSM, 687, Marquette's autograph map. The replica in Thwaites, *JR*, LIX, 108, shows printed cards covering place names. They were not attached to the original. Marquette's script is unobscured on a photocopy of 1953, in AMU, Map Collection. Other reproductions are in John G. Shea, *Discovery and Exploration of the Mississippi Valley* (New York, 1852), after unn. p. 267; James Lenox and John G. Shea, eds., *Recit des Voyages et des Decouvertes de R. Père Jacques Marquette* (Albany, N. Y., 1855), after *Avant-propos*; de Montézon, *Rel. Inédites*, II, unn. p. 330, followed by *Appendice* and the map; Louise P. Kellogg, "Marquette's Authentic Map Possibly Identified," *Proceedings of the State Historical Society of Wisconsin, 1906*, LIV (1907), 186–87; Kellogg, *The French Regime in Wisconsin and the Northwest* (Madison, Wis., 1925), p. 200; Nellis Crouse, *Contributions of the Canadian Jesuits to the Geographical Knowledge of New France, 1632–1675* (Ithaca, N. Y., 1924), pp. 112–13; Sara J. Tucker, *Indian Villages of the Illinois Country, Pt. 1, Atlas* (Springfield, Ill., 1942), pl. V.

37. Archives Nationales, Paris, Le Service Hydrographique, B 4044–74; Karpinski reproductions in the Edward F. Ayer Collection of the Newberry Library, Chicago; Thwaites *JR*, LV, 94–95. See also, Jean Delanglez, "Marquette's Autograph Map of the Mississippi River," *M-A*, XXVII (1945), 31–35. Dablon's letter transmitting the *Relation . . . les Années 1670–1671*, modestly says the chart was made by two Jesuits, Thwaites, *JR*, LV, 254–55. Louis Karpinski, *Bibliography of Printed Maps of Michigan with a Series of Over One Hundred Reproductions of Maps Constituting an Historical Atlas of the Great Lakes and Michigan* (Lansing, Mich., 1931) p. 99, says, "Not until the second quarter of the nineteenth century was any cartographical work of the magnitude and character of this Jesuit map executed in the Great Lakes area."

to have copied the drawing in the form which is known as the Manitoumie map.[38] All search for the Jolliet original has so far been fruitless.[39] But a man like Dablon would be eager to have its outline in the "Relation . . . les Années 1672–1673"; and the wording taken from the title of the Manitoumie map, "Carte de la Nouvelle Decouverte que les Peres Iesuites Ont Fait en l'Année 1672, et Continuée par le P. Jacques Marquette . . . en l'Année 1673 [Map of the New Discovery which the Jesuit Fathers Have Made in the Year 1672, and Continued by Father Jacques Marquette . . . in the Year 1673]," further associates it with the Relation. It is in this document that Allouez' earlier contact with the Illinois, at the Mascoutin Village on the Fox River, finds place; it also contains Jolliet's dictation about the exploration which brought him and Marquette to the same site and then to the original home of the Illinois.[40]

Dablon would have asked Marquette for a facsimile of his "very exact chart," which Jolliet had lost, together with the missionary's journal.[41] Since Marquette had no need for the map on the trip he was undertaking in 1674, there is no reason for his not having complied with this request. If this document set out with the duplicate journal, its presence in the Collège

38. BN, Vd. 30, Estampes; Karpinski reproductions in the Ayer Collection at the Newberry, "Carte de la Nouvelle Decouverte que les Peres Iesuites Ont Fait en l'Année 1672, et Continuée par le P. Jacques Marquette de la Mesme Compagnie Accompagné de Quelq' Francois en l'Année 1673 Qu'on Pourra Nomme en Francais la Manitoumie a Cause de la Statue Qui S'Est Trouvée, dans Une Belle Vallée et Qui les Sauvages Vont Reconoistre pour Leur Divinité, Quils Appellent Manitou, Qui Signifie Esprit ou Genie."

39. Jean Delanglez, "The Jolliet Lost Map of the Mississippi," *M-A*, XXVIII (1946), 102.

40. Thwaites, *JR*, LVIII, 28–31 and APF, Fonds Brotier 155 (Canada–1), 11–13 tell of Allouez and Jolliet. Kellogg, *French Regime*, p. 200, n. 29, abandoned the conjecture advanced in Kellogg, "Marquette's Map," pp. 184–85, which would have Marquette draw this map.

41. APF, Fonds Brotier 155 (Canada–1), 12.

Sainte-Marie today is proof of their arrival at their destination without mishap.

Strangely enough, Jean Delanglez, who wrote so well about most things of the French regime in North America, over-looked the testimony of the map, when he made a study of the Récit. He insisted that Marquette kept a diary separate from the one by Jolliet, that Dablon sent for a second copy of it when the original was lost, and that it started on its way to him in the fall of 1674.[42] At this point, Delanglez slipped into the blunder which accounts for his other oversights. Following the example of writers who overemphasize the first chapter of Dablon's Récit, Delanglez did the same thing.[43] He built his study on the Chantilly manuscript and of it he said, "the *Récit* proper extends from the middle of page [26] to the lowest third of page [52]."[44] A glance at the original discloses him as quoting the pagination of only chapter one. This im-proper amputation of a part from the whole made Delanglez see Dablon saying to his friend Father Boucher, when he wrote about his "little work," that he had turned to "all the memoirs of the Deceased Fr. Marquette," to describe the discovery of the Mississippi.[45] Surely, says Delanglez, it would not have been necessary to make such a collection, if the journal had been at hand. He suggested an accident similar to the one which overtook its predecessor as answering for its absence.[46]

42. Delanglez, "Recit des voyages," p. 190.

43. Thwaites, *JR,* LIX, 86–163, separated chapter one from the rest, see above, ch. 3, n. 16. Steck thought this first chapter was the whole Récit, and neglected chapters two and three, Francis B. Steck, *Marquette Legends,* ed., August Reyling (New York, 1960), Index, p. 348, " '*Récit*' i.e. the Narrative of the Jolliet 1673 expedition, q.v."

44. Delanglez, "Recit des voyages," p. 177, follows the page num-bering of APF, Fonds Brotier 159 (Canada–5), 25–67, as found at the head of each sheet, see above, ch. 3, n. 1.

45. ARSJ, Gal. 110, pt. 1, 62v, "Lettre du P. Dablon au P. Boucher (Quebec, 25 octobre 1678)."

46. Delanglez, "Recit des voyages," p. 184.

And he fell into this mistake all the more easily because of his extensive research about seventeenth-century New France. He had uncovered so much material related to the discovery of the Mississippi that he asserted there was "no essential fact" about it which could not be traced in manuscripts other than the journal.[47]

Delanglez had hardly formulated his theory when he realized the damage it cast upon Dablon's character. If the first chapter of the Récit was a compilation from sources written by others than Marquette, it should tell what he saw and what he did in the third person, but a generous measure of pronouns in the first person is scattered over these pages: "I" and "we" are employed just as if the narrative was by one who had been on the trip. To save Dablon from the charge of mendacity in this usage, Delanglez appealed to what he dubbed a "literary artifice," taken advantage of by the editor to enliven his style. Said he, "scholars of the era are known to expose policies of historical characters by quoting imaginary speeches embodying their views." [48] However, the things told of in the Récit are not well known policies. Often the first person shows up in the description of unique incidents of actual experience, as when Marquette writes, "j eu la curiosite de boire des Eaux mineralles de la Riuiere qui n'est pas loing de Cette bourgade [Mascoutin village], Je pris aussi le temps de reconnoistre Vn simple qu'un Sauuage qui en Scait le secret a enseigné au P.

47. Ibid. The sources Delanglez considered sufficient for writing about the discovery are: (1) Jolliet's dictation of August 1, 1674; (2) the map Jolliet made from memory; (3) Marquette's autograph map; (4) Marquette's holograph journal of his second trip to the Illinois; (5) the unpublished Relations for the years 1672 to 1678; (6) various volumes of the printed Relations; and (7) conversations with Jolliet or other men who had been on the exploration. Ibid., p. 211.

48. Ibid., pp. 219–20. He called as witness Charles V. Langlois and Ch. Signobos, *Introduction aux Études Historiques* (Paris, 1899), p. 258.

Alloües auec beaucoup de Ceremonies . . . [I had the curiosity to drink some mineral waters further up the river, yet not far from this village, I also took time to investigate a medicinal plant which a savage, who knew its secrets, had discovered to Father Allouez with much ceremony]." [49] This remark follows a long description of the Fox River Valley in the third person. In the seventeenth century, when quotation marks were unknown, such a switch meant a change from indirect to direct discourse.[50] In the present instance there is no excuse for denying this practice. Nor may Dablon's prudent character be overlooked in a consideration of this passage. In the "Relation . . . les Années 1672–1673," he told how Allouez, who had been among the Mascoutin Indians, joined Marquette at the mission of St. Ignace in the summer before the exploration, and how the two priests traveled in company to the Sault. However, such a superior would not have felt a "literary artifice" constituted sufficient justification for fabricating any conversation between the priests. Known documents fail to supply evidence for the topics of their discourse as they journeyed together.[51]

When Jolliet and Marquette arrived at the Mascoutin village, guides were obtained who led them to a portage opening on westward flowing waters. The Récit traces their success in the first person, "nous conduisirent-ils heureusement jusqua vn portage de 2700 pas . . . pour entrer dans Cette riuiere [suc-

49. ACSM, 296, 8; Thwaites, *JR*, LIX, 100–101. Though, as a rule, only the original Récit at Montreal will be cited, when speaking of what Dablon wrote in his "little work," the page numbers for identical passages in the Chantilly Récit are to be found in Appendix II.

50. Lewis Hanke, *Bartolomé De Las Casas Historian, an Essay in Spanish Historiography* (Gainesville, Fla., 1952), p. 82, tells why the "I" portions in Las Casas' abstract of the 1492–93 diary, kept by Columbus, are quotations.

51. APF, Fonds Brotier 155 (Canada–1), 28; Thwaites, *JR*, LVII, 250–51, tells of Marquette traveling with Allouez, and his visit to the Mascoutins is ibid., LVIII, 24–25.

cessfully, they conducted us to a portage of 2700 paces long
. . . by which we might enter this river]." A few lines later
on, he names the river *Meskousing* ("Wisconsin").[52] Simple
as this sounds, it would be hard to explain how Dablon could
attribute these words to Marquette without his journal. If he
was depending on Jolliet's dictation to determine the length
of the path, he would have repeated what is found there: in
it, the measurement is said to be "une demi-lieue."[53] The
"2700 paces" of the Récit are in no way a common synonym
for half a league; hence, they point to a different estimate in
a different manuscript. In like manner, the Manitoumie map
and the map with the arms of Frontenac, which certainly were
drawn with Jolliet's help, call the Wisconsin River, "R. de
Messiösing" or "R. de Miskous," but the Récit speaks of it
by neither of these names. Dablon would not have departed
so far from Jolliet's terms as to caption it "Meskousing" unless
he felt he had a better authority for doing so. Owing to Marquette's fluency in Indian dialects, he deserved to be so considered.

The Récit pays slight heed to what happened as the canoes
sped down the Wisconsin River because the hoped-for discovery came so quickly. Marquette says of it, "apres 40 lviuës
sur Cette mesme route, nous arriuons a l'embouchure de nostre
Riuiere et nous trouuant a 42 degrez et demy D'eslauation,
nous entrons heureusement dans Missisipi Le 17e Juin auec
vne Joye que je ne peux pas Expliquer [after 40 leagues on
this same route we arrived at the mouth of our River, and
being at 42 degrees and a half above the equator, we happily
paddled into the Mississippi, the 17 June, with a joy which
I am unable to make known]." Here, more than anywhere
else, it is the wording of the quotation which proves it was

52. ACSM, 296, 10–11; Thwaites, *JR*, LIX, 104–7. Marquette's
autograph map does not name the river.
53. APF, Fonds Brotier 155 (Canada–1), 11, is Jolliet's dictation of
August 1, 1674.

not invented by Dablon, whose written style inclines toward
the dramatic. The scene of the successful arrival of the exploring canoes, borne from the Wisconsin onto the bosom of
the Father of Waters, could never have been told so simply by
him. However, it seems quite appropriate for a fervent missionary, who for five years had been praying for a chance to
carry the Gospel to this river, to experience, at the moment of
fulfillment, a spiritual exultation overstepping the power of
mere language to express.[54]

After traveling through uninhabited lands until June 25,
the expedition first encountered the Illinois.[55] The Indians
welcomed Jolliet and Marquette to their encampment. After
a single night among them, the exploration had to go forward,
so the priest promised to return and spend more time with
them later on. Then, he says, "Nous prenons congé des Ilinois
. . . nous descendons suivant le courant dela Riuiere apellee
Pekitonoui qui se descharge dans Missisipi venant du norouest
delaqᴵᴵᵉ Jay quelq' chose de considerable a dire aprezq' jauray
raconté ceq' jay remarqué sur cette Riuiere [We take leave of
the Illinois . . . we float down following the current of the
River called Pekitonoui which empties into the Mississippi
coming from the northwest concerning which I have considerable to say after I shall have recounted what I noticed on this
latter River]." [56] These words could hardly stand as they do
unless they came from Father Marquette's journal. If Dablon

54. ACSM, 296, 11. Thwaites, *JR,* LIX, 106–7, translates this passage, "We safely entered Missisipi, on The 17th of June, with a Joy
that I cannot Express." APF, Fonds Brotier 159 (Canada–5), 16v,
employs the word "exprimer," instead of "Expliquer." Dablon probably inserted the former word because he understood it would better
convey Marquette's real meaning.

55. ACSM, 296, 15; Thwaites, *JR,* LIX, 114–17.

56. ACSM, 296, 24v; Thwaites, *JR,* LIX, 136–37. These words are
on the second page substituted for the missing 23–24 of the Montreal
Récit. The passage is identical, however, with the one in the original
in France, APF, Fonds Brotier 159 (Canada–5), 22.

had been making up the narrative, he would not have introduced the incongruity found here. He had the autograph map
which places the Illinois village on the Mississippi close to
the fortieth degree north. On the same map, the mouth of the
Pekitonoui is close to the thirty-eighth degree. From this, he
could see the impossibility of floating away from the savage
rendezvous on "the current of the River called Pekitonoui."[57]
The inclusion in the Récit of such an error indicates an honest
effort to transcribe the words found in a document whose
author was no longer within reach. The only inaccessible chronicler of the trip was Marquette. Therefore, his journal must
have occasioned this misunderstanding. Such a conjecture is
fortified by a consideration of the stylistic pecularities found in
his autograph narrative of the second trip to the Illinois.[58] It
has a very few sentences which begin with capital letters, while
the ending of one thought is hardly ever separated from the
beginning of the next by the proper punctuation marks. Con-
sequently, the passage "we float down following the current
of the River called Pekitonoui" may be assumed to have been
written in the original without such aids to clarity. Dablon took
the whole thing for one sentence. If he had pondered it a little
more closely in relation to the geographical data on Marquette's
autograph map, he would have seen the words were intended
to be divided into two. If a period is placed after "we float
down following the current," the new thought, "Of the [de la]
River Pekitonoui," has the sense "Concerning the River." Then,
the memoir fits in with what must have been in the mind of its
author. It now reads, "We take leave of the Illinois . . . we
float down, following the current. Concerning the River called
Pekitonoui, which empties into the Missisipi, coming from the
northwest, I have considerable to say about it after I shall

57. ACSM, 687, Marquette's Autograph Map. Laenas G. Weld,
"Jolliet and Marquette in Iowa," *The Iowa Journal of History and
Politics*, I (1903), 3–16, locates the Indian camp.

58. ACSM, 296, 63–68.

have recounted what I noticed on this latter [Mississippi] River." Without a period, the meaning is obscure. It would have been left so by an editor determined not to intrude his own interpretations into the text he was transcribing, if and when he did not understand it.

Just before the promised description of the Missouri River commences, an allusion is made to some rocks with Indian painting on them. The attempt to impart a notion of these weird glyphs is all in the first person and ends, "voicy apeupres La figure de ces monstres Comme nous L'auons Contretirée [here is approximately the shape of these monsters, as we have made the tracing of them]," but no sketch is to be found at this place or elsewhere in the manuscript. The only adequate argument for this omission is to believe that the likenesses of these beasts had been drawn on the pages of the original relation alone. When it went to the bottom of the St. Lawrence with Jolliet's wreck, Dablon had to resort to the duplicate. Lacking the prototype, he left the lacuna rather than substitute an illustration of his own imagining.[59]

When the explorers finally came in contact with the Illinois Indians, the priest, because only he was fluent in their language, delivered them a speech. He salted it with "I" and "we." A study of it will suffice to close the case in favor of Dablon's having literally quoted from the missionary's journal whenever his biography employs direct discourse. Delanglez says the speech is a capital specimen of the "literary artifice" attributed to Dablon, since it contains "a statement which Marquette could not possibly have made." This is, "Je leur parlay . . . que Le grand Capitaine des françois leur faisoit scauoir que c'est luy qui mestoit la paix partout et qui auoit dompté L'Jroquois [I told them . . . that the great Captain of the French informed them, that it was he who restored the peace everywhere and who had subdued the Iroquois]." [60]

59. ACSM, 296, 26; Thwaites, *JR*, LIX, 138–41.
60. Delanglez, "Recit des voyages," p. 236, discusses the speech,

Delanglez applied the term "Captain of the French" to Frontenac and the subduing of the Iroquois to his visit, in July of 1673, to the Cataraqui River, where he built a post in their neighborhood.[61] If such was the meaning of the words in the Récit, Marquette in June, 1673, could not have told the Indians of exploits which were not to take place until a month later. Therefore, Delanglez accuses Dablon of improvising the whole oration, when he edited the Récit in 1678. This supposition ignores the absurdity of improvising an anachronism and of labeling a summer excursion to a friendly council with the red men at Cataraqui as a conquest.[62] On the other hand Daniel de Remy, Seigneur de Courcelle, the governor whom Frontenac had superseded only after Talon's orders for the Mississippi exploration were issued, can be looked on as one who put the Iroquois in their place. Marquette knew of the measures this officer had taken against them because, in September, 1666, when he first arrived in Quebec, he found the whole town pushing preparations for a final drive to terminate a twelve-month campaign against the Five Nations.[63]

---

which may be read fully in ACSM, 296, 17; Thwaites, *JR*, LIX, 118–21.

61. Archives Nationales, Paris, Archives des Colonies, C11, A4, 14–24, journal of Count Frontenac's voyage to Lake Ontario in Preston and Lamontagne, *Royal Fort Frontenac*, p. 106; also in Margry, *Découv. et Étab.*, I, 195–238, or in English translation in Edmund B. O'Callaghan, ed., *Documents Relative to the Colonial History of the State of New York* (Albany 1853–61), IX, 95–114.

62. Margry, *Découv. et Étab.*, I, 210; O'Callaghan, *Documents*, IX, 112. Abbé Lascaris d'Urfe and abbé François de Fenelon had a mission on the nearby bay of Quinté, and their chiefs took part in the meet.

63. BN, Collection Moreau, 842, 34, "extrait d'un lettre escritte de Kebec par le P. Thierry Beschefer . . . au P. Antoine Chesne (2 octobre, 1666)," and D. H. Laverdière and H. R. Casgrain, eds., *Le Journal des Jésuites* (Quebec, 1871), p. 350, reprinted in Thwaites, *JR*, L, 201–2.

De Courcelle was leading 1,200 French soldiers and both
Huron and Algonquin allies into the hostile country. Alexandre
de Prouville, Marquis de Tracy, just then in Canada, was to
accompany the invasion, which moved to the attack on October
3, 1666.[64] Such a formidable offensive terrified the savages;
they fled without offering opposition. The French set the torch
to all the Mohawk towns, their winter food supply, and the
unharvested grain in the fields. In the meantime, Father Marquette had joined Fr. Gabriel Druillettes at Three Rivers to
study the native languages.[65] There he witnessed the triumphal
return of the army. From there, in the summer of 1667, in
one of the few letters he wrote to friends back in France, he
spoke of this military success which led the Iroquois to beg for
a lasting peace.[66] Father Le Mercier, in the *Relation . . . les
Années 1666–1667,* praised de Courcelle for having wrested
submission from these barbarians through "la terreur des armes
de sa Majesté [the terror of the arms of His Majesty]." [67] At
the Sault in 1671, when St. Lusson took possession of the West
in the name of Louis XIV, Father Allouez, in his sermon to
the assembled tribes, proclaimed "Onnontio, ce celebre Cap-
taine de Quebec" to be "la terreur des Iroquois . . . depuis

64. Ibid., pp. 138–47. De Tracy was viceroy of the West Indies,
George M. Wrong, *The Rise and Fall of New France* (Toronto, 1928),
I, 373–75.

65. Laverdière-Casgrain, *Le Journal des Jésuites,* p. 351; Thwaites,
JR, L. 202, "Octobre, 1666 Le P. Iacques Marquette mont aux Trois
Riuieres." There, Druillettes was superior until the fall of 1667, ARSJ,
Franc. 23, 219v, "Catalogus Provinciae Franciae, 1666 Exeunte."

66. BN, Collection Moreau, 842, 37v, "Lettre du P. Marquette au
P. Pupin (4 aoust, 1667)," the Iroquois "n'auoient iamais creu que
les Francois peussent aller faire la guerre en leur pais [never imagined
that the French could carry the war into their country]." The intendant announces the victory, "Lettre de Talon au ministre Colbert
(10 novembre, 1666)," *RAPQ, 1930–31,* p. 51; and dwells on its
importance, ibid., p. 52 and pp. 60–61. This is partially transcribed,
O'Callaghan, *Documents,* IX, 56–57.

67. Thwaites, *JR,* L, 236–37.

qu'il a desolé leur Päis [Onnontio, that celebrated Captain of Quebec . . . the terror of the Iroquois . . . now that he has laid waste their country]." [68] In the letter of transmission accompanying the Relation that fall, Father Dablon, Le Mercier's successor as superior, mentions a new expedition of de Courcelle through Lake Ontario to let the western units of the confederation see the might of the French.[69] Finally, when Frontenac entered on his administration, the *Relation . . . les Années 1671–1672* carried a last eulogy. "Eternellement nous nous souviendrons dupremier [le gouverneur] pour avoir si bien rangé les Iroquois à leur devoir [We shall eternally remember the former (governor), for having so well straightened out the business of the Iroquois]." [70] All this was vividly clear to the two young explorers. Without any knowledge of Frontenac's ability to restrain the aborigines, they had to turn to his predecessor for examples of prowess executed by "the celebrated Captain of Quebec." Marquette was justified in speaking of him as he did. He could only hope he was right in expecting similar protection from de Courcelle's successor.

Delanglez refused to be embarrassed by the difficulty arising from the pronouns. In his article about the Récit, it was dismissed in thirty-seven lines. Sixty-eight pages did not prove adequate for his jumping from one to the other of the seventeenth-century sources which he had brought together to supply a description of the Mississippi exploration without the aid of Marquette's journal.[71] And to be sure, he found so much pertinent material that it would have required more diligence than was his to keep its mass from burying something of importance. However, since he maintained there was "no essen-

68. Ibid., LV, 110–11.
69. Ibid., LIV, 252–55. Dollier de Casson was de Courcelle's chaplain, Margry, *Découv. et Étab.*, I, 169–92; O'Callaghan, *Documents*, IX, 81.
70. Thwaites, *JR*, LV, 234–35.
71. Delanglez, "Recit des voyages," pp. 173–94 and 211–58.

tial fact" about the discovery which could not be drawn from
his documents, the impact of any such incident, not included
there, is enough to cause disaster to his conjecture.[72]

A precautionary measure, which all the members of the
expedition considered important enough to be repeated very
often throughout the trip, and which the finished monograph
of their success openly acknowledges as accessory to its accomplishment, must stand among the essential facts recounted.
The Frenchmen adopted the precaution after their portage
from the Fox to the Wisconsin River. Before they boarded
their canoes to descend this unknown stream into unknown
peril, the manuscript affirms, "nous commencames tous en-
semble une nouuelle deuotion a la S^te. Vierge Jmmaculée que
nous pratiquâmes tous les jours [We, with full accord, commenced a new devotion to the Holy Virgin Immaculate which
we practiced every day]." This was the recitation of a special
prayer invoking the protection of the Mother of God and
asking her help toward the happy outcome of the exploration.[73] The open acknowledgment of the help received from
this spiritual device is made near the Indian village of Mitchi-
gamea. As it came in sight, war-whooping savages rushed to
the shore. War clubs began to fly through the air. Some came
close to the mark. The Récit concedes, "Nous Eusmes recours
a Nostre Patrone et a nostre conductrice La Ste Vierge Jmmaculée, et nous auions bien besoin de son assistance [We had
recourse to Our Guardian and Leader the Holy Virgin Immaculate, and we had dire need of her assistance]." Things did
come out well.[74]

Dablon's conversation with Jolliet is the only one of Delanglez's sources which might have made known these prayers.
But not even Jolliet could have known why Father Marquette
happened to choose this particular attribute of the Virgin as

72. For Delanglez's sources see above, ch. 5, n. 47.
73. ACSM, 296, 10; Thwaites, *JR,* LIX, 106–07.
74. ACSM, 296, 30; Thwaites, *JR,* LIX, 150–51.

the one for the party to depend on. Here is where the first chapter of the Récit reveals what had gone on in the missionary's own mind in a way which one might easily state in one's own journal, but which, in the present case, no other document could supply. The passage reads:

Le jour de L Immaculée Conception de la Ste. Vierge, qui I'auois tousjours Inuoquée depuisque je suis en ce paÿs des outaoüacs, pour obtenir de Dieu La grace de pouuoir visiter les nations qui sont sur la Riuiere de Missisipi, fut justement Celuy au quel arriua Mr Jollyet auec Les ordres de Mr. L Comte de frontenac nostre Gouuerneur Et de Mr. Talon nostre Intendant, pour faire auec moy Cette découuerte.[75]

[The day of the Immaculate Conception of the Bl. Virgin, whom I have ever invoked since I came to the Ottawa country, to obtain the grace from God to visit the nations who are on the Mississippi River, was the very one on which M. Jolliet arrived with the orders of M. the Count De Frontenac our Governor and M. Talon our Intendant, which commissioned him with me to make this discovery.]

Here, because by coincidence it was the feast of the Immaculate Conception when Jolliet came to St. Ignace and the long desired permission to be off for the Illinois country reached Father Marquette, the missionary makes an intimate confession that he had been praying to the Blessed Virgin, under this title, for this favor ever since he had established the mission at Sault Sainte-Marie in 1668.[76]

Having obtained the permission, he continued:

Sur tout je mis nostre Voyage soubs le protection de la Ste. Vierge Immaculée, Luy promettant que si elle nous faisoit la grace de découurir la grande Riuiere, Je luy donnerois Le nom de la

75. ACSM, 296, 2; Thwaites, *JR*, LIX, 88–89.
76. Ibid., LIV, 190–95 for Marquette's beginnings at the Sault. APF, Fonds Brotier 155 (Canada–1), 34, and Thwaites, *JR*, LVII, 262–63, are earlier expressions of Marquette's desire to undertake the trip, but do not hint at his prayer.

Conception et que je ferois aussi porter ce nom a la premiere mission que j établyrois chez Ces nouueaux peuples.[77]

[Above all, I put our voyage under the protection of the Bl. Virgin Immaculate, promising her that if she granted us the privilege of discovering the Great River I would give it the name Conception and that I would also assign this name to the first mission which I should establish among these new people.]

Thus, when Marquette prevailed upon his companions to choose their patroness, he was carrying out a resolution made months before. It would be unnatural to tell them this; it was natural to mention it in his diary. Delanglez bypassed this whole episode with the inadequate remark, which he did not expand, "Dablon knew of Marquette's great devotion to the Blessed Virgin." [78] Such knowledge does not include how long Marquette had prayed, or the time at which he had invoked her mediation.

Delanglez was in a hurry to piece together the clippings from his research. Such haste alone accounts for his overlooking the obvious: he was too much the scholar to dissimulate once he became aware of an obstruction to his theory. An obstruction to it was presented by what Dablon wrote of the Indians with guns whom Marquette met shortly below the Ohio River. These savages were found to have not only guns, but

des haches, des houës, des Cousteaux de La rassade des bouteilles de verre double ou ils mettent Leur Poudre, . . . [il disaient] quils acheptaient Les estoffes et toutes autres Marchandises de Europeans qui estoient du Costé de L'est, que ces Europeans auoient des chapletz et des images, quils joüoient des Jnstrumentz qu'il y en auoit qui estoient faitz comme moy, et quils en Estoient bien recu.

[hatchets, hoes, knives, glass beads, bottles of double glass in which they keep their powder, . . . (and they said) that they buy

77. ACSM, 296, 3–4; Thwaites, *JR,* LIX, 90–93.
78. Delanglez, "Recit des voyages," p. 223.

cloth and all other wares from Europeans who live toward the east, that these Europeans have rosaries and statues, that they play instruments, that some who look like me live there, and that they were well received by them.]

These Indians knew of no white men to the south and thought it was not more than ten days' journey to the sea.[79] Their revelation pricked the nerve which set the expedition in motion. To anticipate all other Europeans in getting to the Mississippi River was the marrow of the exploration; hence, this is an essential fact. Jolliet's map called these natives Monsouperia. The Récit assigns them no name. In a previous article, Delanglez had admitted his inability to find a satisfactory hypothesis for the anonymity of these Indians.[80] His final word on the subject admitted the problem was "well-nigh insoluble." And, within the bounds of his conjecture, so it is.[81] If he had considered the evidence for the safe arrival of Marquette's duplicate journal and Dablon's dependence on it, rather than attempting to build the first chapter of the Récit from "all the memoirs of the deceased Fr. Marquette," he would have seen there was no need for his misgivings.

The present chapter will close by pointing to some of "the memoirs" which concern affairs covered in the second and third chapters of Dablon's biography of Father Marquette. Dablon's recourse to them for this purpose supplies the right interpretation of his meaning when he said he had "arranged them" to draw upon their contents for his "little work."

79. ACSM, 296, 29–30; Thwaites, *JR*, LIX, 146–53.
80. "I am well aware that none of these hypotheses is satisfactory." Delanglez, "Joliet Lost Map," pp. 111–12.
81. Delanglez, "Recit des voyages," pp. 245–47. Elsewhere, Delanglez thought Dablon might have copied a "lost account of the voyage," which omitted the name employed by Jolliet, ibid., pp. 249–50. See also Jean Delanglez, "The Discovery of the Mississippi, Secondary Sources," *M-A,* XXVIII (1946), 8, and Delanglez, "Jolliet Lost Map," p. 108. He never made clear what this account would be.

The first document Dablon utilized for the "Chapitre Second Récit du second voyage que le Pere Jacques Marquette a fait aux Jlinois . . . [Chapter Two. Recital of the second voyage which Father Jacques Marquette made to the Illinois . . .]" was the journal kept by the missionary on this trip.[82] Here day by day as the months went by, his southern progress, frequently interrupted by necessary delays was set down. It is not a very colorful story until he reached the mouth of the Chicago River. Dablon epitomizes it, but without the original he could not have written as he did. His second paragraph dates Marquette's departure thus, "Il partit pour cela dans le mois de Nouembre de l'année 1674 de la Baye des puantz [He left the Bay of the Stinkers (Green Bay), for there in the month of November of the year 1674]." [83] It requires a little study of the journal itself to understand how he figured this out. It says the mission house of St. Francis Xavier was left earlier, on "25 oct. 1674," but wind held the canoes in the Fox River for twenty-four hours. Then on the twenty-sixth, at the Potawatomi village, where the river meets the bay, some Illinois visitors proposed to form a convoy for the explorer as he made the trip to the land of their fathers. The question had to be settled Indian fashion, by a council. Two days passed before the proposition was agreed upon and the whole party was ready to depart. It was October 28 when the Sturgeon Bay portage was reached. Here the twenty-ninth and thirtieth were consumed in getting things across the peninsula from bay side to lake side. Under October 31, an entry is made describing the very great difficulty of this operation. It may be presumed this day was devoted to rest, because on November 1, the expedition harbored for the night in the mouth of a river which entered Lake Michigan twenty-six miles south of the portage.[84] The distance can be estimated, though it is not actually given in the

82. ACSM, 296, 63–69v.
83. ACSM, 296, 38; Thwaites, *JR*, LIX, 184–85.
84. ACSM, 296, 63–64.

manuscript, because there is mention of a westward trail from the spot overland to the Potawatomi village at the mouth of the Fox. The present city of Kewaunee at the mouth of a stream twenty-six miles south of Sturgeon Bay is very close to being on the same parallel of latitude with the home of the Potawatomi. Since thirty miles a day on lake water is taken as average for canoe travel of the period, Dablon, with the journal for evidence, had every reason for transcribing Marquette's final departure from the bay and first day's trip on the lake as "in the month of November." Without the journal, it would be very hard to explain why he selected this date.

Because Father Marquette's health began to fail and the snow commenced to fall, it was decided to winter on the site of present-day Chicago. There until March 29, 1675, he and his two donnés, Pierre Porteret and Jacques Largillier, remained.[85] Dablon allotted only a few lines to what happened during these months from early December, 1674, until the end of March, 1675, when winter quarters were deserted. Incidentally, this passage contradicts Delanglez' conjecture that the "first person" was employed by the editor to "enliven his style," insofar as here, Dablon changes the journal's direct discourse, "I set out," into the third person, saying, "he set out." [86]

The Récit passes on to a description of Marquette's arrival among the Illinois and his founding the mission of the Conception in the village of the Kaskaskia. The ceremonies lasted from Maundy Thursday, April 11, 1675, until Easter Sunday.

85. ACSM, 296, 63, the holograph journal has no surname after "Jacques," Marquette probably left the space, which comes at the end of the line and of the sentence, to be filled according to Jacques' preference for, "Largillier," "Largilier," "l'Argilier" or "le Castor," which were various titles applied to him. Apparently, he forgot to make the addition immediately and, because of the location of the lacuna, his attention was not attracted to it later on.

86. ACSM, 296, 39; Thwaites, *JR,* LIX, 186–87.

By then, the missionary was prostrated. He realized the shadow
of death was upon him and determined to be on his way
toward St. Ignace before his illness could spread gloom to the
Indians. He promised them the mission would not be abandoned. Next, Dablon narrates details from the few remaining
days left to Marquette on this earth, of his death, and of his
burial in the wilderness. All this had been put on paper for
the first time in the letter which Father Cholenec wrote on
October 10, 1675, as he transcribed the dictation of Pierre and
Jacques.[87] After their stop with him at La Prairie de la Madeleine, the two donnés went to Quebec and Dablon received
Marquette's unfinished autograph journal from them together
with their story. On October 13, 1675, he penned an obituary
which he sent to headquarters in Rome.[88] This death notice
and the part in chapter two of the Récit, dealing with these
things, are so similar to Father Cholenec's letter as to suggest
dependence on it for their content.[89]

The passing of the missionary's soul and the burial of his
body are sketched according to the words of the canoe men
who had been with him at the end. Their description of these
last days is simple but graphic. It ends with their leaving his
death site, in the wilderness, with regret and after having set
"une grande Croix proche de son tombeau pour seruir de
marquer aux passans [a large cross close to his grave to serve
as a marker to passersby]." Father Cholenec's letter, which
deals with these things, supplies the hint necessary to explain
how Father Nouvel, superior of the western missions, became

87. APF, Fonds Brotier 166 (Canada–12), no. 4, 26v, "Lettre du
P. Cholenec au P. Fontenay (10 octobre 1675)."

88. ARSJ, Gal. 110, pt. 2, 195–196v, "Lettre circulaire du P.
Jacques Marquette."

89. *Institutum Societatis Iesu* (Florentiae, 1892–93), III, 111, "Regulae Rectoris, no. 35," allots authority to the superior to inspect his
subject's writing. "Videat scripta et litteras omnes . . . quas ipsi alliis
scribunt [He may look at writings and all letters . . . which they write
to others]."

Dablon's informant about the reburial of Marquette's bones in the church of St. Ignace, which in 1675 had become the headquarters for the area.[90] Father Cholenec writes of Pierre Porteret and Jacques Largillier, who put up the large cross, "ces deux memes domestiques donnés estoint descendus cet esté des Outouacs pour Quebec, et y estans ensuite retournés, ie les ay Vu icy allans Et reuenans [these same two donnés had come down to Quebec from the Ottawa, and having returned there immediately, I saw them, here, both coming and going]." This means that some time prior to October 10, 1675, the date of Cholenec's letter, the men who had been at the scene of the missionary's death had passed La Prairie de la Madeleine, on their return trip to Michilimackinac. Father Nouvel's course of action, a few weeks later, would indicate that the donnés brought a message from Dablon, expressing his solicitude over Marquette's exposed grave and a wish that the body might be transferred to the mission cemetery.[91]

In November, some Christian Indians on the way to their winter hunting ground stopped at St. Ignace and asked for a chaplain to accompany them. The superior had them sketch out the neighborhood where they expected to spend the cold months. They outlined a trip south, along the Lake Huron shore on the east side of what is now the state of Michigan. Well down the coast, they marked a big bay. Thence, they planned to ascend a river deep into the country toward the west. This placed their winter quarters close to Father Mar-

90. ACSM, 296, 46; Thwaites *JR*, LIX, 200–1 tells of the cross. The move of Nouvel is described in Raphael N. Hamilton, "St. Mary's Mission at Sault Ste. Marie," *Michigan History*, LII (1968), 122–32.

91. APF, Fonds Brotier 166 (Canada–12), no. 4, 26v, "Lettre du P. Cholenec au P. Fontenay (10 octobre, 1675)." In 1649, the body of Fr. Jean de Brebeuf, killed by the Iroquois in Huronia, had been removed from his death site and buried at Fort Ste. Marie in a similar manner, see *Report Concerning the Canadian Archives, 1884*, n. E, lxiii–lxvii; *Woodstock Letters*, XIV (1885), 331–40.

quette's grave. Nouvel decided he himself would act as chaplain. He took along "two Frenchmen," which suggests his having the companionship of Pierre and Jacques. They knew the place where Marquette was buried.[92] There is much in the commentary on his trip which would justify the supposition that his going was motivated by a hope of learning more about the site, with the possibility of transferring the bones to St. Ignace. For instance, just after the arrival at the place of wintering, it was December 7, he was impelled to say:

> Je ne peux pas expliquer la consolation que j'eus le lendmain de célébrer nos adorables mystères dans nostre chapelle, en un lieu si esloigné, au milieu de ces grandes forets, . . . Oh que le feu père Marquette, d'heureuse mémoire, qui est mort assez proche d'icy, a eu raison de s'obliger par voeu à ne quitter jamais ces rudes mais aymables missions que lorsque la S^{te}. Obeissance l'en retireroit. Dieu luy a accordé la grace d'y mourir, ô quel bonheur! [93]

> [I am not able to explain the consolation which I had the next day (the feast of the Immaculate Conception) while celebrating the sacred liturgy in our chapel in a place so remote, in the heart of primeval forests . . . Oh, how sure it is that the late Father Marquette of happy memory, who died quite close to this place, was wise in binding himself by vow never to leave these rough but lovable missions unless holy obedience would recall him from them. God accorded him grace to die here, Oh, what goodness!]

After Christmas, Nouvel began a series of exploratory

92. [Claude Dablon], *Relation de Ce Qui S'Est Passé de Plvs Remarqvable avx Missions des Peres de la Compagnie de Iesvs en la Novvelle-France és Années 1676 & 1677*, ed., James Lenox, (Albany, 1854), p. 50. See also Thwaites, *JR, LX*, 214–29. For the location of Marquette's temporary grave see Raphael N. Hamilton, "The Marquette Death Site: The Case for Ludington," *Michigan History*, XLIX (1965), 228–48.

93. Dablon (ed., Lenox), *Relation . . . és Années 1676 & 1677*, p. 59.

marches. He set out "le 29 décember d'aller au Costier des Nipissiriniens 8 ou 10 lieues dans le bois [the 29th of December in order to go to the camp of the Nipissiriniens, 8 or 10 leagues in the forest]." After visiting them, he heard of another tribe in a different direction, so, "Je fis une 2de excursion jusque chez les Misissakis a quelques journées de nostre demeure [I made a second excursion all the way to the Missakis, several days' journey from our place]." Here he stayed several days. Despite the fact that the cold was terrific, he managed to make a few other sallies into the snow-piled forest, then he had to be contented to settle down, in the winter quarters, until mid-March, 1676, when the members of his savage flock decided to start home. Their chaplain was constrained to go along with them empty-handed.[94]

Nouvel seems to have failed to write his letter in 1677.[95] It was the summer of 1678 before Dablon received from him the intelligence he had been waiting for. On the return from their winter hunt of 1677, the Kiskakon Ottawa visited the death scene of their favorite missionary, intent on returning his remains to St. Ignace. They found Father Marquette's corpse practically incorrupt despite two year exposure:

> suiuant ce qu'ils ont Coustume de faire Envers ceux pour qui ils ont bien du respect; ils ouurent donc la fosse, ils deuelopent le Corps, et . . . ils lauerent les os et les exposerent a l'air pour les secher, apres quoy les ayant bien arranges dans une Caisse d'ecorce de bouleau, ils Se merent En chemin pour nous les apporter en nostre Maison de st. Jgnace.
>
> Ils estoit prez de 30 Canotz qui faisoint ce Conuoy auec une tres bel ordre . . . quand ils aprocherent de nostre maison, Le P. Nouuel qui y est superieur, fut au deuant d'Eux auec L P.

94. Ibid., pp. 63–66.
95. Ibid., pp. 1–165; Thwaites, *JR*, LX, 168–309. See above, pp. 78–79, where a reason is assigned for including 1676 and 1677 in one Relation; but in this long narrative there is no account of the Ottawa mission after the Spring of 1676.

Pierson accompagné: de ce qu'il auoit de françois et de sauuages, et aÿant fait arrester le Conuoy, il fit Les interrogations ordinaires pour Verifier que cestoit ueritablement le corps du Pere qu'ils apportoient.[96]

[in conformity with the Custom which they have toward those for whom they have great respect; they open the grave, they uncover the body, and . . . they wash the bones and expose them to the air to dry, thereupon, packing them carefully in a chest of birch bark, they resumed their journey to bring them to us at our residence of St. Ignace.

There were almost 30 canoes, spaced in good order, which made up this convoy . . . when they approached our house, Father Nouvel who is superior there, confronted them with Father Pierson accompanied by the French and savages of his flock, and having made the convoy stop, he conducted the customary interrogations to verify that it was truly the body of the Father which they were bringing.]

Pierre Porteret and Jacques Largillier were almost certainly beside Father Nouvel to assist in the enquiry. According to a letter of October 13, 1676, Father Jean Enjalran, giving a French friend his impressions of New France upon his arrival, says among other things that he had seen the two men who were with Father Marquette at his death and that in 1676 Father Albanal went back to the Outaouacs with the donnés who serve the fathers who are there.[97] If this does not mean that Pierre and Jacques spent the entire winter of 1676–77 at Michilimackinac, they had at least been there enough of the time to supply Father Nouvel with all the particulars about Marquette's grave, its geographical surroundings and the cross which marked it. With such knowledge, he questioned the Indians to verify the remains. Their answers satisfied him and so "apres cela on porte le Corps a l'Eglise gardant tout ce que le rituel marque En Semblable Ceremonies. [After this the

96. ACSM, 296, 51.
97. Thwaites, *JR*, LX, 104–47, prints Enjalran's letter.

body was carried to the church to the accompaniment of everything which the ritual lays down for such ceremonies]." The day on which Father Marquette's relics came home is spoken of in technical ecclesiastical terms as "la 2de feste de la pentecote"; this means the Monday after the feast. The next day, Tuesday June 8, 1677, the reburial took place "dans un petit Caueau au milieu de L'Eglise [in a little vault in the center of the church]."[98]

Now, in an atmosphere of joy, Dablon could have written finish to his Récit. However in the same packet which had supplied the details of Marquette's final resting place, there was a letter from Father Allouez. Among other things, it told of a trip he had made to the Illinois in 1677. It brought him to "Kachkachkia" on April 27. Everyone there was eager to receive him as the successor to their deceased black robe. His letter says, "Jentray d'abord dans la Cabane ou auoit logé le Pere Marquette [I immediately entered the cabin where Father Marquette had lived]," and having taken possession, he immediately commenced instructing the Indians. He had intended this only as a preliminary visit. And after setting up a huge cross on May 3, he started for Green Bay, adding, "je les laissay dans un grand desir de me reuoir auplustost, ce que je Leur ay fait Esperer [I left them anxious for my return, as soon as possible, the which I had encouraged them to expect]." Dablon was sure his readers would be pleased to hear that Father Marquette's mission was to be continued; hence, he expanded the Récit by the addition of a third chapter. He began it with this expository paragraph:

Le P. Jacq' Marquette estant mort dans les trauuaux apostoliq' de La Mission des Ilinois Il ne pouuoit auoir vn meilleur successeur q' Le P. Claude Alloües qui a vne parfaite connois' de toutes les Missions des Outaoüacs & vne gde Intellice dans toutes leur langues come Il est plein d vn Zele que ne laisse point en repos.

98. ACSM, 296, 51.

[Since Fr. Jacq Marquette died in the apostolic work of the Mission of the Illinois he could not have had a better successor than Fr. Claude Allouez who had a perfect knowledge of all the missions of the Ottawa and a great insight into all their languages, and since he is full of zeal which knows no rest.]

Thereupon, he transcribed Allouez' letter in toto.[99] Surely this final inclusion of yet another document, added to all the sources he had cited, justifies Dablon's remark to Father Boucher about turning to "all the memoirs of the deceased Fr. Marquette," in writing of his life, with "his discoveries . . . and the establishment of the Mission of the Illinois," all of which he included in the Récit.

99. APF, Fonds Brotier 159 (Canada–5), 31–34; ACSM, 296, 52–60; Thwaites, *JR*, LX, 158–67. This introduction does not find a place in the Montreal manuscript.

CHAPTER 6

The Truth About
the Discovery

B Y the evidence uncovered in the present study, the Marquette documents seem well established as produced by the people, at the time, and in the places usually attributed to them. There still remains the possibility that those people, in the seventeenth-century in Canada and France, forged the data advanced by them as facts. The de Tonti narrative, fabricated in 1697, which was mentioned in the preface, is not the only fake published by Marquette's contemporaries. There were several who were willing to improve upon the truth in return for the price paid by European readers, curious to have details of the mysterious new lands drained by the Mississippi River. In 1697, Father Hennepin, who in early editions of his first book had told of Marquette's exploration, now asserted, in the new *Nouvelle Decouverte* that he himself should rightfully be called the discoverer of the river. The story he told con-

153

tains extensive sections pirated from known sources, together with episodes which are purely fictional.[1] Another instance of counterfeiting is found in Chrestien Le Clercq, *Premier Etablissement de la Foy dans la Nouvelle France*. It came from the press of Amable Auroy of Paris in 1691 and contains a journal of de La Salle's voyage of 1682 attributed to Fr. Zénobe Membré and another about the de La Salle colony on the Gulf of Mexico ascribed to Fr. Anastase Douay. The Membré narrative has actually been demonstrated to be a plagiarism of memorials concerning de La Salle's journey to the mouth of the Mississippi, which his Paris agent, abbé Bernou, wrote for presentation to the French Court. The account by Douay is actually a copy of the dictation obtained from an interview with de La Salle's brother, Fr. Jean Cavelier, and saved by the cartographer, Guillaume Delisle. The manuscripts originating with Bernou and Cavelier are still available in Paris archives and have been used to expose the fraud.[2] The existence of such trumped-up works demands a further investigation of the Marquette documents to determine how true they are in what they tell about the discovery and the discoverer.

1. Louis Hennepin, *Nouvelle Decouverte d'Un Tres Grand Pays Situé dans l'Amerique, entre le Nouveau Mexique et la Mer Glaciale,* . . . (Utrecht, 1697), is analyzed in Jean Delanglez, "Hennepin's Voyage to the Gulf of Mexico 1680," *M-A,* XXI (1939), 32–81. Hennepin's first book is discussed above in ch. 2. The title of the apocryphal de Tonti is *Dernieres Découvertes dans l'Amerique Septentrionale De M. de la Salle; Mises au Jour par M. le Chevalier Tonti Gouverneur de Fort Saint Louis, aux Islinois* (Paris, 1697). Tonti's criticism of the book is in a letter to his brother from Fort Mississippi, March 4, 1700, ASH, 115–10, no. 14. This is translated by Jean Delanglez, "Tonti Letters," *M-A,* XXI (1939), 220–35.

2. Chrestien Le Clercq, *Premier Etablissement de la Foy dans la Nouvelle France,* . . . (Paris, 1691), was probably written by abbé Bernou and his friend Renaudot, see, Jean Delanglez, "The First Establishment of the Faith in New France, Chapters XXI to XXV," *M-A,* XXX (1948), 187–214. See also, Jean Delanglez, "The Authorship of the Journal of Jean Cavelier," *M-A,* XXV (1943), 220–23.

Map of the Territory in North America Explored by
Père Marquette and Sieur Jolliet

There is little need to dwell at length on proving the existence of what Dablon calls the "most notable peculiarities" of
the unknown lands contacted by the expedition. In subsequent
years, the arrival of Europeans substantiated what Jolliet and
Marquette had been first to see. The Mississippi River was
awesome, but has a slow and gentle current, just as described.
The Missouri was different. The Récit says, "Je n'ay rien veu
deplus affreux, vn embaras de gros arbres entiers, de branches,

disletz flotans, sortoit de Lembouchure de La riuiere peki["s"
crossed out]tanouï auec tant d'impetuosite qu'on ne pouuoit
s'exposer a passer autrauerse sans grand danger [I have seen
nothing more frightening, a barrier of entire large trees, of
branches, of floating islands belched from the mouth of the
river Peki("s" crossed out)tanoui with such violence that it
was only with great danger that one might take the risk to pass
through]," and so it is today.[3] Food was abundant. There were
great herds of buffalo on the shore. In the stream were "des
poissons monstreux, vn des quels donna sj [*sic*] rudement
Contre nostre Canot que je Crû que C'estoit un gros arbre que
L'alloit mettre en pieces [tremendous fish, one of which
bumped our canoe so roughly I thought it was a big tree which
would smash it in pieces]," said Marquette. He was not exag-
gerating. Captain Meriwether Lewis, who passed this way in
1803, told of a catfish landed near the mouth of the Ohio
which weighed 128 pounds, and says he had been told of
similar catches tipping the scale at 200 pounds.[4]

The friendly tribe of the Wild Rice had given a frightening
portrayal of a demon on the Mississippi "qu'on entend de fort
loing qui enferme Le passage et qui abysme Ceux qui osent en
approcher [who was heard for a great distance, who barred
the way and swallowed up all who ventured to approach]."
As the French drew near the Ohio River, they encountered
what they took to be the basis of this belief:

> Voicy ce demon, cest une petite anse de rochers haulte de 20 pieds
> ["qui le suit" crossed out] ou se dégorge tout Le Courant de la
> riuiere Le quel estant repousse contre celuy qui Le suit et arreste
> par une jsle qui est proche, est contraint de passer par un petit
> Canal, cequi ne se fait pas . . . sans un grand tintamarre qui
> donne de la terreur a des sauuages . . . .

3. ACSM, 296, 26–27; Thwaites, *JR*, LIX, 140–43.
4. ACSM, 296, 12; Thwaites, *JR*, LIX, 108–9, has Marquette's
description and the verification is in Richard H. Dillon, *Meriwether
Lewis, a Biography* (New York, 1965), p. 67.

[Here is this demon, it is a little cove of rocks rising about twenty feet above the water, into which the whole current of the river rushes and, thus, is whirled back against the oncoming stream which (just here) is funneled into a narrow channel by a nearby island. (The water) cannot execute this feat . . . without setting up a great clangor, which terrifies the savages . . . .]

Fr. Jean François de St. Cosme, who made the Mississippi voyage a few years later, addressed the bishop of Quebec from the "Akanseas" on January 2, 1699, telling of the whirlpool he had found at the same place. In the nineteenth century the wall of rock was known as the "Devil's Bake Oven" and the opposite obstruction as the "Grand Tower."[5]

During the months of his wintering on the site of Chicago, Marquette jotted down some geographical data which would help future priests who might come to these parts. When he left, he thanked a spring flood for making it possible to reach the Des Plaines River "sans trouuer aucun portage, on traisna peutestre enuiron un demy arpant [without finding any portage, you drag (the canoe in shallow water) only for perhaps a half an arpent (20 yards)]."[6] Robert Knight and Lucius Zeuch, in their *The Location of the Chicago Portage,* analyze the missionary's notes, and discredit the possibility of their having been invented by someone who had not been there.[7]

5. ACSM, 296, 5 and 296, 27–28; Thwaites, *JR,* LIX, 96–97 and 142–45, recount the warning and the basis for it. St. Cosme's letter is in Archives Nationales, Paris, K, 1374, Leonard Papers, no. 81, 15; reprinted in Louise Kellogg, *Early Narratives of the Northwest, 1634–1699* (New York, 1917), pp. 386–87. Willard Glazier, *Down the Great River, Embracing an Account of the True Source of the Mississippi* (Philadelphia, 1891), p. 334, supplies the nineteenth-century names.

6. ACSM, 296, 65 and 296, 68; Thwaites, *JR,* LIX, 178–81. This portage is identified by H. Hansen, *The Chicago River* (New York, 1942), p. 53.

7. Robert Knight and Lucius H. Zeuch, *The Location of the Chicago Portage Route of the Seventeenth Century* (Chicago, 1928), pp. 61–62, with a map of the route, dated 1821, ibid., 107.

If contact with reality exemplifies the lack of exaggeration where the first chapter of the Récit describes natural phenomena, there are other portions which may sound a bit heroic. Thus, in his prelude to the trip, Dablon expresses Jolliet's delight over the assurance by Frontenac and Talon that Father Marquette might be his partner. Speaking of the appointments made in Quebec, he says, "ces Messieurs, dis-ie, Nommerent en mesme temps pour Cette entreprise Le Sieur Jolyet quils jugerant tres propres pour ["cette entreprise" crossed out] si grand dessein estant bien aise que Le P. Marquette fut de la partie [These officials, I say, commissioned the one with the other for this enterprise, whom they judged very fit for so great a design, the Sieur Jolliet being very glad that Father Marquette was assigned to the project]."[8] The word order in the original French is a bit involved. When the Parisian editor, de Montézon, tackled the clause, he saw no reason for Jolliet's enthusiasm and decided to clarify the meaning by a few grammatical changes. He switched the adjective *propres* ("fit") into the singular and *bien aise* ("very glad") into the plural. This makes Frontenac and Talon glad to have Marquette go on a trip for which only Jolliet was fit. Thwaites transcribes the correct French from the Montreal Récit, but makes his English translation coincide with de Montézon's version. A cursory glance at the contemporary manuscripts will demonstrate why both the explorers were fit for the exploration and why Jolliet was very glad to have Father Marquette for his partner.

Jolliet, himself, assigns a reason for his satisfaction over the partnership in the dictated account of his discovery made to Father Dablon on August 1, 1674. He says he "sejoignit au pere Marquette [he had associated himself with Father Marquette]" because he had "depuis long temps premeditoit cette entreprise, l'ayant bien des fois concertée ensembles [for a long time planned the endeavor, it being frequently discussed be-

8. ACSM, 296, 1–2; Thwaites, *JR*, LIX, 88–89.

tween them]."[9] The frequent discussion has been mistakenly assigned to the winter of 1672–73 by some scholars.[10] This can hardly have been the case. Jolliet probably spent this winter close to his headquarters in Sault Sainte-Marie.[11] It is certain Marquette was at Saint Ignace most of the time.[12] Moreover, the Récit, in the prelude just mentioned, implies that it was in the autumn of 1672 that Jolliet expressed to Talon and Frontenac the contentment he felt in having Father Marquette go with him. If at that time he could say that his pleasure in having Marquette for a partner arose from frequent discussions with him about the trip, then these planning sessions must have taken place before that fall. A survey of Jolliet's whereabouts in the years immediately before 1672 will reveal that he and Marquette had several meetings, over a long time, in those years.

Jolliet met Marquette for the first time in 1666. He was a student at the college in Quebec when the latter arrived there.[13] His second contact was after his overseas visit when he went to Sault Sainte-Marie for the beginning of his career as a trader. While abroad, he had been close to Louis XIV's imperialistic wars.[14] Two Jesuit-college-trained men, reunited on the rim of

9. APF, Fonds Brotier 155 (Canada–1), 11.

10. Louise P. Kellogg, "Father Jacques Marquette, A Tercentenary Tribute," *Catholic World*, CXLV (1937), 270.

11. [Nicholas Perrot], *Memoire sur les Moeurs, Coustumes et Religion des Sauvages de l'Amerique Septentrionale . . .*, ed. Jules Tailhan (Leipzig, 1864), p. 128.

12. APF, Fonds Brotier 155 (Canada–1), 27v; Thwaites, *JR*, LVII, 248, Father Marquette begins a letter, in the spring of 1673, which is full of the activities of the previous winter.

13. D. H. Laverdière and H. R. Casgrain, eds., *Le Journal des Jésuites* (Quebec, 1871), p. 351; Thwaites, *JR*, L, 202, Marquette spent three weeks in Quebec, in 1666.

14. Jean Delanglez, "Louis Jolliet, Early Years, 1645–1674," *M-A*, XXVII (1945), 5 and 8. Jolliet left Canada about October, 1667 and was back by mid-August, 1668. The War of Devolution, begun in 1667, closed May 2, 1668.

civilization, would probably find time to discuss the fate of the empty continent outside their window. This unoccupied empire was the most precious booty at stake in the dynastic struggle then exhausting France, England, and Spain. Jolliet and Marquette could do no more than speculate on how far settlers had gone into the wilderness from Virginia and New Mexico. The question was still unanswered when at the beginning of September, 1669, Marquette had to leave to assume charge of the mission on Chequamegon Bay.[15] However while he was still at the Sault, Father Allouez stopped by, arrivng June 6. He was the man through whom Europe had first heard the Indian name "Messipi." In his letter of 1667 for the Relation, he told of a visit from savages called Illinois. They described the great size, length, and general direction of the stream along which some of their people lived. He decided from what they said that it emptied into the sea near Virginia. If he was right, it offered a route by which the English might outflank New France.[16] If he was wrong, because the river took an unexpected western turn, then its course led to New Spain. In the *Relation . . . les Années 1661–1662,* Fr. Jerome Lalemant had written of Iroquois raids to the southwest of Lake Ontario by which they came to a beautiful river. The Indians who lived there told the invaders that they went down this stream to the sea, where they traded with Europeans. Father Lalemant surmised they were Spanish.[17] Two young Frenchmen, like the Canadian-born Jolliet and the missionary Marquette, could very well have begun discussing a possible exploration of the Mississippi in this summer of 1669.

Marquette's activity, when he was moved to a new location,

15. ARSJ, Franc. 23, 261, "Catalogus Provinciae Franciae, 1669 Exeunte." Two weeks sufficed to reach the Bay. Marquette arrived there September 13, 1669, Thwaites, *JR,* LIV, 168–69.

16. Ibid., LI, 42–43, and 52–53. Allouez tells of visiting the Sault in the *Relation . . . Les Années 1668–1669,* ibid., LII, 198–203.

17. Ibid., XLVII, 146–47.

indicates how deeply he had been impressed with the idea of solving the mystery of the Mississippi. At Chequamegon Bay in the fall of 1669 he found a young Illinois slave, took him into his cabin and made him his instructor in the language which was common to the Indians who had told Allouez about their southern home. He plied him with questions about the country. When the youth told him he knew a tribe called Chaouanou (Shawnee) who had glass beads, it revived Marquette's fear that Europeans who were not French might be the first to enter the Mississippi Valley. As soon as he could, in the spring of 1670, he made his way back to the Sault. From there, he addressed his letter for the *Relation . . . les Années 1669–1670*. In it he asked permission to go "dans cette Riviere tant que nous pourrons, avec un François, & ce junne homme qu'on m'a donné qui scait quelques-unes de ces langues [to go down the river as far as we can, with a Frenchman, and the boy who was given me and knows several of those languages]." Again Jolliet and he were able to plan their endeavor.[18]

This third meeting with Jolliet lasted several months in the summer of 1670. Oddly enough, it has been overlooked by Marquette's biographers. His letter for the *Relation . . . les Années 1669–1670*, written in the early spring of the latter year, could only have been addressed from the Sault. It was begun "aprés les Festes de Pâques [after the Feast of Easter]" because of an order received "du P. Dablon, depuis mon arrivée icy, aprés une Navigation d'un mois dans la neige, & dans les glaces qui nous ont fermé le passage, & dans des dangers de mort presque continuels [from Father Dablon since my arrival here, after a navigation of a month, and in almost constant peril of death, through snow and ice which blocked our way]."[19] The locality designated as "here" could not have

18. Ibid., LIV, 188–89.
19. Ibid., pp. 168–69, and 184–85. Joseph P. Donnelly, *Jacques Marquette, S. J., 1637–1675* (Chicago, 1968), pp. 151–58, is the first

been the mission of the Holy Spirit because Marquette's trip
there in early September, 1669, could not have been blocked
by "snow and ice." In 1670, Easter fell on April 6. There was
plenty of "snow and ice" on Lake Superior then. Moreover,
Father Dollier and M. Galinée, in their exploration of Lake
Huron, arrived at the Sault May 25, 1670. There they rested
three days. Renewing their journey, Galinée mentions their
taking leave of "des Peres d'Abon [Dablon] et Marquette qui
estoient pour lors en ce lieu [the Fathers Dablon and Marquette, who were then at this place]."[20]

The duration of Marquette's visit is settled by another part
of his letter to Le Mercier. It says, "Tous les Sauvages se
seperent [de la Mission du Saint-Esprit] pour aller chercher à
vivre . . . & me supplioient fort qu'un de nos Peres les allât
retrouver l'Automne. quand ils seroient r'assemblez [á La
Pointe] [all the savages scattered (from the Holy Spirit Mission) to try to find a supply of food . . . & they strongly sup-
plicated me that one of our fathers would come to recontact
them in the autumn when they would reassemble (at La
Pointe)]." That is to say, the Indians had watched their chaplain and his tutor at work on the Illinois language during the
winter. If he did not tell them his plans, they must have surmised his design and made him promise to return himself or
send a missionary in the fall. The letter goes on to say, "s'il
plaist à Dieu nous envoyer quelque Pere, il prendra ma place,
tandis que pour executer les ordres du Pere Superieur, j'iray
commencer la Mission des Ilinois [if it pleases God to send a
father, he will take my place, while to carry out the order of

biographer of Marquette to recognize where he spent the summer of
1670. He proposes several conjectures about Marquette's activities
while at Sault Sainte-Marie, but overlooks the probability of meetings
with Jolliet for discussing the Mississippi.

20. BN, Mss. fr., n.a., 7485, 24v; [de Bréhant, de Galinée], *Exploration of the Great Lakes, 1669–1670*, tr. and ed. James H. Coyne,
Ontario Historical Society Papers and Records, IV, pt. 1 (1903), 73.

Father Superior, I shall go to begin the Mission of the Illi-
nois]." Since all depended on the coming of a substitute when
the autumn flotilla returned from Quebec, Marquette had to
stay where he was until then.[21]

Jolliet should have been at Sault Sainte-Marie during the
summer of 1670. This was the season when the leader of a
fur company had to be at headquarters to pick up any pelts
which Indians brought in from their winter hunting. Galinée
had counted about twenty-five Frenchmen in the white man's
village at the Sault. Among them were some who sang high
mass and vespers on saints' days and Sundays. Jolliet had
musical skill. He was the *bourgeois* ("manager of the trappers") since Adrien's going away. This all points to his being
among the "twenty-five" with time to do some planning, while
Father Marquette waited for Father Le Mercier to send that
substitute.[22] Jolliet's willingness not only to plan but to act as
Marquette's donné in founding the mission of the Illinois may
be inferred from the words used by the latter in asking permission to set out for the Mississippi. His letter to Le Mercier
for inclusion in the *Relation . . . les Années 1669–1670* said
a "Frenchman" and the Indian-boy tutor were ready to go
with him; it would be idle to fancy that any other Frenchman
than Jolliet was intended. In the Relations it was a general
policy to refrain from naming the Canadians who might come
to the wilderness missions. Médard des Groseilliers had been
a donné.[23] Pierre Esprit Radisson had served in the same ca-
pacity.[24] Though most Canadians recognized their adventures,

21. Thwaites, *JR*, LIV, 184–85. Dablon approves the plan, ibid.,
pp. 136–37.

22. BN, Mss. fr., n.a., 7485, 24v; de Galinée, *Exploration of the
Great Lakes,* p. 73.

23. Laverdière-Casgrain, *Le Journal des Jésuites,* p. 64; Thwaites,
JR, XXVIII, 228–29.

24. [Marie de L'Incarnation], *Lettres de la Révérende Mère Marie
de l'Incarnation (née Marie Guyard) Première Supérieure du Monastère des Ursulines de Québec, Nouvelle Édition,* ed. l'abbé Richau-

these activities were recounted only as exploits of "French-men," so the Relations could not be used as evidence against them.[25] There could be no blame cast on Jolliet for accompanying Father Marquette as a donné, but the priest was writing for publication and according to form, hence he would refrain from mentioning the name.

When fall came, the Ottawa flotilla returned. There was no replacement for Father Marquette so, faithful to his promise, he left the conquest of the Mississippi to Providence and went back to the mission of the Holy Spirit to carry on his priestly ministrations for the Indians "when they would reassemble."[26] He found them gathering with unwonted haste, apprehensive of a new danger.

During their summer wanderings, some of the Ottawa from Chequamegon Bay had been captured by the Sioux. By pleading the existence of peace between the tribes, they obtained leniency only to betray the chief who spared them. Winter brought retaliation. In 1671, with the first signs of spring, Marquette's flock fled eastward toward the protection of the French. He followed them.[27] At the Sault, he paused until his Indians were persuaded to settle down at St. Ignace.[28] This allowed another visit with Jolliet; his presence is testified to by his signature on the claimer to the empty part of North America which Sieur de St. Lusson affixed to a tree at the mission this year in

deau (Paris, 1876), II, 129. These letters were originally published in Paris in 1681.

25. Thwaites, *JR*, XLII, 218–19; XLIV, 236–37; XLV, 216–17, 232–35. In 1670, these men helped establish the Hudson Bay Co., which took the fur trade of this northern sea to England.

26. ARSJ, Franc. 23, 275, "Catalogus Provinciae Franciae, 1670 Exeunte."

27. Perrot-Tailhan, *Memoire sur les Moeurs*, pp. 101–2; Thwaites, *JR*, LV, 168–71; LVI, 114–17.

28. Gilbert J. Garraghan, "Some Hitherto Unpublished Marquettiana," *M-A*, XVIII (1936), 23, Marquette remained at the mission Sainte-Marie until July 2, 1671.

June.[29] As the king's ambassador St. Lusson was under orders from Talon, not only to make claims, but to find mines and "quelque communication avec la mer du sud qui separe ce continent de la Chine [some communication with the sea of the south which separates this continent from China]."[30] After leaving the Sault, he did take a look for copper on the Ontonagon River, but he made no attempt to find a route toward the Pacific Ocean.[31] In the *Relation . . . les Années 1670–1671* which describes this visit, Father Dablon expresses optimistic speculations about such explorations to be undertaken by way of the Mississippi. Father Marquette was still anxious to go. Jolliet preceded St. Lusson to Quebec this summer with no other apparent purpose than to arrange things so that he might be the one to look for the sea of the South. All this may be taken to mean that more discussions with Marquette were had while the king's ambassador was at Sault Sainte-Marie, and that such talk had persuaded the official that he need look no further for a way across the continent until the possibilities of the Mississippi River had been investigated. By 1671, then, all indications point to a period of three years in which Marquette and Jolliet had frequently discussed the expedition. Three years is a "long time" for two young men to feel the attraction of adventure without doing something about it. Hence, when Jolliet was commissioned to seek the Mississippi it was natural for him to request Father Marquette for his partner and be "very glad that . . . [he] was assigned to the project."[32]

29. Perrot-Tailhan, *Memoire Sur les Moeurs*, p. 128.

30. *RAPQ, 1930–1931*, p. 136, "Mémoire de Talon sur la Canada au Ministre Colbert (10 novembre 1670)." In 1670 Father Le Mercier probably held up Father Marquette's Mississippi plan so that the Jesuits would not anticipate St. Lusson's reconnoiter.

31. Ibid., p. 159, "Memoire de Talon au Roi sur le Canada (2 novembre 1671)." St. Lusson was in Quebec by August 26, 1671.

32. Thwaites, *JR*, LV, 94–224, is where Dablon tells of the possible

It is fine to demonstrate Jolliet's desire for Father Marquette's companionship on the expedition; more important in proving the truthfulness of the Récit is the reaction of the governor to this wish. In the narrative Marquette says that when Jolliet arrived at St. Ignace he brought "Les ordres de M^r. L Comte de frontenac nostre Gouuerneur Et de M^r. Talon nostre Jntendant pour faire auec moy Cette decouuerte [the orders of M. the Count de Frontenac our Governor and of M. Talon our Intendant (which commissioned him), with me to make this discovery]."[33] In 1897, the possibility of such an appointment was questioned by H. Lorin, a French biographer of Frontenac. His doubt arose from his knowledge of the lack of rapport between the governor and the Jesuits. Lorin sought to strengthen his opinion by advancing a further theory that members of the religious Order concealed Marquette's presence on the exploration from the government officials in Quebec.[34] All the components of such a conjecture are discounted by Frontenac's contemporary activity. In the year 1672, he began his first term as governor. This year Louis XIV had launched his fusiliers into the Dutch War. Also, this year, Father Albanel returned to Quebec from a trip to the North where he had found English forts on Hudson Bay.[35] The English were still at peace with France, but friendly to the Dutch. Frontenac knew it would be well for the king's cause if he could persuade the British trespassers to leave their outposts in a peaceful manner. The Jesuit, who had just made a voyage from the Bay,

exploration. ACSM, 296, 1–2; Thwaites, *JR*, LIX, 88–89. Dablon puts these words into Jolliet's mouth.

33. ACSM, 296, 3–4; Thwaites, *JR*, LIX, 90–93. Again Dablon says Frontenac and Talon appointed Marquette, in the *Relation . . . les Années 1671–1672*, see below, pp. 167–68.

34. Jean Delanglez, "The 1674 Account of the Discovery of the Mississippi," *M-A*, XXVI (1944), 312, cites H. Lorin, *Le Comte De Frontenac* (Paris, 1897), ch. 3 for the opinion.

35. Thwaites, *JR*, LVI, 156–57, 184–85.

was best equipped to carry a message; hence, without show of prejudice Albanel was sent back as the governor's representative.[36] A few months earlier in 1672, Talon had received a letter from Colbert expressing anxiety for Canada in the new war. At one place the minister wrote, "Il n'y a rien de plus important pour ce pais la, et pour le service de sa Ma^té que la descouverte du passage dans la mer du Sud [There is nothing more important for that land, and for the service of his majesty than the discovery of the passage into the South Sea]."[37] When Talon proposed the names of those best qualified for the discovery, he was acting as special defendant of the royal interests; hence, again for the king's cause, the governor could not hesitate to approve one of the two men simply because he was a member of the Society of Jesus. Frontenac wrote Colbert that he was sanctioning Talon's choice.[38]

On the part of the Order, Marquette's selection was advertised with total lack of secrecy. The last of the printed Relations, the one for 1671–72, tells of Albanel's discovery of Hudson Bay and goes on to say:

Nous n'esperons pas moins de celuy que Monsieur le Comte de Frontenac, & Monsieur Talon, pour satisfaire aux intentions de sa Majesté, ont fait entreprendre pour la découverte de la mer du Sud, qui probablement nous donneroit entrée aux grandes mers de la Chine & du Japon Le Pere & les François qui sont envoyez pour cette hazardeuse expedition, ont besoin de beaucoup de courage . . . .[39]

[We expect no less from the one whom Monsieur the Count de Frontenac & Monsieur Talon, carrying out the wishes of his

36. *RAPQ, 1926–1927,* p. 50, "Lettre du Gouverneur . . . au Ministre (13 novembre 1673)."
37. Ibid., *1930–1931,* p. 168, "Lettre du Ministre Colbert à Talon (4 juin 1672)."
38. Ibid., *1926–1927,* p. 18, "Lettre du Gouverneur . . . au Ministre (2 novembre 1672)."
39. Thwaites, *JR,* LV, 234–36.

Majesty, have made try for the discovery of the South Sea, which probably will give entrance to the great seas of China and Japan. The father & the Frenchman who are sent on this hazardous expedition, have need of much courage.]

In the body of the Relation, it makes clear this is the expedition by which "nous esperons bien que dans peu de temps nous la [Foy] porterons jusqu'à la fameuse riviere nommée Missisipi, . . . [We are confidently hoping that in a short time we will bring (the Faith) as far as the famous river bearing the name Mississippi . . .]."[40]

When in the spring of 1673, the printed *Relation . . . les Années 1671–1672* was delivered in Quebec, Frontenac surely read it. He was in the process of gathering data to fulfill a clause in the royal instructions handed him when he took office. Louis XIV had told him:

> Les Pères Jésuites qui sont establis à Quebec . . . ayent contribué à l'establissement . . . de cette colonie, Sa Majesté desire que ledit sr de Frontenac ayt beaucoup de consideration pour eux; mais en cas qu'ils voulussent porter l'autorité ecclésiastique plus loin qu'elle ne doibt s'entendre, il est nécessaire qu'il leur fasse connoistre . . . et donner advis de tout à Sa Majesté, ...[41]

> [The Jesuit fathers who are established at Quebec . . . , having contributed to the establishment . . . of this colony, His Majesty desires that the said Sieur de Frontenac have much consideration for them; but in case they seem to carry ecclesiastical authority beyond legitimate bounds, he must make this clear to them . . . and give notice of all to His Majesty . . . .]

The first step in tracing the direction taken by the activities of "the Jesuit fathers" was to read their publication. There, Frontenac would have come upon the announcement that one

40. Ibid., LVI, 146–47.
41. *RAPQ, 1926–1927,* p. 5, "Mémoire du Roi pour Servir d'Instruction au Sieur Comte de Frontenac . . . (7 avril 1672)." See also, W. J. Eccles, *Frontenac, The Courtier Governor* (Toronto, 1959), p. 52.

of the priests had been appointed by him to go with Jolliet seeking for "the great seas of China and Japan." Had this not been true, there could be no doubt that the Jesuits were "carrying ecclesiastical authority beyond legitimate bounds." Furthermore, since it was in May, 1673, when the explorers moved into the wilderness, Marquette would have gone in violation of a decree which Frontenac had recently promulgated, unless the latter had made an exception for this voyage. The decree required passports for anyone going into the woods, even if they be priests. Fr. François de Crépieul, setting out for Tadoussac, had been forced to apply for a visa. He did so, but appealed the case to the Court. No decision came from Versailles until 1675.[42]

In the years immediately following the discovery of the Mississippi, Frontenac did not have to read the literature of the Jesuits to be reminded that Father Marquette had been Jolliet's partner in the 1673 exploration. Three times, between 1675 and 1677, abbé Bernou sent questionnaires to Quebec asking information about the Mississippi discovery. Two of them contain the request for "une relation entiere sil se peut auec la Carte du uoyage du R. p. Marquette et du S^r. Jollyet [a complete relation if possible, with the map of the voyage of Rev. Fr. Marquette and S^r. Jolliet]."[43] In 1681, Thevenot's

42. *RAPQ, 1926–1927*, p. 20, "Lettre du Gouverneur . . . au Ministre (2 novembre 1672)" announced the test case of "P Crespien [*sic*], Jesuite." When the king's answer came, April 22, 1675, it told the governor to permit all ecclesiastics the liberty to go and come anywhere in Canada without obliging them to have passports, ibid., p. 82.

43. BN, Clairambault, 848, 168–69, Bernou addresses Frontenac's secretary Barrois. "Monsieur Dalera," ibid., pp. 848, 363–64, who is mentioned by de La Salle, Margry, *Découv. et Étab.*, II, 253, and identified as Jean Daleyrac by Jean Delanglez, "The Discovery of the Mississippi, Secondary Sources," *M-A*, XXVIII (1946), 12; and "Sr. De St. Martin, mathematicien Professor séculier chez les PP Jesuites à Quebec passant en france cette année 1677 [Sr. De St. Martin, mathematician, lay professor at the (college of the) Jesuit fathers in

"Voyage & decouverte du P. Marquette & Sr Jolliet dans l'Amerique Septentrionale" came out.[44] The importance allotted the missionary by these persons caused Frontenac no concern. Conversely, he might well have taken it amiss if anyone had denied that either Marquette or Jolliet went exploring without his commission; for, his own report of the Mississippi discovery, sent to Colbert in 1674, links their names together as his choice to be the leaders of the expedition.[45]

Almost at the end of the Récit's portrayal of the Mississippi discovery, it comments on the explorers' determination to turn back, just a few days' journey from the river's mouth. With straightforward simplicity the reader is informed that Marquette and Jolliet felt they had come far enough to prove that the Mississippi emptied into the Gulf of Mexico instead of the Pacific, and that it would be imprudent for them to go closer to the sea and Spanish settlements lest they be captured as French spies. This matter-of-fact recital is devoid of those heroics common to counterfeited romances of adventure. However, strangely enough, one of the earliest attempts to throw doubt on the first chapter of the Récit has to do with this passage. Father Hennepin's fanciful *Nouvelle Decouverte d'Un Tres Grand Pays,* mentioned at the beginning of the chapter, attacks the assertion that Marquette and Jolliet ever came so close to salt water. Hennepin published this book in Utrecht, Holland, in 1697 and dedicated it to William III, the Dutch king who with his wife, Queen Mary Stuart, shared the throne of England after the Glorious Revolution of 1688 drove James II into exile. The book was immediately translated into English, and with the title *A New Discovery of a Vast Country*

Quebec, who is coming to France this year, 1677]," also received the queries, BN, Clairambault 1016, 396–97.

44. Melchisedech Thevenot, *Recueil de Voyages,* (Paris, 1681), p. 7.
45. ASH, 5, no. 16, 3.

in America . . . by L. Hennepin so appealed to British readers
that two printings were made during the year 1698.[46] The
book interprets Hennepin's travels of 1680 quite differently
than in his earlier writing. It has him start from de La Salle's
Fort Crèvecoeur, go to the mouth of the Illinois River, then
turn south on the Mississippi to the Gulf of Mexico. Hennepin
is then said to have turned back up the river and to have
traveled its length to a spot beyond the Falls of St. Anthony.
In accomplishing this trip, Hennepin takes to himself the distinction of being the first European to have seen the Mississippi.
The English publisher may have felt this extravagant assertion
needed a counterbalance. To serve as such he added a summary
of Thevenot, with the title "A Discovery of some new Countries and Tribes in North America by Father Marquette."[47]
Hennepin had realized that the Jesuit narrative contradicted his
own pretensions; so, in *A New Discovery* he insists he sought
out Jolliet to ask him about his previous voyages, and "that
Gentleman answer'd me . . . that he had never gone further
than the Hurons and Outtaouats [they lived round the upper

46. [Louis Hennepin], *A New Discovery of a Vast Country in
America Extending over Four Thousand Miles between New France
and New Mexico . . . by L. Hennepin* (London, 1698). The first
English issue is cited in the present work. In The Edward F. Ayer
Collection of the Newberry Library, Chicago, it is distinguished by a
code number 1698-C. The second issue, with different page numbers,
is 1698-E. This is the one from which *A New Discovery of a Vast
Country in America by Father Louis Hennepin,* ed., Reuben G.
Thwaites (Chicago, 1903), was taken.

47. [Hennepin], *A New Discovery of a Vast Country in America,*
pt. 2, pp. 318–49. Grace L. Nute, "Father Hennepin's Later Years,"
Minnesota History, XIX (1938), 393–98, advances a conjecture that
the English king, William III, had persuaded Father Hennepin to
fabricate the deposition of discovery so that he might lead Captain
William Bond back to the Mississippi to establish an English settlement there. In 1699, Dr. Daniel Coxe promoted such an expedition
and his plans were thwarted only by the timely arrival of D'Iberville
in the same territory, in the same year.

Great Lakes] with whom he remain'd to exchange commodities with their Furs."[48]

Assertions such as this in *A New Discovery* supply cause for its severe criticism. In the present instance the evidence of the seventeenth-century documents clearly demonstrates the fictitious nature of the limitations it puts on Jolliet's explorations. Abbé Bernou, in pushing de La Salle's first expedition to the Mississippi Valley, wrote a "Memoire pour la decouverte et la conquéte des pays de Quivira et de Theguayo [Memorial for the Discovery and Conquest of Quivira and Theguayo in North America]," wherein he incorporated testimony to the truth.[49] He was proposing a plan for the advancement of King Louis' war against Spain, which would help his client. He advised an invasion of Mexico through the great mid-American valley, where opposition was lacking and transportation easy. These assertions were substantiated by calling on the journey of "le pere marquette et le Sr Jolliet." They learned "que l'on n'ira pas bien loin audela des grands lacs sans trouuer des chevaux et des mules [that one does not go far beyond the great lakes before they find horses and mules]" and they encountered no trouble from the Indians when they made their way "parmy des peuples inconnus jusques aupres du golfe de mexique [among unknown people almost to the Gulf of Mexico]."[50]

After de La Salle had made his way to the mouth of the Mississippi, he was commissioned in 1684 to establish a colony on the Gulf of Mexico. Bernou, seeking to contribute to its prestige, petitioned *Propaganda Fide* to bestow episcopal power

48. [Hennepin], *A New Discovery of a Vast Country in America,* pt. 2, [xix.]

49. BN, Clairambault, 1016, 211–19.

50. Ibid., 1016, 213–213v. A similar memorial, in Delisle's papers, has critical annotations by an unknown person with answers by Bernou. The length of the exploration is not challenged, ASH, 115, IX, no. 11, 1–12.

on one of the chaplains who was to take care of the colonists.[51] Laval, Marquette's ordinary and metropolitan of Quebec, addressed a protest to Rome because his see embraced all the territory of North America belonging to New France.[52] He asserted that a bishopric at the mouth of the Mississippi would invade this area, since the new bishop and his priests "n'ont qu'environ quatre vingt lieües a faire jusqu au golf de Mexique pour pousser leur decouuerte au dela du terme ou le Pere marquette et le sieur joliet avoient deja poussé la leur, . . . [have not more than eighty leagues to make from the Gulf of Mexico to advance their explorations into the vicinity where Father Marquette and Sieur Jolliet have already pushed their own]." Thus the prelate, who carefully followed the work of the few priests in his diocese, becomes a witness to the extent of the Jolliet-Marquette expedition.[53] When de La Salle's colony failed in 1687, Bernou and Renaudot are believed to have undertaken the rehabilitation of its promoters by publishing, *Premier Etablissement de la Foy*, a book attributed by them to Chrestien Le Clercq. In it, the Jesuits were made the whipping boy for the fiasco. The importance of the Marquette-Jolliet explorations are belittled, but the abbé did not retract his assertion that the explorers had gone almost to the Gulf of Mexico.[54]

Fr. Thierry Beschefer, who succeeded Dablon as superior of the Jesuits in 1680, wrote his first letter about the Canadian missions shortly after. In it he mentions Marquette's contact with the Illinois Indians in this way: "Il alla pour la premiere fois dans leur pays Il y a dix ans dans un grand voyage quil

51. BN, Mss.fr., n.a., 7497, 204v, "Lettre de l'abbé Bernou au M. Renaudot (8 janvier 1685)."

52. August H. Gosselin, *Vie de Mgr. De Laval* (Quebec, 1890), II, 262–63.

53. BN, Clairambault, 1016, 630, "Mémoire enuoié par M. L'Abbé De St Vallier nommé a l'Euéché de Quebec." Since Laval was seeking to resign, the memorial composed by him was submitted in the name of his chosen successor, August Gosselin, *Vie de Laval*, II, 283.

54. Le Clercq, *Premier Etablissement de la Foy*, II, 364–66.

fit auec le sieur Joliet, deux cens lieües par dela les premieres
Bourgades des Jlinois en descendant sur La grande Riuiere
Mississipi [Ten years ago, he visited their country for the
first time, while on the long expedition which he made with
Sieur Jolliet going down the great River Mississippi two hundred leagues beyond the first Villages of the Illinois]." This
would bring the exploration very close to the Arkansas River.[55]
Other testimony of the extent of the discovery comes from a
comptroller general of the Marine and fortifications in New
France who knew Jolliet. He asserts, "La découverte de la Mer
du Sud tenoit fort à couer à Mr Talon, qui jetta les yeux sur
le sieur Joliet pour en faire la tentative . . . . il penetra jusques
aux Akancas . . .[56] [The discovery of the South Sea was a pet
project of M. Talon, who saw in Sieur Jolliet the man to undertake it . . . he opened a route all the way to Akancas . . .]."

Governor Jacques René Marquis de Denonville and King
Louis, concerned about a treaty with England in 1686, asserted
French rights to the interior of America because "la rivière de
Mississipi et . . . peuples incognus aux Europeans furent découverte par le Sieur Jolliet avecq le P. Marquette, jésuite, qui
furent jusqu'an trente-deuxieme degré [the Mississippi River
and . . . people unknown to Europeans were discovered by
Sieur Jolliet with Father Marquette, a Jesuit, who descended as
far as the thirty-second degree]." [57] Thus the witnesses against

55. Thwaites, *JR*, LXII, 210–11.

56. Claude C. de B. de La Potherie, *Voyage de l'Amerique*
(Amsterdam, 1723), II, 130–31. This passage is among those in
Emma H. Blair, ed., *The Indian Tribes of the Upper Mississippi
Valley and Region of the Great Lakes as Described by Nicolas Perrot,
French Commandant in the Northwest; Bacqueville De La Potherie,
French Royal Commissioner to Canada; Morrell Marston, American
Army Officer; and Thomas Forsyth, United States Agent at Fort
Armstrong* (Cleveland, 1911), I, 348.

57. Ernest Gagnon, *Louis Jolliet* (2nd ed., Montreal, 1913), p. 147,
"Lettre du Marquis de Denonville au Ministre (6 nouvembre 1687),

Hennepin pile up. Even his patron, de La Salle, was among them. He accused the priest of inaccuracy because "il parle plus conformement a ce quil veut qu'a ce qu'il scait [he talks more in line with what he wants than what he knows]." [58] At the same time, Tonti cautioned his brother in France lest he place any trust in the yarns of the priest.[59] Also, the abbé Bernou, in correspondence with Renaudot, spoke "du mechant livre du Pere Hempin [of the sorry book of Father Hennepin]"; and again, thought well to add, "Je ne dis rien . . . du livre du pere Henipin parce qu'il m'a mis en trop grande colere [I say nothing . . . about Father Hennepin's book because it made me too angry for words]." [60] Some scholars have suggested that perhaps the sufferings which he underwent during his imprisonment by the Sioux affected Hennepin's mind.[61]

Had Marquette and Jolliet lacked all contemporary witnesses for the extent of their exploration, the precise log of distances traveled day by day as found in the Récit would bring them very near to the mouth of the Arkansas River. Their trip begins with their leaving the mission of St. Ignatius at Michilimakinac on May 17, 1673. The narrative in the archives of the Collège Sainte-Marie has the "17" superimposed on some illegible pen marks.[62] This is one of the many corrections which Dablon

---

Archives Canadiennes cor. gen., vol. 9, p. 326"; and O'Callaghan, *Documents*, IX, 383–84.

58. BN, Clairambault, 1016, 187, "Lettre du Sr. de La Salle à l'abbé Bernou (22 aoust 1681)"; Margry, *Découv. et Étab.*, II, 259–60.

59. Jean Delanglez, "Hennepin's Voyage to the Gulf of Mexico, 1680," *M-A*, XXI (1939), 39; or Delanglez, "Tonti Letters," p. 234.

60. BN, Mss.fr., n.a., 7497, 10v, "Lettre de l'abbé Bernou au M. Renaudot (18 mai 1683)"; and ibid., pp 101–3; Margry, *Découv. et Étab.*, III, 74.

61. Delanglez, "Hennepin's Voyage, 1680," p. 76; Justin Winsor, *Cartier to Frontenac, Geographical Discovery of the Interior of North America in Its Historical Relation, 1534–1700* (Boston, 1894), pp. 278–79.

62. ACSM, 296, 3.

made after a scribe with a very clear hand had written the finished draft of Dablon's rough copy.[63] A bit of dissidence arises from this, since Viger, who in 1844 protested he was making a faithful transcript of this document, wrote down "13" instead of "17." [64] May 13 is also in Thevenot's *Recueil de Voyages,* where he designates it as the day for starting the trip.[65] A careful perusal of the Récit in the original is necessary for disclosing the cause of this mix-up.

Sometime in the course of his editing, Dablon must have noticed the day of the departure, the day of entrance into the Mississippi, and the day of embarkation for the return from Akansea were all "17's," of May, of June, and of July respectively. This similarity was enough to cause any editor to wonder whether it was owing to a coincidence or to carelessness. If Dablon attempted to make sure of the correct days by asking Jolliet for the date on which the exploration began, the latter would most naturally respond with his mind on the morning he had left Sault Sainte-Marie, which was somewhat over a hundred miles from St. Ignace. Seventeenth-century canoe travel ordinarily averaged thirty miles a day on lake water, so he would have had to leave the headquarters of his fur business several days before his rendezvous with Father Marquette at Michilimackinac. If the trip began for the priest on May 17, it probably began for Jolliet on May 13, and this would have been his answer to Dablon's question.[66] Fortunately, before the latter sent the final draft of the Récit to France, the confusion between the two beginnings of Jolliet

63. Ibid., p. 60; Thwaites, *JR,* LX, 166–67, Dablon added a full paragraph.

64. Archives du Séminaire des Missions Étrangères, Quebec, Viger, *Ma Saberdache Rouge,* F, 103 and 28.

65. Thevenot, *Recueil de Voyages,* p. 1.

66. Jean Delanglez, *Life and Voyages of Louis Jolliet, 1645–1700* (Chicago, 1948), pp. 112–13, studies the speed of seventeenth-century canoe travel under various conditions.

and Marquette was detected and the right order established. This accounts for the superimposed "17" in the Montreal Récit and, also, for the presence in the Chantilly Récit of the date, "le 17ᵉ de May 1673," in a script which has not been tampered with.[67] Thevenot must have had access to an earlier, uncorrected version. Perhaps it was the missing part of one of the fragments of the Récit which got into his hands.[68] Viger, who did not think he was going against his promise of accuracy by adding punctuation, modernized spelling, and capital letters, would hardly have scrupled to follow Thevenot when marks on the Montreal Récit suggested Dablon's uncertainty over the date. Of course, the unmutilated Chantilly Récit was unknown to him. Therefore, despite the confusion, it is safe to say that simple coincidence led the trip from St. Ignace to begin on May 17, the discovery of the Mississippi River to come on June 17, and the return trip from Akansea to start on July 17 in the year 1673.

The route from Father Marquette's mission to the Mascoutin Indian village on the Fox River, southwest of the present Berlin, Wisconsin, was well known to the Jesuits. Allouez had erected a large cross among the lodges of these friendly natives and Dablon had come this far in 1670. Beyond this village lay an unknown continental midland. When Marquette and Jolliet would enter this area, there was no possibility of plagiarism in their estimates of the time required to go the distance from one point to another. The many channels of the Fox, overgrown with wild rice, presented the first barrier to westward progress. On the evening of June 7, the Mascoutin headmen invited the explorers to a council for the purpose of

67. APF, Fonds Brotier 159 (Canada–5), 13v.
68. APF, Fonds Brotier 158 (Canada–4), pt. 4, 10, is one of the four fragments of the Chantilly Récit which lacks chs. 1 and 2. If they are missing because Thevenot obtained these pages, it is possible he found May 13 there for the day of the departure, owing to a careless correction of these duplicate copies.

considering a request for guides.[69] Three nights and two days of parleys and exchanges of gifts led to a favorable decision. "Le Lendemain qui fut le dixieme de Juin, deux Miamis qu'on nous donna pour guides s'embarquerent auec nous [The next day, which was the tenth of June, two Miamis who were assigned us for guides embarked with us]," says the Récit.[70]

The distance by river from the Mascoutin hamlet to the portage path, which ends on the bank of the Wisconsin River, is thirty leagues.[71] A canoe going against the stream averaged six and a half leagues a day.[72] Therefore, it would be the afternoon of June 14 when the guides dropped the Frenchmen at the trail which led over the height of land. When they launched forth on the Wisconsin, they were just about 110 miles from the confluence of this stream with the Mississippi. A speed of thirty-seven miles a day was normal for canoes going with the current. Hence, three days' travel would bring Marquette and Jolliet to their goal on the afternoon of June 17, just as the Récit dates the arrival. By the same method of reckoning, since the days from June 17 to July 17 are thirty and the distance from the Wisconsin River to the Quapaw-Akansea village is 1112 miles, an advance of thirty-seven miles a day would accomplish the journey with mathematical pre-

69. ACSM, 296, 8, 10; Thwaites, *JR*, LIX, 100–1, 104–5.

70. Jean Delanglez, "The 'Recit des voyages et des decouvertes du Pere Jacques Marquette,'" *M-A*, XXVIII (1946), 228, thought "the next day" should have been June 8. He overlooked the drawn out procedure of an Indian council. A similar one in which Galinée tried to obtain guides lasted a week, BN, Ms.fr., n.a., 7485, pt. 1, 8v–13; de Galinée, *Exploration of the Great Lakes,* pp. 24–29.

71. The Récit has three leagues instead of thirty. John J. Wood, "The Mascoutin Village," *Proceedings of the State Historical Society of Wisconsin, 1906,* LIV (1907), 173, n. 14, finds thirty leagues comes within three-and-two-tenths miles of the portage; so the zero of the thirty was dropped by mistake. Arthur E. Jones, "The Site of the Mascoutin," ibid., pp. 175–83, suggests that the explorers were misinformed.

72. See above, ch. 6, n.66.

cision. Below the mouth of the Missouri, the strength of the
current is sufficient to forestall an objection which might arise
over the twenty-four-hour delay among the Illinois at their
camp on the shore of what is the present state of Iowa.[73] De La
Salle made an average speed of thirty-nine miles a day after
his flotilla received the additional push of this turbulent
stream.[74] Such speed would allow for the day of inaction and
still bring the expedition to Akansea on July 16, in broad day-
light.[75] This leaves time for the ceremonies conducted by the
Indians until evening, for spending most of the morrow in
rest, and yet beginning the homeward journey on the 17th of
July.[76]

It is almost certain that the last leg of the voyage was begun
from the mouth of the Illinois River on August 25, which
is the feast of St. Louis, king of France. Catholic explorers
were wont to attach to geographical finds the name of the
saint whose feast was being celebrated on the day of discovery.
Jolliet commonly spoke of the stream as "Riuiere de St.
Louis." [77] Furthermore, his estimate that the combined current
of the Missouri-Mississippi proved such a handicap "qu'en

73. Delanglez, "Recit des voyages," p. 235, mistakes the length of
this visit. It began on "le 25ᵉ Juin," Thwaites, *JR,* LIX, 112–13. The
Récit says, "le lendemain, nous prismes Congé [on the following day
(June 26), we took leave]," ibid., pp. 124–25. This means they left
on June 26, but at this point in the narrative there is a digression to
describe a calumet dance, thus distracting attention from the calendar
date of the departure, when the Récit returns to the trip by saying
"Nous prenons congé de nos Illinois sur la fin de Juin, vers les trois
heures apres midy [We take leave of our Illinois toward the end of
June, about three o'clock in the afternoon]," ibid., pp. 136–37.

74. Delanglez, *Life of Jolliet,* pp. 112–13.

75. ACSM, 296, 32; Thwaites, *JR,* LIX, 152–53, the Récit measures
the last day's journey as only twenty to twenty-eight miles.

76. ACSM, 296, 36; Thwaites, *JR,* LIX, 160–61.

77. APF, Fonds Brotier 155 (Canada–1), 12v, in his dictation, on
August 1, 1674, Jolliet speaks of the Illinois River three times as
"Riuiere de St. Louis."

remontant on ne peut faire que quatre a 5 lieues par jour [That
on returning we could only make about four or five leagues a
day]," fits this supposition because it allows forty days for
paddling 530 miles.[78] From the mouth of the Illinois to the
Des Plaines portage is 330 miles. Allowing for a short stop
which the explorers made at Old Kaskaskia village would
leave time for them to be on the site of the present city of
Chicago by mid-September. From there to Green Bay is 270
miles. This could be accomplished easily in the remaining days
of the month. This part of the Récit concludes with the voyage
completed by the return to the Mission of St. Francis Xavier,
which is located on this bay. "Nous sommes rendus dans La
baye des puanz sur La fin de Septembre . . . [We made our
way back to the Bay of the Stinkers about the end of Septem-
ber]." [79]

The date of the expedition's return is given as November,
"S'estans rendus sur la fin de Nouembre a la baye des puants
[having returned to the Bay of the Stinkers toward the end
of November]," in the "Relation de la decouverte de la Mer
du Sud . . . Enuoyée de Quebec . . . la 1er Iour d'Aoust 1674,"
which was dictated to Dablon by Jolliet and which forms the
introduction to the "Relation . . . les Années 1672–1673." [80]
It is unnatural to think that Jolliet could have made a mistake
of two months in a date which must still have been deeply impressed on his mind, when in Quebec less than a year after
the occurence, he first announced the success of his discovery.
It is also unnatural to think that if Jolliet had given Dablon
the November date, the announcement in Father Marquette's
journal that the explorers turned into Green Bay at the end of
September could have slipped past Dablon without his checking

78. APF, Fonds Brotier 155 (Canada–1), 11–12; Thwaites, *JR*,
LVIII, 94–97.
79. ACSM, 296, 37.
80. APF, Fonds Brotier 155 (Canada–1), 12.

the discrepancy. The natural solution of the difference lies in Dablon's poor penmanship and his having probably used the abbreviation for the month, as he jotted down what Jolliet told him. The common French symbols for the two months in question are "9ᵇʳᵉ" for November and "7ᵇʳᵉ" for September. A circular stroke on the bar of the 7 would make it look very much like a carelessly made 9.[81] Thus the scribe who made the final copy of the "Relation . . . les Années 1672–1673" must have found it hard to distinguish between "9ᵇʳᵉ" and "7ᵇʳᵉ" in Dablon's handwriting and he must have guessed wrongly; so, his is the fault for transcribing November instead of September as the date for the expedition's return.[82]

Together, Jolliet the pioneer and Marquette the missionary planned the discovery and exploration of the Mississippi River. Talon the intendant appointed the two young men to carry out their plans in the name of France. Frontenac the governor approved the partnership. The three persons most intimately affected by the European entrance into the Mississippi Valley testify that priest and layman united brought their plans to a felicitous accomplishment.

In 1700, Fr. Jacques Gravier was assigned to continue the mission work among the Kaskaskia of Illinois. Pierre Le Moyne D'Iberville had begun a settlement at Biloxi the year before, so the missionary set out immediately to establish communications with the Louisiana French. He took along a journal of the 1673 exploration which would enable him to compare his

81. Fernand Lefebvre, "Introduction a la paleographie canadienne," *Revue de l'Université d'Ottawa,* XXVIII (1958), 491–521, warns those editing manuscripts of pitfalls to be avoided in making copies; and this particular set of abbreviations is placed among those most often requiring careful criticism, ibid., pp. 518–21.

82. ASH, 5, no. 16, 7, Frontenac's report of the discovery has November for the date of Jolliet's return to Green Bay, which adds weight to the conjecture in chapter 4 of the present book that he copied from the "Relation . . . les Années 1672–1673."

own findings with those of Father Marquette.[83] After he had
encountered his fellow countrymen at "Fort de Mississipi a
17. Lieües de sa decharge dans le Golfe ou mer Mexique le 16ᵉ
Feuvrier 1701" [Fort Mississippi, 17 Leagues from where it
empties into the Gulf or Sea of Mexico, the 16th February,
1701]," he sent back a "Relation" of his voyage. In it, he tells
of asking the chief at Akansea, "S'il se souuenoit d'auoir
autrefois vû un françois vetû de noir dans leur village, habille
comme [moy] [If at any other time he could remember having
seen in his village a Frenchman clothed in a black garment
like mine]." The answer was an affirmative, but the Indian
said this had happened "qu'il y auoit si longtems qu'il ne
pouuoit pas compter les années [this had happened so long
ago that he could not count the years]." Gravier told him it
was about twenty-eight years before and the chief went on to
say that his people had honored the black robe, and "qu'ils luy
auoient dancé le Calumet de Capitaine [that they had danced
for him the calumet of a Captain]." At first Gravier did not
understand what was meant because he had in mind the calumet "que les Kaskaskia auoient donné au Pere Marquette"
[which the Kaskaskia had given to Father Marquette]." However, his confusion did not last long. He says, "j'ai trouvé dans
le journal du Pere qu'ils luy auoient en effet dance le Calumet
. . . [I found in the journal of the father that they had indeed danced the calumet]." [84] The incident is related in the
Récit and Thevenot as taking place the night before the explorers made their start home.[85] Thus the aborigine who with
a dance of peace had welcomed the coming of the first white

83. APF, Fonds Brotier 165 (Canada–11); Thwaites, *JR*, LXV,
100–179. Probably the printed book by Thevenot, *Recueil de Voyages,*
was what Gravier meant when he spoke of a journal.

84. Thwaites, *JR*, LXV, 118–21.

85. ACSM, 296, 35; Thwaites, *JR*, LIX, 158–59; and Thevenot,
Recueil de Voyages, p. 40.

men to mid-America places Marquette beside Jolliet as their quest was accomplished.

Frontenac's report of the Akansea welcome discloses a lack of friendly unanimity among the savage audience at the calumet dance. The French, apprised of possible Indian treachery and of possible European hostility where the Mississippi emptied into the Gulf of Mexico, slept little on the night after the ceremonial. The governor says, "Le pere & le Sr Jollyet delibrerent sur ce qu'ils auoient affaire [the father & the Sieur Jolliet deliberated about what they ought to do]." They decided to begin the homeward voyage at once. Since Jolliet had dictated the words about his consultation with Marquette, he becomes witness to the latter's presence with him at the farthest extent of the discovery.[86]

Finally, Marquette's journal of his second trip to the Illinois contains an observation which could hardly be interpreted with any plausibility, if, in 1673, he had not traveled on the whole exploration. On March 31, 1675, he had just crossed from his winter home at Chicago to the Des Plaines River when he wrote, "ce fust d'icy que nous commencasmes notre portage Il y a 18 mois; . . . [it was from here that we commenced our portage, 18 months ago]." [87] Eighteen months before this date was September, 1673. This is the very month when the Récit says the Jolliet-Marquette expedition crossed from this spot to the Chicago River and Lake Michigan.[88] It is hardly believable that Marquette could have been with Jolliet at this point unless he had been with him all the way, because neither a previously planned rendezvous nor a chance meeting in the

86. ASH, 5, no. 16, 6. Jacques Largillier, one of Jolliet's hired men who was on the whole exploration, also told Father Cholenec that Father Marquette was among the explorers, APF, Fonds Brotier 166 (Canada–12), no. 4, 26; Camille de Rochemonteix, *Les Jésuites et la Nouvelle-France,* (Paris, 1895–96), II, 607.

87. ACSM, 296, 68; Thwaites, *JR,* LIX, 180–81.

88. ACSM, 296, 37; Thwaites, *JR,* LIX, 162–63.

wilderness may be called upon to bring them together. It was owing to their first stop among the Indians on the Mississippi that the explorers came to the portage. There, the natives had not only presented them with a calumet, but had entrusted an Indian boy to their care as a pledge of confidence. It was this lad who let Jolliet know about the short cut to Lake Michigan by way of the Illinois River. This is why the expedition turned aside from the route of its outward voyage, when it again came to the mouth of this stream.[89] If Marquette had not been with Jolliet at this turn-off, but had gone out by himself to found a mission among the Illinois tribes, he would have sought them, according to previous plans, on the Mississippi. Only when the great Kaskaskia town was contacted, on the Illinois River, did the French discover that here was the largest population center of these people, accessible by a portage from Lake Michigan.[90]

Nothing essential to the narrative of the discovery remains to be verified. However, Marquette's responsibility for the truth of the Récit ends almost simultaneously with the close of its first chapter. Thereafter, in chapters two and three, Dablon becomes the biographer of the missionary; hence, the present consideration of the Marquette documents cannot be concluded without probing them, to make sure their composer does not depart from reality in his word-portrait of the discoverer.

For the second chapter of the Récit, Dablon drew upon those

89. APF, Fonds Brotier 155 (Canada–1), 12v; Thwaites, *JR,* LVIII, 100–3. Jolliet makes certain the route was not premeditated. He tells why he selected it in La Potherie, *Voyage de l'Amerique,* II, 131; Blair, *Indian Tribes,* I, 348.

90. Gilbert J. Garraghan, "The Great Village of the Illinois: A Topographical Problem," *M-A,* XIV (1931–32), 142–43; and Marion A. Habig, "The Site of the Great Illinois Village," *M-A,* XVI (1933), 4.

events prior to Easter Sunday, 1675, which led to the establishment of the mission among the Illinois; and the sequence of
seven weeks thereafter, which led to the priest's death on May
18, to recreate Marquette, the man. Here, Jolliet's partner in
the discovery of the Mississippi is made to come aside from
the adventure and reveal his own aspirations, the particular
motive force which drove him toward their accomplishment,
the personal endowments which were characteristically his as
a missionary adventurer.

With this aim in view, it is understandable why Dablon's
account of Marquette's return to Old Kaskaskia, in 1674–
75, omits so many things which are found in the holograph
journal of his second trip to the Illinois Indians. Marquette
kept track of possible food supplies, the conditions of the
weather, the attitude of neighborhood Indians, and other small
happenings in the hope that future missionaries might derive
advantage from such information. Dablon passed over all of
this and stressed Marquette's solicitude for the spiritual wel-
fare of his donnés, a prophecy he made about his impending
death and a novena of Masses he said, during which "il fut
exauce Contre toute les espparances humaines, et se portant
mieux il se uit en estat d'aller au bourg des Jlinois [was heard
beyond all human expectations, and becoming better, he found
himself in a condition to set out for the town of the Illi-
nois]." [91] When Marquette arrived in the large Indian town,
where he and Jolliet had paused in the September of 1673,
Dablon again stresses the spiritual things he did, dwelling

91. ACSM, 296, 39; Thwaites, *JR,* LIX, 186–87. One thing
skipped by Dablon, but in the holograph journal, is Marquette's statement that he said Mass every day except one while on the site of
Chicago. On that occasion, the cold prevented him from doing so,
see ACSM, 296, 65 and 67; Thwaites, *JR,* LIX, 172–73, 180–81. This
passage indicates what Marquette meant by "dire la messe." Coldness
did not cause the missionary to discontinue his prayers. Frozen water
is unfit material for the consecration in the Mass. See Appendix I.

especially on the fervor with which "Le Pere . . . dit ensuitte
la Ste. Messe," on Holy Thursday and how on Easter Sunday,

> les choses estant disposées de la mesme maniere que le Jeudy, il
> celebra les SS. Mysteres pour La 2de fois, et par ces deux sa-
> crifices qu'on y Eut jamais offerts a Dieu il prit possession de cette
> terre au nom de Jesvs Christ.[92]

> [The Father . . . then said the Holy Mass . . . Easter Sunday,
> things being arranged in the same manner as on Thursday,
> he celebrated the Holy Mysteries for the second time, and by
> these two sacrifices, such as had never been offered to God
> before at this place, he took possession of this land in the name
> of Jesus Christ.]

Here, by the way, Dablon uses words for the celebration of
Mass which are equivalent to the most technical language of
the Council of Trent when it speaks of this service.[93] That he
had a right to do so is sustained by what the donnés, who
participated in this solemnity, told Father Cholenec. They
mentioned their having received Holy Communion from Father
Marquette after he had offered the sacrifice on the altar.[94] This
is very pertinent, because the Council distinguishes between
the Communion made *ad divinam hanc mensam* ("at the holy
altar"), which is consecrated bread administered by a priest;
and Communion made *spiritualiter* ("spiritually"), which is
merely an act of desire to share in the Eucharist.[95]

In speaking of what the Récit narrates about the events
which took place on the bank of the Illinois River that Easter
day of 1675, Louise Kellogg in her *French Regime in the*

92. ACSM, 296, 40; Thwaites, *JR,* LIX, 190–91.

93. See Appendix I, n. 37.

94. APF, Fonds Brotier 166 (Canada–12), no. 4, 26v. Rochemonteix, *Les Jésuites et la Nouvelle France,* III, 609, omits part of this
passage in his transcription. He indicates the lacuna by five dots.

95. H. L. Schroeder, *Canons and Decrees of the Council of Trent*
(St. Louis, 1950), pp. 354–56, Sessio decima-tertia, De Eucharista,
Die XI Octobris, MDLI.

Northwest raises the question whether Marquette should be
named the founder of the mission of the Conception, since
the Relations seemed to indicate that Father Allouez had been
at Old Kaskaskia before him. She was led to this conclusion
by what she found in the fifty-eighth volume of Thwaites' reprints of the Jesuit periodical. There, Allouez' letter about his
work for the year 1673–74 mentions his being among some
"Caskakias" in the summer at least a month before the Jolliet-
Marquette expedition arrived on the Illinois River. Her chronology was correct but by an oversight she neglected the location
at which Allouez found his Caskakias in 1673. He was on the
Fox River, among the Miami, when he encountered them.
Kellogg could not have been drawn into such an oversight
had not Thwaites separated the third chapter of the Récit from
the other two. The present work has called attention to Kellogg's dependence on him which led her to omit this part of
the Récit from her *Early Narratives*. Had she used it she would
have read Allouez' own admission that he took over in 1677
the mission of the Conception which Father Marquette had
founded in 1675. There is also a letter from Fr. Thierry
Beschefer, written during Allouez' lifetime, which says of the
Illinois mission, "Le Premier qui Jamais trauaillé a leur
Jnstruction a esté le Pere Jacques Marquette [The first who
ever worked for their instruction was Father Jacques Mar-
quette]." [96]

Pursuing his evaluation of Father Marquette the man, Dablon inserted in the Récit a short treatise on his virtues.[97] As
head of the missions, he was in a unique position to do this,
for according to Jesuit rule each member of the Order is

96. Louise P. Kellogg, *The French Regime in Wisconsin and the
Northwest* (Madison, Wis., 1925), p. 166, n. 62. Her omission of ch.
3 is mentioned above, ch. 3, n. 16. For Allouez' letter of 1674, see
APF, Fonds Brotier 157 (Canada–3), 75; Thwaites, *JR*, LVIII, 264–65
and ibid., LXII, 210–11, for Beschefer.

97. ACSM, 296, 51; Thwaites, *JR*, LIX, 210–13.

obliged to open his soul to his superior at the beginning of his religious life, at frequent intervals during his studies, just before his final vows are taken, and yearly thereafter in connection with his retreat.[98] Father Dablon had been on the receiving end of such manifestations of conscience since 1671, the year he was appointed superior of the Canadian missions. This year, too, he was at Sault Sainte-Marie when Father Marquette stopped by, before going to initiate the mission of St. Ignace. During the pause, he made his final Jesuit vows. On this occasion certainly, the two men took time for such spiritual colloquy as the founder of their Order had advised.[99] Thereafter, the missionary in the field fulfilled the obligation by letter. For example in 1674 after his retreat in the wilderness of Illinois, Marquette's journal records his sending "lettres pour nos PP. [Pères] de st Francois" by the hand of friendly Indians going that way.[100] It seems very probable his manifestation of conscience was in one of these. Such a message is included in the second chapter of the Récit as "Vne des dernieres lettres quil a escriptes au P. Superieur des Missions, auant son grand uoyage [One of the last letters which he (Marquette) wrote to the Fr. Superior of the Missions before he passed away]." [101] The whole quotation from it lays bare his spiritual

98. *Institutum Societatis Iesu* (Florentiae, 1892–93), II, 14, Examen, cap. 4, no. 36, 38 and 40. The time for the annual manifestation is set, ibid., p. 94, Const. pars 6, cap. 1, no. 2.

99. Perrot-Tailhan, *Memoire sur les Moeurs,* p. 128.

100. ACSM, 296, 67; Thwaites, *JR,* LIX, 178–79, Marquette is speaking of the mission of St. Francois Xavier, now De Pere, Wisconsin. He says the Indians will follow "le chemin des Pout," the trail to his "Potawatomi" friends at the mouth of the Fox River. For this trace, see Bessie L. Pierce, *A History of Chicago* (New York, 1937–57), I, 5; or W. D. Stone, *Map of Wisconsin Territory Compiled from Public Surveys* (Washington, n.d., ca. 1840).

101. ACSM, 296, 50–51; Thwaites, *JR,* LIX, 208–11. Thwaites translates "auant son grand uoyage" into "before his great voyage." This is vague. Actually, the French idiom means "before his great voyage into eternity."

hopes and desires.[102] Such candor towards Dablon qualified him to recount the virtues of his subject. Now, Marquette's death unsealed his lips and since he knew the readers of the *Relations*, if and when publication might resume, would find edification in what he could tell, he wrote down a summary of his knowledge. The good points he enumerates fall under four headings: a compelling zeal, a chivalrous devotion to the mother of God, a selfless adaptability which made him all things to all men, and a dependence on God which had been his shield in the midst of pagan immorality. By supplying actual instances of these things from Marquette's life, he removes this classification from the sphere of eulogistic platitude.[103]

In 1668, Father Marquette came among the Indians with a robust physique.[104] By the time he founded his third mission, seven years later, he was worn out with his work, and in this same year, May 18, 1675, he died.[105] For twenty-five years

102. APF, Fonds Brotier 155 (Canada–1), 43–45, "Mors p. Iacobi marquette" treats this letter more fully than does the Récit. The inclusion of a Jesuit's virtues is called for in his manifestation, *Institutum S. I.,* II, 45, Const. pars 3, cap. 1, no. 12.

103. ACSM, 296, 48–51; copied in de Montézon, *Rel. Inédites,* II, 303. Thwaites, *JR,* LIX, 204–11, substitutes the text of John G. Shea and Felix Martin, *Cramoisy No. 12, Relation . . . 1673–1679* (New York, 1860), pp. 115–20, which was transcribed from ACSM, 314, 52–54, "1673–1679 Relation, Original."

104. ARSJ, Franc. 14, 126, after Marquette arrived in Canada, the first triennial catalog (1669) estimated his physical strength as "powerful" (*vires firmae*). Three years later (1672) as he was thinking of the Mississippi exploration, he was still in "good condition" (*vires integrae*), ARSJ, Franc. 14, 285.

105. ARSJ, Gal. 110, pt. 3, 373v–374, speaks of Marquette as "immensis jtinerum laboribus exhaustus . . . populis, quos detexit ipse primus [spent with measureless toil . . . for people, whom he himself was the first to discover]." This quotation is from a letter by Dablon, which he addressed to *Propaganda Fide* in 1679 and is incorporated in an unpublished book by Honoratus Fabri, *Questiones*

after his death, his memory was kept fresh at St. Ignace.[106]
Then, the chapel which had sheltered his grave was burned
by the Jesuits themselves, and it never was rebuilt. Briefly,
the steps which led to this course of action were these: in
1690, during King William's War, a hundred soldiers had
been quartered near the mission to retain the Indians on the
French side.[107] Because the soldiers had little to do, the traditional disorders of idle campaigners began to corrupt them.[108]
The missionaries protested to Governor Louis Hector de Callières.[109] His solution to the problem was delivered in a letter
of September 25, 1702, in which he ordered the Jesuits and
Indians of Michilimackinac to repair to the settlement at Detroit, founded only a year before by Antoine de La Mothe
Cadillac.[110] Though the Minister of Marine intervened to free
the priests from any obligation to make this change, his dispensation reached St. Ignace after most of the Indians had moved
away. The fathers found it useless to remain longer at the
post.[111] In 1705, they decided to abandon the Ottawa country

---

Canadenenses, 1681, noted by Carlos Sommervogel, ed., *Bibliothèque
de la Compagnie de Jésus* (Bruxelles-Paris, 1890–1932), III, Col.
511–21.

106. Archives du Séminaire des Étrangères, Quebec, Lettres, Carton
N., no. 132 and APF, Fonds Brotier 165 (Canada–11), contain contemporary references to Marquette.

107. La Potherie, *Voyage de l'Amerique,* II, 233–36, reprinted in
Blair, *Indian Tribes,* II, 45–49.

108. Rochemonteix, *Les Jésuites et la Nouvelle-France,* III, 487–
503.

109. Thwaites, *JR,* LXV, 192–93, "Lettre du P. Carheil au Gouverneur Callières (30 aout 1702)."

110. Pierre-Georges Roy, *Ordinnances, Commissions, etc. etc. des
Gouverneurs et Intendants de la Nouvelle-France, 1639–1706* (Beauceville, 1924), I, 310, "Reglement de M. de Callières au sujet des plaintes
de M. de La Motte Cadillac, . . . contre les missionnaires, 25 Sept.
1702."

111. Margry, *Découv. et Étab.,* V, 304, "Lettre du Ministre De
Ponchartrain au M. De Lamothe-Cadillac (14 juin 1704)."

and before they left, their religious buildings were consigned to the flames lest they be desecrated. It appears they left Marquette's tomb undisturbed in the ashes. Young Charlevoix was a teacher at the college in Quebec when the missionaries of St. Ignace arrived there. The disheartening failure of their efforts made a deep impression on him. When he wrote his *Histoire et Description,* he dwelled on the incident at some length but did not mention anything about their having saved Marquette's bones.[112]

In the winter of 1711–12, what came to be known as the Fox War broke out. Its battles spread to the west of Lake Michigan.[113] Two years later, the government returned some troops to guard the passage through the Straits of Mackinac. For greater safety, they built their fort with a mission chapel beside it, to the south where Mackinaw City is today.[114] Five miles of water separated the Jesuits from the unmarked grave of Father Marquette.[115] Then came the final struggle between

112. [Pierre F.-X.] de Charlevoix, *Histoire et Description de la Nouvelle-France* (Paris, 1744), IV, 5; [Pierre F.-X. de Charlevoix], *History and General Description of New France,* tr. and ed. John G. Shea (New York, 1866–72), V, 182.

113. Charlevoix, *Histoire et Description,* IV, 94; Charlevoix and Shea, *History of New France,* V, 257.

114. Kellogg, *French Regime,* pp. 280–93, assigns 1714 for the return. Antoine I. Rezek, *History of the Diocese of Sault St. Marie and Marquette* (Houghton, Mich., 1907), II, 114–16, misread the title of a 1741 baptismal ledger, "suite de Register des nouveaux Mackinac," which means "Register of new [baptisms] at Mackinac continued." He mistook the adjective "nouveaux," which is in the plural number, as modifying "Mackinac," which is in the singular; hence, he called Mackinaw City new, or just founded in 1741.

115. The position of the new fort across the Straits from "Cap St. Ignace," where a cross indicates the "Mission détruite," is outlined on the *"Carte du Détroit entre Lac Superieur et le Lac Huron avec le Sault Sainte Marie et le Poste de Michillimackinac Par N. Bellin* [*Map of the Strait between Lake Superior and Lake Huron with the Sault Sainte Marie and the Post of Michillimackinac. By N. Bellin*]," in Charlevoix, *Histoire et Description,* V, 414–15.

France and England for North America. The black robes were
exiled and their Order suppressed. The victorious Union Jack
waved for a space at Michilimackinac. It, in turn, gave way
to the Stars and Stripes and the western surge of independent
Yankees. Such a torrent of events sweeping over the Ottawa
country all but obliterated the memory of days when the Bourbon banner shook its lilies from its staff at St. Ignace. Then,
two hundred years after Father Marquette's burial, evidence
came to light establishing the truth of what the Récit tells of
his reburial at St. Ignace.[116]

For a generation after the Northern Peninsula of Michigan
became part of the United States, no Catholic priests were
stationed in the area. When they returned, there were no
Jesuits among them. In 1873, Fr. Edward Jacker, appointee
of Bishop Frederic Baraga, assumed the care of souls of St.
Ignace. To him, some ancient Ottawa told the legend of a
great priest who had been buried near the inlet now known as
East Moran Bay. Aware that his parish had once been the scene
of Father Marquette's mission, the pastor began fishing for
facts which might be hidden below the ripple of this rumor.[117]

The French Jesuits had built two Indian chapels along the
Straits of Michilimackinac. One, dedicated to St. Francis
Borgia, had been erected in the autumn of 1677 to accommo-
date the increasing number of Christian Ottawa. The other,
under the title of St. Ignatius, was three quarters of a league
away. It dated from the beginning of the mission, in 1671,
and was appropriated by the Hurons. At it, the Jesuits had
a residence.[118] Since Marquette was buried in the spring of

116. ACSM, 296, 51.

117. Harry H. Heming, *The Catholic Church in Wisconsin* (Milwaukee, 1895–98), pp. 247–48 and n. 1.

118. ACSM, 314, 25; Shea and Martin, *Cramoisy No. 12, Relation
for 1673–1679*, pp. 58–59, "La lettre que m'escrit le P. Jean Enjalran
[The letter which Fr. Jean Enjalran wrote me]," says Dablon, in
1679, establishes these facts.

1677, his remains must have found shelter in the older church. Its relationship to recognizable geographical features at Point St. Ignace was established by the de La Salle expedition. On August 27, 1679, here on board the *Griffon,* he anchored in a cove with six fathoms of water. The cove was sheltered from the east wind by "the island of Missilimakinac" about a league off shore. Bordering the strand were the cornfields of the Indians and the buildings of the mission.[119] The next pertinent bit of evidence about the grave site is in Henri Joutel's journal. In 1688, he, in company with Father Cavelier and Father Douay, rested at the Straits, after an overland flight from the scene of de La Salle's assassination. The Jesuits' quarters accommodated four resident fathers and still had room to house the fugitive priests. The layman was pleased with the beauty of the adjacent oratory, built with logs in the Canadian style, which was to sink posts in the ground side by side with a stone cradle at their base. The exterior was then covered with boards and whitewash applied without and within.[120] Such a structure leaves post stains in the ground; the stone footings would help to trace the space once inclosed by its walls. Finally, Lahontan

119. Margry, *Découv. et Établ.,* I, 448, "Relation des decouvertes et voyages du Sr. de La Salle . . . 1679–80–81," reprinted in Melville B. Anderson, ed., *Relation of the Discoveries and Voyages of Cavelier De La Salle from 1679 to 1681* (Chicago, 1901), p. 37. De La Salle describes the bay and the island. Its name is added by his chaplain, Hennepin, *Description de la Louisiane,* reprinted in *Father Louis Hennepin's "Description of Louisiana Newly Discovered to the Southwest of New France by Order of the King,"* tr., Marion E. Cross (Minneapolis, 1938), pp. 35–36. Later on, Cadillac localized "le couvent des Jésuites" in "le fond de l'anse [the convent of the Jesuits (in) the center of the cove]," Margry, *Découv. et Établ.,* V, 75, "Relation de Sieur de Lamothe Cadillac."

120. Ibid., III, 513; [Henri Joutel], *Joutel's Journal of La Salle's Last Voyage, 1684–7 . . .* ed. and tr., Henry R. Stiles (Albany, N.Y., 1906), pp. 199–200. A church of this style, built in 1799 and still standing, is depicted in Joseph P. Donnelly, *The Parish of the Holy Family, Cahokia, Illinois, 1699–1949* (n.p., 1949), p. 38.

in his *New Voyages* not only tells how the missionaries lived
in a "little House or Colledge adjoining a sort of church and
inclos'd with Pales," but spoke of a small settlement of "cou-
reurs-de-bois" to the south and added a map, "Lake of Huron
The Mouth of ye Ilinese Lake," which confirms the details
found in the other sources.[121]

Father Jacker had acquired this documentary evidence
slowly and had not hesitated to share his findings with his
parishioners. Mr. David Murray, who owned the farm at the
head of East Moran Bay, began clearing the brush at the
approximate position of the church. On May 5, 1877, Peter
Grondin, working for him, uncovered a rectangular frame
thirty-six by forty feet square, outlined in stone. This started
a summer-long search for other components represented on
Lahontan's map. A pile of rocks, just outside of the northwest
corner of the square, was investigated by Mr. Murray. When
he found a small crucifix and other fragments of domestic
utensils in the ground close by, the stones were reconstructed
into the fireplace of the Jesuits' house. Bits of iron in various
forms were unearthed among the remains of a similar hearth to
the southwest. This might have been a quasi-forge in a work-
room. A little further away were the remains of a "root-
house." [122]

John G. Shea, who had done so much to make the Récit
available to scholars, heard of the activity at St. Ignace and
wrote, "If these buildings were the Jesuit church and house,
the French village was at the right; and there, in fact, could
be traced the old cellars and small loghouse foundations. On

121. Thwaites, *New Voyages*, I, 145–46. The map is reproduced
in the same volume, p. 36, but Lahontan's identification, calling it
the one sent a friend in 1688, does not appear in the text until p. 319.

122. Samuel Hedges, *Father Marquette Jesuit Missionary and Explorer, the Discoverer of the Mississippi, His Place of Burial at St.
Ignace Michigan* (New York, 1903), pp. 99–121. Hedges was present
during the investigations.

the other side was the Huron village; the palisades can even now be traced. Further back the map shows Indian fields. Strike into the fields and small timber, and you can even now see signs of rude Indian cultivation years ago and many a relic tells of their occupancy." [123] Finally, Father Jacker chose September 3, 1877, as the date on which the actual excavation of the foundation should begin.

The diggers started their work where they believed the altar had been. At the depth of three feet below the ground level, they came upon "just the things that you would expect to meet within the cellar of a building destroyed by fire, such as powdered charcoal mixed with subsoil, spikes, nails, an iron hinge, pieces of timber . . . partly burned and very decayed." The floor of the shallow crypt seemed to have been reached.[124] Below this plane, there was no indication of disturbances to the natural clay deposit. However, as the excavators worked toward the center of the chapel, they again came on signs of a former cavity, which had gone below the established base level. Here, after removing a foot of dirt, they uncovered a large and well-preserved piece of birch bark. It was resting on three sills of cedar, disintegrating from age. All present were convinced they had found Father Marquette's grave.

The workers had approached their task with intelligence and care. They were not trained archaeologists. When they found the little vault had been broken open and was empty of bones, they realized that they had worked a bit too fast. Diligently, they sifted the earth which had been removed from the vicinity of the grave. Several bits of bone-like substance were recovered.[125] Father Jacker writes, "experts to whom these frag-

123. John G. Shea, "Romance and Reality of the Death of Marquette and Recent Discovery of His Remains," *Catholic World*, XXVI (1877), 275.

124. Hedges, *Father Marquette*, pp. 123–27.

125. Ibid., p. 129, thirty-six fragments were found, ranging "in size from an inch in length to a mere scale."

ments were handed for examination—one of them unaware of
the time of the discovery and circumstances—declared them
to be human, very old and acted upon by intense heat." [126]
Various explanations have been offered for what may have
become of the larger parts of the skeleton. Father Jacker, on
the advice of some of his Indian friends who had witnessed
the dig, concluded the tomb had long before been plundered
by their ancestors. The tradition of a great person's sepulcher,
the superstitious customs of the aborigines, the box torn asunder
with fragments of its contents scattered on the ancient floor,
all these things point to pilfering by eager but irreverent hands
in search of talismanic stuff from which the American Indians
fashioned amulets to shield themselves from evil.[127] The sum
of this data enabled Shea to end his article thus, "The detailed
account [in the Récit] of the final interment of Father Marquette, the peculiarity of the bones being in a bark box, the
fact that no other priest died at the mission who could have
been similarly interred, leads irresistibly to the conclusion
we are justified in regarding the remains found as a portion
of those committed to the earth two centuries ago." [128] Here,
archaeology in the service of history throws its weight behind
Dablon's truthfulness in his description of Marquette's
burial.[129]

126. Chrysostom Verwyst, *Missionary Labors of Fathers Marquette,
Ménard and Allouez, in the Lake Superior Region* (Milwaukee, 1886),
pp. 136–43, quotes Father Jacker's recollections, nine years after the
event. George S. May, "The Discovery of Father Marquette's Grave
at St. Ignace 1877 as Related by Father Edward Jacker," *Michigan
History*, XLII (1958), 267–87, is a modern evaluation of Verwyst's
material.
    127. Hedges, *Father Marquette*, pp. 131, 140.
    128. Shea, "Romance and Reality," p. 281.
    129. Father Jacker retained the eighteen fragments of Father Mar-
quette's bones, until 1882 when he learned that a Jesuit-staffed college,
named after the seventeenth-century priest-explorer of the Mississippi,
had just been opened in Milwaukee, Wisconsin. Such an institution

At this point, it seems that what this book set out to do has been accomplished. Not every assertion in the Récit has been considered. Some things which are told there and omitted here have been treated quite fully in easily accessible periodicals.[130] To dwell on other incidents would have been to transgress the limits set for the present research, which was to weigh the evidence bearing on the validity or invalidity of the primary sources relating to Père Jacques Marquette. This book was not intended to put an end to all investigations about the priest-explorer of the Mississippi River. He, among all the early French missionaries, has in a special manner caught the fancy of the American people. They like to read about him and to talk about him. One of the best ways to start a conversation is to ask a trenchant question. If the reader thinks of such a one which is unanswered in the present work, he probably will not have to look too far to find somebody ready to discuss it with him.[131]

---

appealed to him as the safest depository for his treasure. He consigned the bones and a testimonial letter to the rector of the school. A handsome case was made and the bones and Father Jacker's testimony were sealed therein. Today, Marquette University still guards the fragmentary remains of its patron. See Raphael N. Hamilton, *The Story of Marquette University* (Milwaukee, 1953), pp. 119–21.

130. See articles by Hamilton in the bibliography of this book.

131. On September 15, 1965, President Lyndon B. Johnson signed into law a joint resolution establishing a "Tercentenary Commission to Commemorate the Advent and History of Father Jacques Marquette in America," *United States Statutes at Large,* LXXIX, 781. The discussion of the joint resolution which led to this act is in the *Congressional Record* (89 Congress, 1 Session), pp. 13068–69, 19686–88. The years of the celebration extend from 1968–1973.

Reference Matter

APPENDIX I

Concerning Marquette's Ordination

THE January, 1949, issue of *La Revue de l'Université Laval* contains an article by Fr. Joseph C. Short, then pastor of St. Francis Xavier parish in De Pere, Wisconsin, which discusses Marquette's missionary career, and questions whether he worked as a priest.[1] In his research, Short became aware of the abbreviated studies made by Marquette in the field of Catholic dogma, and was baffled by the problem which he saw in this. The current canon law of the Church requires four years formal study of speculative theology in preparation for the priesthood.[2] How, then could any bishop ordain a man who did not come near fulfilling this requirement? Short suggested in his article that the young Jesuit, becoming tired of academic confinement, had probably changed his grade to that of a lay brother, and had done his work in Canada as a lay catechist.

The March, 1949, issue of the same journal contained two refu-

1. Joseph C. Short, "Jacques Marquette, s.j. catechist," *Revue de l'Université Laval*, Quebec, III (1949), 436–41. Father Short became interested in the seventeenth-century French Jesuits because his parish was very close to the site where, in 1671, Father Allouez built the first chapel in honor of St. Francis Xavier on the Fox River. Short had intended to publish a book, but his death came, June 30, 1951, before he had finished the manuscript. See below, Appendix I, n.10, for other publications by him.

2. *Codex Juris Canonici*, Canon 1365, par. 2, requires four years theological study for the priesthood. However, this decree was not promulgated until 1919.

tations of this theory. One was by Fr. Paul Desjardins, archivist of
the Collège Sainte-Marie, Montreal. He turned to the administration
of the sacraments of baptism and penance by the missionary as proof
for Marquette's being in holy orders.[3] A Tridentine decree forbids
lay folk to baptize, except "in danger of death, baptism may be
performed by anyone . . . however, if a priest is on hand, he is to
have preference over others." When Marquette baptized "a woman
who was instructed for more than a year," he was doing what only
a priest could do, that is, baptize a person not in danger of death.[4]
Also, only a priest can hear confessions and grant absolution. Marquette's letter in the "Relation . . . les Années 1672–1673" tells
how he spent the winter. "This autumn I commenced to instruct
some in making their general confessions." When they finally were
ready, "they begged me not to give them absolution until they had
told me everything." Others who recited their faults asked, "that
I give them absolution [and] they let me know they had only told
me what they could not remember having ever confessed before."[5]
The words of this description are the technical ones found in the
Roman ritual and the limitations placed by some of the Indians on
their manifestations of conscience make sure that this self revelation
was for the purpose of fulfilling the penitent's part in the sacrament,
since in this instance they need submit to the priest only those sins
which have not been absolved by a former confessor. Had the
Indians merely been seeking counsel for self improvement, the right
procedure would not permit any limitation on the catalog of their
transgressions. Nor may it be said that, if Marquette administered
the sacrament on this occasion, he violated the so-called "seal of

3. Paul Desjardins, "Jacques Marquette était-il prêtre," *Revue de
l'Université Laval,* Quebec, III (1949), 634–39.

4. *Rituale Romanum, Paul V Pontificis Maximi Jussu Editum*
(Ratisbon Reprint, 1926), p. 8, Titulus II, cap. 1, par. 16, contains the
rule. Thwaites, *JR,* LVII, 260–61, mentions the woman who spent
twelve months preparing for baptism, which indicates she was not
in immediate danger of death. Thwaites' many volumes of Jesuit
documents are discussed in ch. 3 of this book.

5. *Rituale Romanum,* p. 91, Titulus III, cap. 1, par. 1, says only
priests may absolve from sin. Thwaites, *JR,* LVII, 256–57, tells of
Marquette acting as confessor.

confession" by dwelling with admiration, as he does here, upon the care exercised by the Indians in the examination of their lives and the innocence he found in certain ones among them. By professional secrecy, the confessor is only obliged to refrain from disclosing anything which might either injure the reputation of a penitent or add to the difficulty which the latter might feel in telling his sins.[6]

The second article supporting Marquette's priesthood placed considerable reliance on the holograph copy of Marquette's final vows, which had accidentally come to light in 1935 when Fr. Gilbert J. Garraghan was in Europe gathering archival material for his history of Jesuits at work in the United States after 1818. The formula was the one proper to spiritual coadjutors of the Society; hence, it was argued, he must have been a priest.[7] At the end of this article, the editor of the review announced the close of the controversy in the pages of his periodical. However, the opposition turned to another Garraghan document to continue the dispute. In 1937, the tercentenary of Marquette's birth was celebrated. This afforded an occasion for a brief paper-bound pamphlet, *Marquette, Ardent Missioner, Daring Explorer,* in which Garraghan presented some new manuscripts he had happened upon during a trip to Europe.[8] One reference he had come upon was from the "Catalogus Secundus" of the Champagne Province for 1655. This is the part of the catalog sent to Rome once every three years, in which superiors evaluate the character of the men under them. Marquette's novice master, after twelve months' observation, described his temperament as a mixture of melancholic and sanguine.[9] Father

6. Antonio M. Arregui, *Summarium Theologiae Moralis* (Editio Septima, Bilbao, 1922), pp. 422–23.

7. Raphael N. Hamilton, "Father Jacques Marquette, S.J., Priest," *Revue de l'Université Laval,* Quebec, III (1949), 640–42. Gilbert J. Garraghan, "Some Hitherto Unpublished Marquettiana," *M-A,* XVIII (1936), 23, printed a replica of the vow formula, saying it was in Paris. This error was copied by Hamilton. Actually, the holograph document is in ARSJ, Gal. 28, 42.

8. Gilbert J. Garraghan, *Marquette, Ardent Missioner* (New York, 1937), p. 5, n. 2.

9. ARSJ, Camp. 11, 87v, describes the frame of mind in Latin,

Short found in the word "melancholic," which he interpreted according to the meaning it has in present colloquial speech, a new basis for his conjecture about Marquette's lack of ordination. Thus, he pictured the young Jesuit as the sullen, spoiled child of a well-to-do family, tired of the common life and pining for the excitement of the Canadian wilds, while his superiors dared not cross him lest they lose his family's patronage. In this plight, they were glad to be rid of him; so, they quietly dispatched him to North America and concealed his lack of ordination from the family by a bit of fiction about his zeal as a missionary.[10]

In the seventeenth century, it was common to assign human temperaments to four basic divisions and combinations thereof. A man's natural inclination was said to be choleric if he was energetic and self-reliant. He was phlegmatic if he was calm and composed. The melancholic man was sensitive and inclined to put himself out of the picture. The sanguine person was generous and eager to please others. Therefore, when Marquette's master used these technical terms, he was simply stating, in the impersonal language always found in the "Catalogus Secundus," that this boy overlooked himself in the service of his companions.[11] In the years to come,

---

"Melanchol. sanguinea." The part of the triennial catalog known as the "Catalogus Secundus," wherein Jesuits are evaluated, is released from the Roman Archives of the Society of Jesus only with the permission of the general. Very Rev. John L. Swain, vicar-general, arranged for the present withdrawal, AMU, N. Amer., Fr. Reg., 12, Burrus to Hamilton, Rome, May 9, 1961 and Hamilton to Very Rev. John L. Swain, May 25, 1961.

10. Since the editor of *La Revue de l'Université Laval* had closed its pages to further argument on the topic, Father Short released this new hypothesis through a number of Wisconsin newspapers. *The Sheboygan Press,* February 15 and February 21, 1951, allotted space to the story. Father Short secured reprints of this material as a broadside which he distributed generously. The copy is in AMU, N. Amer., Fr. Reg., 19 [cited hereafter as "Short, *Reprint, Sheboygan Press*"].

11. Conrad Hock, *The Four Temperaments* (Milwaukee, 1934), pp. 18–53, writes about these early classifications of human psychic inclination; and dwells on their combinations, their advantages, and disadvantages.

several other superiors were obliged to express their estimate of his social attitude in similar publications. In 1658, Fr. Jacques Pupin found his disposition to be a combination of choleric and melancholic.[12] The same combination of words expressed Fr. André du Perrier's view in 1661. In 1665, Fr. Charles-François Deharaucourt was his superior and thought the single term sanguine enough to describe the attitude of the young man as he entered upon his theological studies. In Canada in 1669, the same characteristic attitude was observed by Father Le Mercier. When Fr. Claude Dablon called him all things to all men he, too, was dwelling on this sort of temperament.[13]

In 1949, Jean Delanglez, who has been classed among the foremost twentieth-century students of the French regime in America, was very actively producing the literature which established his reputation. He did not let the Marquette ordination controversy pass unheeded. His article in the March issue of *Revue d'Histoire de l'Amérique Française* hinted that he had turned to this magazine because the announcement that *La Revue de l'Université Laval* would not continue the discussion came before he had his material ready for publication.[14] The delay was owing to a request he had made to the Archivum Romanum Societatis Jesu for a photocopy of the official record of Marquette's ordination and by March he had not received it.

The official roster of seventeenth-century Jesuit ordinations was included in the last section of the triennial catalog, known as the "Supplementum." The triennial catalog, always written in longhand before the invention of the typewriter, is looked upon as the best

12. ARSJ, Camp. 11, 132v.

13. ARSJ, Camp. 11, 180v, "Melanch et chol."; ibid., 11, 239v, "Sanguinea"; ARSJ, Franc. 14, 219, "Sanguinea"; ibid., 14, 340 and 15, 107v are Dablon's reports which are discussed in Chapter 6. Francis B. Steck, *Marquette Legends,* ed. August Reyling (New York, 1960), pp. 4–5, adopts Short's cynical attitude toward these appraisals of Marquette's character, and Timothy Severin, *Explorers of the Mississippi* (New York, 1968), p. 87, influenced by Steck (see his select bibliography), continues the misunderstanding.

14. Jean Delanglez, "Le Reverend Père Jacques Marquette, était-il Prêtre?" *Revue d'Histoire de l'Amérique Française,* II (1949), 581–83.

source for Jesuit history and its preservation is legislated for in the *Institutum Societatis Iesu*.[15] The "Supplementum" consists of several numbered subdivisions pertinent to events which do not necessarily take place each year. In 1669, the sixth subdivision certified to those who had been raised to holy orders during the period from 1666 to 1669. Delanglez' knowledge of Jesuit practice made him hopeful that the notation about Marquette would not be too hard to find.[16]

In June, 1949, the *Revue d'Histoire* carried the assurance which Delanglez had not been able to include in his first article about Marquette's ordination. Here, he tells what had been done about obtaining the official document. His remarks conclude, "Rome interrogated has made reply. Father Marquette was ordained at Toul the 7 of March, 1666. That is the fact which puts an end to the controversy." The same edition carried the notice of Delanglez' sudden death, May 9, 1949.[17] His office was found piled high with all sorts of manuscripts, together with longhand (even some shorthand) notes, all distributed in a most individualistic order. Without the key to his method of classification, it was easier to obtain a new copy of the Roman ordination entry than to attempt to uncover this particular item midst the welter of documents in the disorderly room; hence, a facsimile in print was not made available until January, 1950.[18]

15. *Institutum Societatis Iesu* (Florentiae, 1892–93), II, 542, Cong. IV (A.D. 1581), canon 12 and III, 57 Cong. VII (A.D. 1615–16), Regulae Secretarii Societatis, no. 7, punctum decimum.

16. The divisions of the "Supplementum" are: Primum, naming the Jesuits loaned to other provinces; Secundum, naming those returned from such assignments; Tertium, naming the deceased; Quartum, naming those dismissed from the Order; Quintum, naming novices received; Sextum, naming Jesuits ordained; Septimum, naming those admitted to the grade of "professed"; Octavum, naming those admitted to the grade of "spiritual coadjutors"; Nonum, naming those admitted to the grade of "temporal coadjutors."

17. Delanglez, "Jacques Marquette, était-il prêtre?" pp. 73–74, 165–71.

18. Jerome V. Jacobsen, "Documents: Marquette's Ordination," *M-A*, XXXII (1950), 50–51. See AMU, N. Amer., Fr. Reg., 23, Jacobsen to Hamilton, Chicago, July 26, 1949 for the delay.

For this book, a photo of the official document was obtained directly from the Archivum Romanum Societatis Jesu.[19] Even after such evidence was at hand, Father Short was unsatisfied and took advantage of local newspapers to argue further. The duplicated date before "P. Ioannes Hardy" persuaded him that, in recent times, this manuscript had been deceitfully tampered with to make room for the addition of Marquette's name. To bolster his suspicion, he called attention to the lack of any mention of a Mass offered by Marquette during the whole summer of his exploration with Jolliet. He demonstrated the similarity between the early French script "F.," abbreviation for *Frère* ("Brother") and "P.," contraction for *père* ("Father") to show how Marquette's admirers might easily have mistaken the epithet proper to a layman for the one associated with a priest.[20]

A careful scrutiny of the penmanship in "Sexto" of the "Supplementum" for 1669 should persuade anyone that all the names were written at one time by the same quill in the same hand of the same person, leaving no room for forgery.[21] In addition, there is a Jesuit rule which requires a copy of the ordinations to be retained in the provincial archives.[22] This suggested the possibility that a similar list of Jesuits ordained in 1666 might be uncovered in Nancy, France, where Fr. Nicolas Roger, who was Marquette's provincial from 1664 to 1668, had lived. This clue was tracked down and the discovery made that, although most of the Society's documents disappeared during the French Revolution, the archives of the Bib-

19. ARSJ, Camp. 11, 282, "Suplementum Catalogi Provinciae Campaniae Anno 1669." In the original, the last numeral of the second "1666" covers a "7."

20. Short, *Reprint, Sheboygan Press* and Joseph C. Short, "Communication," *Wisconsin Magazine of History,* XXXIII (1949), 92–95.

21. Fr. E. J. Burrus of the Jesuit Historical Institute in Rome with Fr. Edmund Lamalle, Librarian, and Fr. Pou y Marti, O.F.M., made a special study of the Marquette documents at the Jesuit archives, because of Short's charges. All were "absolutely convinced that they were authentic," AMU, N. Amer., Fr. Reg., 7, Burrus to Hamilton, Rome, May 30, 1955.

22. *Institutum S.I.,* III, 92, Regulae Particulares, Socii Provincialis, no. 23, imposes the obligation.

liothèque Publique de Nancy did have a few original annals of the Champagne province, and among them an official catalog of ordinations.[23] A photograph of the page which lists Jesuits receiving the sacerdotal dignity over the twelve years between 1655, when Marquette had no more than begun his novitiate, and 1667, when he had just begun his priesthood has "P. Jacobus Marquette Tulli 7Martii [*sic*] 1666" as the second man to receive holy orders during this year.[24] When the entry was first made, the month of March was spelled with a small "m" and the "7" was placed, in form much like an inverted "v," quite close to it. Subsequently, someone put two loops above the small "m" to change it into a capital letter. In doing so, the "7" was partially obscured. The numeral is still visible if one looks closely.[25]

To conjecture that after 1666 Marquette was addressed by any title other than the one assigned priests is to swim against an overwhelming tide of evidence. All the catalogs of the province of Champagne from 1667 till his death bracket his name with other priests and allot to him the identical capital "P." which stands before their names and the names of priests only. The catalogs of the province of France, to which he was loaned after March, 1666, follow the same practice year by year throughout the rest of his career.[26] Besides this, there are innumerable contemporary docu-

23. J. Favier, "Manuscrits de la Bibliothèque de Nancy," in *Catalogue Général des Manuscrits des Bibliothèques Publiques de France, Departments* (Ministère de l'Instruction Publique, Paris, 1886–1956), IV, 209, no. 560, fol. 16, "Annales des ordinations, 32 feuillets."

24. Archives de la Bibliothèque Publique de Nancy, Nancy, Manuscrit 560 (138), 20, "Répertoire officiel des ordinations champenoises faisant partie des archives provinciales de la Compagnie de Jésus [Official catalog of the Champagne ordinations, constituting a part of the Provincial Archives of the Company of Jesus]."

25. L. Carrez, *Documenta ad Historiam Societatis Jesu* . . . (v.p., 1897–1914), VII, xi, in a volume printed in 1905, places Marquette's ordination in Toul, "mense martio anni 1666 . . . sacerdotio initiatus est [in the month of March of the year 1666 . . . he was raised to the priesthood]." Evidently he overlooked the "7."

26. Bibliography, Section I, "The Marquette Documents," in the present book under the entries "Catalogus Provinciae Campaniae" and

ments which spell out the word, "Pater" in Latin, "Père" in French, for "Father," when they attach a title to his name. Fr. Louis Nicolas, who was at Sillery when Father Marquette first arrived in Canada, dated a baptism performed by him. In so doing, he calls him "Pater."[27] Father Le Mercier, as superior of the Jesuit missions, assigned Marquette to his first post, in 1668, and addressed him as "père."[28] Governor Frontenac, in 1674, employed the priestly title "père" in regard to Father Marquette.[29] Bishop Laval, who

"Catalogus Provinciae Franciae," has the exact references where Marquette's name is placed among other priests with the same title they have. In these catalogs, unordained teachers have the title "M." for "Magister." Names of lay brothers are not preceded by titles but their temporal, domestic duties are enumerated following their names; so, these catalogs offer no similarity in abbreviated titles which might cause confusion.

27. Archives de l'Archevêché de Québec, Quebec, "Liber Baptismatorum a Patribus Societatis Iesu In Residentia seu Reductione Sancti Josephi Vulgo Sillery," p. 16v. After this notice there is a pen mark which is scratched out. Apparently Nicolas began his signature and realized that it was superfluous, since the baptizing priest's name is found in the entry.

28. The word "père," spelled out in full, is found attached to Marquette's name in all the annual letters which were printed between 1669 and 1673. [François Le Mercier], *Relation de Ce Qvi S'Est Passé de Plvs Remarqvable avx Missions des Pères de la Compagnie de Iesvs en la Novvelle France aux Années Mil Six Cens Soixante-sept & Mil Six Cens Soixante-huit* (Paris, 1669), p. 106, tells of "le Pere Iacques Marquette" having gone to the Sault. [François Le Mercier], *Relation de Ce Qvi S'Est Passé . . . les Années 1668. & 1669* (Paris, 1670), p. 102, says, "Le Pere Marquette nous écrit du Sault" etc. [François Le Mercier], *Relation de Ce Qvi S'Est Passé . . . les Années 1669. & 1670* (Paris, 1671), pt. 2, pp. 38 and 40, "le dessein qu'a formé le Pere Marquette" is expanded in a "Lettre du Pere Iacques Marquette." [Claude Dablon], *Relation de Ce Qui S'Est Passé . . . les Années 1670. & 1671* (Paris, 1672), p. 147, tells of "le Pere Marquette" in charge of the Mission of the Holy Spirit. [Claude Dablon], *Relation de Ce Qui S'Est Passé . . . les Années 1671. & 1672* (Paris, 1673), pp. 128–29, twice connects "père" with Marquette's name.

29. ASH, 5, no. 16, 2.

had been Marquette's ordinary, called him "père" in 1685.[30] In 1697, Father Gravier not only wrote "père" before the name, but in telling the retired Bishop Laval of his own appointment as vicar-general by Monsignor St. Vallier, he rejoices in having "the authority which Your Grace had given to Father Marquette and Father Allouez." This means that Father Marquette was entrusted with sacerdotal rights normally exercised by one of the episcopal state, and allotted only to chosen priests for grave reasons.[31] In closing the present commentary on the impossibility of mistaking Marquette's title for anything but the one appropriate to priests, there are several occasions when he is mentioned in mixed groups including lay brothers and when he is distinguished from them by the fully spelled out word. For example, Father Le Mercier spells out Père Iacques Marquette as accompanied by Frère Louys le Boême, when they set out for Sault Sainte-Marie in 1668.[32]

Father Short is correct in saying there is no mention of Masses offered by Marquette in the narrative of the Mississippi exploration. The emphasis is on the novelties of the new country and this pushes all else into the background. But the account of his second trip to the Illinois Indians has frequent allusions to his having said Mass.[33] Short admitted this, but asserted that the words "dire la Messe," which are found in the journal, meant a prayer service to people of the seventeenth century and they employed the words of the Council of Trent, "to offer Mass," when speaking of the renewal of the Lord's supper.[34] Littré's dictionary of the development of the French language, under "la Messe," calls attention to a seventeenth-century prayer service of this nature known as "the dry

30. BN, Clairambault, 1016, 629.

31. Archives du Séminaire des Missions Étrangères, Quebec, Lettres Carton N, no. 132; Thwaites, *JR*, LXV, 53–54, "Lettre du P. Gravier au Msgr Laval (17 september 1697)." John G. Shea, *The History of the Catholic Church in the United States* (New York, 1886–92), I, 313 and n. 1, supports Marquette's commission as vicar for Laval.

32. Le Mercier, *Relation . . . les Années, 1667–1668*, 106; Thwaites, *JR*, LI, 260–61.

33. ACSM, 296, 67; Thwaites, *JR*, LIX, 180–81.

34. AMU, N. Amer., Fr. Reg., 19, Short to Baldwin, September 1, 1950, develops the conjecture about the meaning of "to say Mass."

Mass[,] also called Naval Mass or Hunter's Mass," which was resorted to when conditions made it impossible to consecrate bread and wine, but he insists that the adjective "dry . . ." must be attached to "Mass" when such ceremony is meant.[35] An example of such usage turns up in Garcilaso de La Vega's narrative of Hernando de Soto's expedition, published in 1605. During the battle at Mauvila the Spaniards lost all their flour, wine, and Mass vessels. The chronicler laments that without what was needed *para dicir misa* ("for saying Mass"), they could only participate in ceremonies "the Spaniards referred to as dry Mass [*misa seca*]." He then described the latter service: a priest recited prayers "of the Mass without the consecration [of the bread and wine]."[36] The contrast in this passage between "saying mass" and the ceremonies which the Spaniards called "dry mass" is striking and makes clear that they were speaking of a Mass with the consecration of the bread and wine when they employed the term "dicir misa." As for the Tridentine decrees, they permit a wide selection of synonyms for expressing the renewal of the Lord's supper and no one of these expressions is approved above the rest. "To celebrate Mass" is used most frequently by the Holy Synod and both Littré and *Le Dictionnaire de l'Académie Françoise* of 1694 identify this term with what is meant by "saying Mass."[37]

Since 1949, when the hypothesis which questioned Marquette's priesthood was first advanced, no one, until now, had taken the trouble to investigate the sources of this theory in detail. In a book

35. E. Littré, *Dictionnaire de la Langue Françise* (Paris, 1889), III, 531.

36. Garcilaso de La Vega, *La Florida del Inca* in *Biblioteca de Autores Españoles desde la Fomacion de Lenguaje hasta Nuestros Dias,* various editors (Madrid, 1960), CXXXII, 410. The date, 1605, for the first edition is established, ibid., CXXXII, xlvii.

37. H. J. Schroeder, *Canons and Decrees of the Council of Trent* (St. Louis, 1950), p. 422, Sessio vigesima-secunda, De Sacrificio Missae, Die XVI Septembris, MDLXII, *Missas celebrare* ("To celebrate Masses"). The identity of this term with "saying Mass" is in both *Littré, Dictionnaire,* III, 531, and [Académie Françoise], *Le Dictionnaire de l'Académie Francoise Dedié au Roy* (1st ed., Paris, 1694; reprinted, ed. Paul Dupont, Lille, 1901), II, 50.

where the documentary narratives of the Marquette discoveries are examined, the assertion that they err in calling their author a priest deserved the present study. Its findings seem to establish the absence of any sufficient grounds for doubting Marquette's ordination.

APPENDIX II

References to Similar Passages in Primary and Secondary Sources

Thwaites, *Jesuit Relations and Allied Documents* (new page numbers for each volume)	Quebec Edition, *Jesuit Relations for 1632 to 1672* Reprints (new page numbers for each year)
XLII, 218–19	1655–56, 38
XLIV, 236–37	1657–58, 19
XLV, 216–17	1659–60, 3
XLV, 232–35	1659–60, 12–13
XLVI, 74–75	1659–60, 29
XLVII, 146–47	1661–62, 3
XLIX, 240–51	1664–65, 7–10
L, 138–47	1665–66, 5–9
L, 236–37	1666–67, 2
LI, 42–43	1666–67, 21
LI, 52–53	1666–67, 23
LI, 260–63	1667–68, 21
LII, 198–203	1668–69, 17–19
LII, 212–13	1668–69, 20
LIV, 136–37	1669–70, 80
LIV, 168–69	1669–70, 87
LIV, 168–95	1669–70, 87–92

Thwaites (Continued)	Quebec Edition (Continued)
LIV, 176–77	1669–70, 88
LIV, 180–83	1669–70, 89
LIV, 184–85	1669–70, 90
LIV, 188–89	1669–70, 91
LIV, 190–95	1669–70, 91
LIV, 252–55	1670–71, 2
LV, 94–225	1670–71, 24–50
LV, 110–11	1670–71, 27
LV, 130–31	1670–71, 31
LV, 168–71	1670–71, 39
LV, 170–71	1670–71, 39
LV, 234–35	1671–72, 1
LV, 246–49	1671–72, 1–2
LVI, 114–17	1671–72, 35–36
LVI, 116–19	1671–72, 36
LVI, 146–47	1671–72, 42
LVI, 156–57	1671–72, 50
LVI, 184–85	1671–72, 55
LVI, 216–17	1671–72, 55–56

Thwaites (Continued)	De Montézon, *Relations Inédites* are the *Relations* prepared, 1673–78, but not printed
LVII, 248–63	I, 95–102
LVII, 250–51	I, 96
LVII, 260–61	I, 101
LVII, 262–63	I, 102
LVIII, 24–25	I, 125–28
LVIII, 90–109	I, 193–204
LVIII, 94–97	I, 195
LVIII, 100–3	I, 199
LVIII, 264–65	I, 219–20
LIX, 86–93	II, 241–45

Thwaites (continued)	De Montézon (continued)
LIX, 88–89	II, 242
LIX, 90–93	II, 245
LIX, 96–97	II, 247–48
LIX, 100–1	II, 249–50
LIX, 104–7	II, 252–54
LIX, 106–7	II, 253–54
LIX, 108–9	II, 255–56
LIX, 112–13	II, 258
LIX, 114–17	II, 259–60
LIX, 124–25	II, 265
LIX, 136–37	II, 274
LIX, 138–41	II, 275
LIX, 140–53	II, 277–83
LIX, 150–51	II, 282
LIX, 152–53	II, 283
LIX, 158–59	II, 287
LIX, 160–61	II, 288
LIX, 162–63	II, 289
LIX, 164–83	II, 318–30
LIX, 172–73	II, 323
LIX, 178–79	II, 327
LIX, 184–85	II, 290
LIX, 186–87	II, 291–92
LIX, 190–91	II, 293
LIX, 200–1	II, 299–300
LIX, 206–7	II, 303
LIX, 208–11	II, 305–6
LIX, 210–13	II, 306
LX, 158–67	II, 312–17
LX, 166–67	II, 317
LX, 168–309	II, 97–191
LX, 214–29	II, 126–35

Corresponding page
numbers in the *Récit,*

ACSM, 296	APF, Fonds Brotier 159 (Canada–5)
1–2	13
2	13v
3–4	13v–14
8	15v
10–11	16–16v
15	18
24v	22
26–27	23
27–32	23–24v
30	24
37	26v
39	27
46	29v
48–51	30–31
50–51	31
51	31
52–60	31–34
56–60	33–34

APPENDIX III
Chronology

1637   June 1, Jacques Marquette is born at Laon, France
1646   Oct. 18, enters Jesuit college at Reims, France
1654   Oct. 7, with A.B. degree, enters Jesuit novitiate, Nancy,
          France
1656   teaches at Jesuit college, Auxere, France
1657   begins study of philosophy at Jesuit college, Pont-à-
          Mousson, France
1659   requests to work on foreign missions, and is told by su-
          perior to wait
1659   teaches at Jesuit college, Reims
1661   teaches at Jesuit college, Charleville
1663   teaches at Jesuit college, Langres
1664   teaches at Jesuit college, Pont-à-Mousson
1665   addresses second request to work on foreign missions
1665   April 28, superior, Father Oliva, writes without granting
          the request
1665   Oct. 18, with M.A. acquired during teaching, Marquette
          begins study again
1665   Dec. 29, Father Oliva, superior, writes that Marquette may
          go to Canada
1666   Marquette concentrates study on moral theology
1666   March 7, Marquette is ordained at Toul, France

1666   May 31, Father Marquette writes from seaport that his
        boat is about to sail

1666   Sept. 20, Marquette arrives at Quebec, Canada

1666   Nov. 10, goes to Trois Rivières to study Indian languages

1667   Aug. 4, writes from Trois Rivières to Father Pupin, a
        French Jesuit

1668   April 21, starts for missionary work at Michilimackinac

1668   May 20, signs baptismal register at Boucherville, near
        Montreal

1668   summer, founds the mission at Sault Ste. Marie, now in
        Michigan

1669   Louis Jolliet comes to Sault Ste. Marie

1669   Sept. 13, Father Marquette transfers to Holy Spirit mis-
        sion, Chequamegon Bay

1670   shortly after Easter, pays visit to Sault Ste. Marie

1670   Sept., returns to Chequamegon Bay to find Sioux threat-
        ening the mission

1671   June 4 to 14, Sieur de St. Lusson posts French claim to
        West, Jolliet signs it

1671   June, retreating Hurons bring Father Marquette with them
        to Sault Ste. Marie

1671   July 2, at Sault Ste. Marie, Father Marquette takes final
        Jesuit vows

1671   July 12, Claude Dablon becomes superior of the Canadian
        missions, Quebec

1671   summer, Louis Jolliet goes to Quebec

1671   summer, Father Marquette founds mission at site of pres-
        ent St. Ignace, Michigan

1672   summer, he visits Sault Ste. Marie

1672   Sept., Talon and de Frontenac appoint Jolliet and Mar-
        quette to explore West

1672   Oct. 2, Jolliet leaves Quebec to go to Sault Ste. Marie

1672   Dec. 8, he arrives at St. Ignace, and informs Marquette
        of his appointment

1673   after March 25, Marquette writes letter to Father Dablon
        for Relation

1673   spring, French Jesuits discontinue publication of Relations

1673	May 13, Louis Jolliet leaves Sault Ste. Marie to explore the West
1673	May 17, Father Marquette joins Jolliet at St. Ignace and the exploration begins
1673	June 17, the explorers arrive at the Mississippi River
1673	June 25, they make contact with the Illinois Indians in present-day Iowa
1673	July 16, they arrive at Quapaw-Akansea village and begin return trip July 17
1673	Aug. 25, the explorers enter the Illinois River
1673	Sept., the center of Illinois population is found at Kaskaskia
1673	Sept., the explorers portage to Chicago River and Lake Michigan
1673	Sept. 30, they arrive at Green Bay, St. Francis Xavier Mission
1674	early in July, Jolliet loses written records of the exploration in a wreck
1674	summer, Father Marquette falls ill
1674	Aug. 1, Jolliet dictates an account of the exploration to Dablon
1674	Oct. 25, Marquette sets out with 2 donnés to return to Kaskaskia
1674	Oct. 25, Dablon dates a letter to the French provincial, mentioning the discovery of the Mississippi
1674	Nov. 14, Governor de Frontenac informs Colbert of the discovery
1674	Nov. 23 to 27, Marquette meets friendly Indians near the mouth of the Milwaukee River
1674	Dec. 4, Marquette and his donnés arrive at the mouth of the Chicago River
1674	winter, Father Marquette and party pause on site of present Chicago, Illinois
1675	March 30, they leave their winter quarters
1675	April 11 to 14, Easter week, Father Marquette founds Conception mission, Kaskaskia
1675	April, his final illness begins
1675	last week of April, Marquette is taken to the east side of L. Michigan then northward toward St. Ignace

1675   May 18, Marquette dies and is buried at the site of present Ludington, Michigan

1675   late summer, the donnés bring news of his death to Quebec

1675   Oct. 10, Father Cholenec tells their story in a letter to a French Jesuit

1677   spring, mission Indians recover Father Marquette's bones from the temporary grave

1677   June 8, his bones are buried in the St. Ignace chapel

1678   Oct. 25, Dablon writes Father Boucher that he has finished a "little work" about Father Marquette

1701   Cadillac founds Detroit and attracts western Indians to his protection

1706   Jesuits, without a congregation, leave St. Ignace and burn the chapel

1712   Fox War causes return of Indians from Detroit to Michilimackinac

1714   Fort Michilimackinac built south of Straits of Mackinac, Jesuits reside there

1763   Treaty of Paris, French and Indian War, cedes Canada to England

1763   English forbid Jesuits to receive new members, and confiscate Quebec college

1800   Father Casot, last Canadian Jesuit dies at Hôtel Dieu, Quebec

1800   a few Jesuit manuscripts, saved by Father Casot, are preserved by the hospital nuns

1842   Jesuits return to Canada and start Collège Sainte-Marie at Montreal

1844   the nuns of Hôtel Dieu restore the Jesuit manuscripts to Collège Sainte-Marie

1873   Father Jacker becomes pastor of St. Ignace, Michigan

1877   he becomes convinced that the old Jesuit chapel was near East Moran Bay

1877   Sept. 3, archaeology uncovers chapel foundation and Father Marquette's bones

BIBLIOGRAPHY

SECTION I

The Marquette Documents.

The manuscripts which have an essential relationship to Jacques Marquette are listed here. Information concerning other manuscripts cited in the notes is not repeated.

"A Mon R. Pere Clud le Moisne de la Comp[agnie] de Jesus, A Reims." Archives de la Bibliothèque Nationale, Paris, Collection Moreau, 842, 31–32v. A copy of "Relation de la decouverte de la Mer du Sud . . . ," which introduces the manuscript "Relation . . . les Années 1672–1673."

Beau Soleil. "Pretantions que le Sieur Beau Soleil a Contre Monsieur Ioliet tant pour luy que p^r La Vefue de feu Sieur Ioliet [Adrien] a present son Espouse." Archives of the Chicago Historical Society, Schmidt Collection, I, 53. The brief of the lawsuit to assure Adrien's widow of her share in the returns from the "Old Association" which began trading at Sault Sainte-Marie in 1669.

Bernou Map. See "Carte de la decouuerte du Sr Jolliet . . . ."

Bernou, Abbé Claude. Miscellaneous papers about North America. Archives de la Bibliothèque Nationale, Paris, Clairambault, 848 and 1016 and Archives du Service Hydrographique, Paris, IX, no. 11. See also Renaudot, Eusèbe and de Laval-Montigni, François.

———. "Memoire pour la decouverte et la conquete des pays de Quivira et de Theguayo." Archives de la Bibliothèque Nationale,

Paris, Clairambault, 1016, 213–213v. Dated as written in 1677 by a reference to Marquette's death as having taken place two years before. A copy with criticism of Bernou is in Archives Nationales, Archives du Service Hydrographique (Dépôt des Cartes et Plans de la Marine), Paris, 115, IX, no. 11, 1–22.

Boucherville Baptism Ledger. See "Livre des Registres, contient Les Baptismes . . . ."

"Carte de la decouuerte du Sr Jolliet ou l'on voit la communication du Fleuue St Laurence auec les Lacs Frontenac, ..." Archives Nationales, Paris, Le Service Hydrographique, la Bibliothèque, B 4044–37. The map with the arms of Frontenac and a dedicatory letter about the 1673 discovery of the Mississippi, drawn by J-B. Franquelin. A small reproduction copied by abbé Claude Bernou is in Archives Nationales, Paris, Le Service Hydrographique, la Bibliothèque, B 4044–49.

"Carte de la Nouvelle Decouverte que les Peres Iesuites Ont Fait en l'Année 1672, et Continuée par le P. Jacques Marquette de la Mesme Compagnie Accompagné de Quelq' Francois en l'Année 1673 Qu'on Pourra Nomme en Francais la Manitoumie a Cause de la Statue Qui S'Est Trouvée, dans Une Belle Vallée et Qui les Sauvages Vont Reconoistre pour Leur Divinité, Quils Apellent Manitou, Qui Signifie Esprit ou Genie." Archives de la Bibliothèque Nationale, Paris, Vd. 30, Estampes.

Carter Brown Library Map. See "Nouuelle Decouuerte de Plusieurs Nations dans la Nouuelle France . . . ."

"Catalog, Triennial," sent to Rome every third year. It contains "Catalogus Secundus" and "Supplementum." Marquette's record is found in Triennial Catalogs of the following years:

1652–1655, Archivum Romanum Societatis Jesu, Rome, Camp. 11, 87v

1655–58, ———, Camp. 11, 132v

1658–61, ———, Camp. 11, 180v

1661–65, ———, Camp. 11, 208v, 239v

1666–69, ———, Camp. 11, 282

1665–69, ———, Franc. 14, 126, 172, 219

1669–72, ———, Franc. 14, 285, 340

1672–75, ———, Franc. 15, 107v.

"Catalogus Provinciae Campaniae," is the title of the annual catalogs announcing Marquette's yearly assignments in the Champagne Province. After 1666, he is said to be out of the province: 1667–68, Archivum Romanum Societatis Jesu, Rome, Camp. 19, 88

1668–69, ———, Camp. 19, 98

1669–70, ———, Camp. 19, 112v

1670–71, ———, Camp. 19, 123v

1671–72, ———, Camp. 19, 148

1672–73, ———, Camp. 19, 163

1673–74, ———, Camp. 19, 175

1674–75, ———, Camp. 19, 183v.

"Catalogus Provinciae Franciae," is the title of the annual catalogs announcing Marquette's yearly assignments in the Province of France. After 1666, he was loaned to this province, which had the responsibility for the Canadian missions.

1666–67, Archivum Romanum Societatis Jesu, Rome, Franc. 23, 218v–219

1667–68, ———, Franc. 23, 232

1668–69, ———, Franc. 23, 245

1669–70, ———, Franc. 23, 261

1670–71, ———, Franc. 23, 275

1671–72, ———, Franc. 23, 287–287v

1672–73, ———, Franc. 23, 301–301v

1673–74, ———, Franc. 23, 320

1674–75, ———, Franc. 23, 337.

"Catalogus Secundus." See "Catalog, Triennial."

"Ce qui s'est passé de plus remarquable dans le voyage de Mrs. D'Ollier et Galinée." Archives de la Bibliothèque Nationale, Paris, Mss.fr., n.a., 7485, 1–25. The journal of the two Sulpicians who set out with de La Salle in 1669 and met Adrien Jolliet near Niagra Falls.

Chantilly Récit. See "Recit Des voyages et Descouuertes du Pere Jacques Marquette . . . ."

Cholenec, Pierre, Letters of. See "Lettre du P. Cholenec . . . ."

Dablon, Claude, Letters of. See "Lettre du P. Dablon . . . ."

Dablon, Claude. "Lettre a Mon R. P. (de Quebec le 25 octob

1674)." Archives de la Province de France, S.J., Chantilly, Fonds Brotier 157 (Canada–3), pt. 1, 2–5v. The summary of events in the missions for the year 1673–74, which Father Dablon sent in place of the regular Relation in the fall of 1674.

"Doc. pour Servir a l'Histoire de l'Eglise du Canada." Archives du Séminaire de Saint Sulpice, Paris, I, pt. 1, 1–12. A copy of "Relation de la decouverte de la Mer du Sud . . .," which introduces the manuscript "Relation . . . les Années 1672–1673."

"Du Premier Voyage qu'a fait Le P. Marquette Vers le nouveau Mexique et Comment s'en est forme le dessin." Archives du Collège Sainte-Marie, Montreal, 296, 1–37. The title of ch. 1 of the "Montreal Récit."

"Du 1ᵉʳ voyage q'a fait le P. Marquette vers le nouueau Mexiq' et comment s'en est forme le dessein." Archives de la Province de France, S.J., Chantilly, Fonds Brotier 159 (Canada–5), 13–26v. The title of ch. 1 of the "Chantilly Récit."

"Fr. Pierre Cholenec to Fr. Jean De Fontenay (de la residence de st francois Xauier ce 10ᵉ octobre 1675)." See "Lettre du P. Cholenec au P. Fontaney . . . ."

"Fragment du Iournal du P. Marquette." Archives du Séminaire des Missions Étrangères, Quebec, "Ma Saberdache Rouge," F, 119–32, Appendice No. 5. An introduction to "The holograph journal of Marquette's second trip to the Illinois Indians," which is thereafter transcribed.

Franquelin Map. See "Carte de la decouuerte du Sʳ Jolliet . . . ."

De Frontenac, Louis de Buade, Gouverneur de la Nouvelle France. "Journal of his voyage to Lake Ontario, 1673." Archives des Colonies in Archives Nationales, Paris, C11, A4, 12–24.

———. "Report of Jolliet's discovery of the Mississippi." See "Relation de La descouverte . . . ."

Galinée, [De Bréhant]. Narrative. See "Ce qui s'est passé de plus remarquable dans le voyage de Mrs. D'Ollier et Galinée."

"The holograph journal of Marquette's second trip to the Illinois Indians." Archives du Collège Sainte-Marie, Montreal, 296, 63–68v. A descriptive title for the day-by-day record of the missionary's return, in 1674, to found the Conception Mission among the Kaskaskia. Vicher called it "Fragment du Iournal du P. Marquette." Shea spoke of it as a "letter begun but not ended by him [Marquette] . . . containing a journal of the voyage on which he died."

"Joliet à Monseigneur (Quebec le 10 octobre 1674)." Archives du Séminaire de Saint Sulpice, Paris, Doc. pour l'Hist. de l'Eglise du Canada, I, pt. 1, 12. A copy of a letter, probably sent to Bishop Laval, to tell of the success of the discovery of the Mississippi.

"Jolliet's dictation made to Dablon on August 1, 1674." This title is applied to three seventeenth-century documents, which are identical in content. (1) The introduction of the "Relation . . . les Années 1672–1673," Archives de la Province de France, S.J., Chantilly, Fonds Brotier 155 (Canada–1), 10–13, see "Relation de la decouverte de la Mer du Sud . . . ." (2) "A Mon R. Pere Clud le Moisne . . .," Archives de la Bibliothèque Nationale, Paris, Moreau, 842, 31–32v. (3) "Doc. pour Servir a l'Hist. de l'Eglise du Canada," I, pt. 1, 1–12. See also "Relation de La descouverte de plusieurs pays Scituës au midy de la Nouvelle france faitte A 1673."

"Jolliet's letter, dated October 10, 1674." See "Joliet à Monseigneur . . . ."

De Laval-Montigni, François. "Mémoire enuoié par M. L'Abbé De St Vallier nommé a l'Euéché de Quebec." Archives de la Bibliothèque Nationale, Paris, Clairambault 1016, 629–31. The document written by Bishop Laval about his diocese which he wished to resign to abbé St. Vallier. On these pages are three columns: (1) Bishop Laval's protest against an intrusion of his diocese; (2) Bernou's answers to Laval; (3) an extract from the Bull which grants the bishop of Quebec jurisdiction over the whole extent of New France.

"Letter begun but not ended by him [Marquette] . . . containing a journal of the voyage on which he died." Archives du Collège Sainte-Marie, Montreal, 296, 63–68v. Shea's descriptive title for "The holograph journal of Marquette's second trip to the Illinois Indians."

"Letters to the general of the Society of Jesus, written by Marquette." Fondo Gesuitico Societatis Jesu, Rome, Indipetae 757, no. 126 and no. 156. The first letter, written in 1665, asks for the assignment to foreign mission work; the second thanks the general for the appointment to Canada.

"Lettre a Mon R. P. (de Quebec le 25 octob 1674)." See Dablon, Claude. "Lettre . . . ."

"Lettre circulaire du P. Jacques Marquette." Archivum Romanum Societatis Jesu, Rome, Gal. 110, pt. 2, 195–196v. An obituary notice of Father Marquette's death, dated October 13, 1675.

"Lettre du P. Cholenec au P. Fontenay (10 octobre 1675)." Archives de la Province de France, S.J., Chantilly, Fonds Brotier 166 (Canada–12), no. 4, 26–27v. The letter about Father Marquette's death, based on the account of the two donnés who witnessed his decease and buried his body.

"Lettre du P. Dablon au P. Boucher (Quebec, 25 octobre 1678)." Archivum Romanum Societatis Jesu, Rome, Gal. 110, pt. 1, 62. The letter which promises that Father Ragueneau will forward Dablon's "little work" about Father Marquette to Father Boucher.

"Lettre du P. Dablon *à Propaganda Fide* (Quebec 1679)." Archivum Romanum Societatis Jesu, Rome, Gal. 110, pt. 3, 373v–374. A seventeenth-century copy of the original.

"Lettre du P. Dudouyt au Msgr. Laval." Archives du Séminaire des Missions Étrangères, Quebec, Lettres, Carton N., no. 62. Among several letters from this priest, who was the bishop's agent in Paris.

"Lettre du P. Gravier au Msgr. Laval (17 septembre 1697)." Archives du Séminaire des Missions Étrangères, Quebec, Lettres, Carton N., no. 132. The letter which calls Father Marquette Laval's vicar-general.

"Lettre du P. St. Cosme au Monseigneur l'Évêque de Quebec (Akanseas, 2 janvier 1699)." Archives Nationales, Paris, K, 1374, Leonard Papers, no. 81, 15. Describes a trip on the lower Mississippi in 1699.

"Liber Baptismatorum a Patribus Societatis Iesu In Residentia seu Reductione Sancti Josephi Vulgo Sillery." Archives du Archevêché de Québec, p. 16v. The baptismal entry assigning "Pater" Marquette as the minister.

"Livre des Registres, contient Les Baptismes, Les Mariages & Les Enterrements qui ont este faits dans La Paroisse de Boucherville, 1669–1696." Boucherville, P.Q., Canada.

"Ma Saberdache Rouge." Archives du Séminaire des Missions Étrangères, Quebec, F, 19–102. Jacques Viger's transcription of the "Montreal Récit"; comments by Viger about the Récit are in Appendices no. 1 to no. 4, 105–19.

"Manitoumie Map." See "Carte de la Nouvelle Decouverte que les Peres Iesuites Ont Fait . . . ."

"Marquette's Autograph Map." Archives du Collège Sainte-Marie, Montreal, 687. The descriptive title used for the map of the Mississippi Valley sketched by Father Marquette at the time of the discovery.

Marquette's Letters. See "Letters to the general . . . ."

"Montreal Récit." See "Recit Des Voyages et Des Découuertes Du P. Iacques Marquette . . . ."

"Mors p. Iacobi marquette." Archives de la Province de France, S.J., Chantilly, Fonds Brotier 155 (Canada–1), 38–45. A free translation of "Lettre circulaire du P Jacques Marquette."

"Nouuelle Decouuerte de Plusieurs Nations dans la Nouuelle France, En L'annee 1673 et 1674." John Carter Brown Library, Providence, Rhode Island. Map on which is a copy of the dedicatory letter about the discovery of the Mississippi, which is on "Carte de la decouuerte du Sr Jolliet ou l'on voit la communication du Fleuue St Laurence auec les Lacs Frontenac . . . ."

"Oliva to Jacques Marquette, Feb. 4, 1659." Archivum Romanum Societatis Jesu, Rome, Epist. Gen., Camp. 8, pt. 2, 257. The refusal Marquette received to his first request for foreign mission work.

"Oliva to Jacques Marquette, April 28, 1665." Archivum Romanum Societatis Jesu, Rome, Epist. Gen., Camp. 8, pt. 2, 428v. The answer of the general of the Jesuits to Marquette's request, dated 1665, in which he asks for foreign mission work.

"Oliva to Provincial Roger, December 29, 1665." Archivum Romanum Societatis Jesu, Rome, Epist. Gen., Camp. 8, pt. 2, 428v. The general's letter suggesting the assignment of Marquette to the Canadian missions.

Ordination Documents. See "Répertoire officiel . . ."; "Catalog, Triennial . . . Supplementum."

"Recit d'un 3e. Voyage fait aux Jlinois par le Pere Claude Allouez."

Archives du Collège Sainte-Marie, Montreal, 296, 52–60. The title of ch. 3 of the "Montreal Récit."

"Recit d vn 3ᵉ voyage fait aux Jlinois par le P Alloüez." Archives de la Province de France, S.J., Chantilly, Fonds Brotier 159 (Canada–5), 31–34. The title of ch. 3 of the "Chantilly Récit."

"Recit de 2 voyage de P. Iacq' Marquette pour porter La foy aux Ilinois. Sa glorieuse Mort." Archives de la Province de France, S.J., Chantilly, Fonds Brotier 159 (Canada–5), 26v–31. The title of ch. 2 of the "Chantilly Récit."

"Recit Des Voyages et Des Découuertes Du P. Iacques Marquette De la Compagnie de Jesvs En l'annee 1673. Et aux Suiuantes." Archives du Collège Sainte-Marie, Montreal, 296, 1–62. The "Montreal Récit." It has three chapters: Ch. 1 narrates the discovery; ch. 2 tells of Marquette's subsequent career; ch. 3 dwells on the continuation of his work by Allouez.

"Recit Des voyages et Descouuertes du Pere Jacques Marquette de la Compagnie de Jesus en 1673 et autres." Archives de la Province de France, S.J., Chantilly, Fonds Brotier 159 (Canada–5), 13–34. The "Chantilly Récit." It has three chapters, which are identical with those of the "Montreal Récit."

"Recit du second voyage que le Pere Jacques Marquette a fait aux Jlinois pr. y portee la foy, et la glorieuse mort du mesme Pere dans les trauaux de cette Mission." Archives du Collège Sainte-Marie, Montreal, 296, 37–51. The title of ch. 2 of the "Montreal Récit."

"Registre des Baptêmes et Sépultures des Sauvages du Lac St. Jean Chicoutimie et Tadoussac de 1669 à 1692." Archives du Séminaire des Missions Étrangères, Quebec, LV, col. 1. The register kept by the Jesuits who had charge of the mission including the Island of Anticosti showing frequent visits to Jolliet's summer home.

"Relation de la decouverte de la Mer du Sud faite par les Riuieres de la nouuelle france Enuoyée de Quebec par le Pere Dablon superieur general des missions de la Compagnie de Iesus le 1ᵉʳ. Iour d'Aoust 1674." Archives de la Province de France, S.J., Chantilly, Fonds Brotier 155 (Canada–1), 10–13. Forms the introduction to the handwritten "Relation . . . les Années 1672–1673." See also "A Mon R. Pere Clud le Moisne." Archives de la Bibliothèque Nationale, Paris, Collection Moreau, 842, 31–32v.

"Doc. pour Servir a l'Histoire de l'Eglise du Canada." Archives du Séminaire de Saint Sulpice, Paris, I, pt. 1, 1–12.

"Relation de La descouverte de plusieurs pays Scituës au midy de La Nouuelle france faitte A 1673." Archives Nationales, Archives du Service Hydrographique (Dépôt des Cartes et Plaus de la Marine), Paris, 5, no. 16, 2. Identical with Father Dablon's "Relation de la decouverte de la Mer du Sud . . ." except that Jolliet's wreck comes on the first page instead of in the middle of the document.

"Relation de La descouverte de plusieurs pays . . . ." Archives de la Bibliothèque Nationale, Paris, Mss.fr., n.a., 7491, 351–55. A copy of the same title is Archives du Service Hydrographique, Paris, 5, no. 16, and is among the papers of Eusèbe Renaudot, editor of the seventeenth-century *Gazette de France*.

"Relation de 1679 abrégé des précédentes." Archives du Collège Sainte-Marie, Montreal, 314, 1–148. Father Dablon's explanation of the rough draft of the "1673–1679 Relation, Original."

"Relation . . . les Années 1672–1673." Archives du Collège Sainte-Marie, Montreal. A rough copy, with many corrections, from which the final copy of the same Relation in Archives de la Province de France, S.J., Chantilly, Fonds Brotier 155 (Canada–1), 10–34, was made.

"Relation . . . les Années 1672–1673." Archives de la Province de France, S.J., Chantilly, Fonds Brotier 155 (Canada–1), 10–34. Noted in the previous reference is the Relation which has, by way of introduction, "Relation de la decouverte de la Mer du Sud faite par les Riuieres de la nouvelle france Enuoyée de Quebec par le Pere Dablon superieur general des missions de la Compagnie de Iesus le 1er. Iour d'Aoust 1674." See "Section II, Printed Relations," in this Bibliography, for Relations published prior to 1672–73.

"Relation . . . les Années 1673–1674." Archives de la Province de France, S.J., Chantilly, Fonds Brotier 157 (Canada–3), pt. 2, 1–97.

"Relation . . . les Années 1674–1675." Archives de la Province de France, S.J., Chantilly, Fonds Brotier 162 (Canada–8), no. 3. Contains a summary of the "Lettre circulaire du P. Jacques Marquette."

"Relation . . . les Années 1676 & 1677." Archives de la Province de France, S.J., Chantilly, Fonds Brotier 160 (Canada–6), 1–31. The Relation which covers events from the fall of 1675 to the spring of 1677.

"Relation . . . les Années 1677–1678." Archives de la Province de France, S.J., Chantilly, Fonds Brotier 159 (Canada–5), 1–34. The Relation which contains the "Chantilly Récit." The title of this narrative is on p. 13, and then ch. 1 covers pp. 13–26v; ch. 2, pp. 26v–31; ch. 3, pp. 31–34.

"Relation . . . [qui] comprend une periode de six annees depuis 1673 jusqu'en 1679." Fr. Felix Martin's descriptive title for "1673–1679 Relation, Original," Archives du Collège Sainte-Marie, Montreal, 314. See this title for contents.

Renaudot, Eusèbe. Personal Papers. See Archives Nationales, Paris, K. 1232, no. 1–98, and Archives de la Bibliothèque Nationale, Paris, Mss. fr., n.a., 7485, 7491 and 7497, for depositories and cartons relevant to Father Marquette.

"Répertoire officiel des ordinations champenoises faisant partie des archives provinciales de la Compagnie de Jésus." Archives de la Bibliothèque Publique de Nancy, Manuscrit 560 (138), 20. The record of Father Marquette's ordination preserved at Nancy, France.

"1673–1679 Relation, Original." Archives du Collège Sainte-Marie, Montreal, 314, 1–148. A summary of former mission activities, plus those of 1679. In the summary, pp. 44–62 contain ch. 2 and ch. 3 of the "Montreal Récit."

"Supplementum Sextum." See "Catalog, Triennial . . . ."

"Vow formula of Fr. Marquette." Archivum Romanum Societatis Jesu, Rome, Gal. 28, 42. The holograph, autographed statement of Marquette's vows as a Jesuit.

SECTION II

The Printed Relations

All italicized titles of Relations in the text of the present book are brought together here. The books they represent are various printed editions of the seventeenth-century Jesuit Relations, and bibliographical treatises about the Relations.

The Jesuit Relations and Allied Documents, Travels and Explorations of the Jesuit Missionaries in New France, 1610–1791. Edited by Reuben G. Thwaites, 73 vols. Cleveland, 1896–1901. Reprints of the forty volumes of the seventeenth-century Relations, French text opposite the English translation, to which are added documents with the same date of origin which are chronologically arranged to supplement information of the yearly volumes. Thwaites' series is carried to 1791 by adding the Relations unprinted after 1673, and other works about the Canadian Jesuits up to this date.

The Jesuit Relations and Allied Documents, Travels and Explorations of Jesuit Missionaries in North America 1610–1791, Selected and Edited. Edited by Edna Kenton. Toronto, 1925. Contains the English translation of data from Thwaites, *Jesuit Relations,* which deals with Father Marquette.

McCoy, James C. *Jesuit Relations of Canada, 1632–1673, a Bibliography.* Paris, 1937. Lists and describes most of the Relations, printed in the seventeenth century.

O'Callaghan, Edmund B. *Jesuit Relations of Discoveries and Other Occurences in Canada and the Northern and Western States of the Union, 1632–1672, from the Proceedings of the New York Historical Society.* New York, 1747 [should be 1847]. The reprint of O'Callaghan's address, in which he tells of the whereabouts of original copies of the Relations. Felix Martin translated this.

Relation de Ce Qvi S'Est Passé de Plvs Remarqvable avx Missions des Pères de la Compagnie de Iesvs en la Novvelle France aux Années Mil Six Cens Soixante-Sept & Mil Six Cens Soixante-Huit. Edited by François Le Mercier. Paris, 1669.

Relation de Ce Qvi S'Est Passé de Plvs Remarqvable avx Missions des Pères de la Compagnie de Iesvs en la Novvelle France avx Années 1668. & 1669. Edited by François Le Mercier. Paris 1670.

Relation de Ce Qvi S'Est Passé de Plvs Remarqvable avx Missions des Pères de la Compagnie de Iesvs en la Novvelle France avx Années 1669. & 1670. Edited by François Le Mercier. Paris, 1671.

Relation de Ce Qui S'Est Passé de Plus Remarquable aux Missions des Pères de la Compagnie de Jesus en la Nouvelle France les Années 1670. & 1671. Edited by Claude Dablon. Paris, 1672.

Relation de Ce Qui S'Est Passé de Plus Remarquable aux Missions des Pères de la Compagnie de Jesus en la Nouvelle France les Années 1671. & 1672. Edited by Claude Dablon. Paris, 1673. The last Relation to be printed in the seventeenth century.

Relation de Ce Qui S'Est Passé de Plus Remarquable aux Missions des Pères de la Compagnie de Jesus en la Nouvelle-France pendant les Années 1672 et 1673. Edited by John G. Shea. New York, 1861. Known as No. 13 in the Cramoisy Series edited by Shea, this is a printing of the manuscript in Archives du Collège Sainte-Marie, Montreal.

Relation de Ce Qui S'Est Passé de Plvs Remarqvable avx Missions des Peres de la Compagnie de Iesus en la Novvelle France és Années 1676 & 1677. Edited by James Lenox. Albany, N.Y., 1854. A reprint of the document narrating the progress of the missions from the fall of 1675 to the spring of 1677, Archives de la Province de France, S.J., Chantilly, Fonds Brotier 160 (Canada–6), 1–31. See above in Section I.

Relation de Ce Qui S'Est Passé de Plus Remarquable aux Missions des Peres de la Compagnie de Jesus en la Nouvelle France les Années 1673 à 1679, par R. P. Claude Dablon Recteur du College de Quebec & Superieur des Missions de la Compagnie de Jesus en la Nouvelle France. Edited by John G. Shea and Felix Martin. New York, 1860. No. 12 in the Cramoisy Series edited by Shea, this is a printing of the manuscript in Archives du Collège Sainte-Marie, Montreal, 314.

Relation de Ce Qvi S'Est Passé de Plvs Remarqvable dans la Mission Abnaquise de Sainct Joseph de Sillery . . . l'Année 1684. Edited by John G. Shea. New York, 1857. No. 2 in the Cramoisy Series edited by Shea.

Relation de la Mission des Illinois, 1693. Edited by John G. Shea. New York, 1857. No. 1 in the Cramoisy Series edited by Shea.

Relation du Voyage Enterpris par Feu M. Robert Cavelier, Sieur De La Salle, pour Découvrir dans le Golfe de Mexique l'Embouchure du Fleuve Mississipy, par Son Frère M. Cavelier, Prêtre de St. Sulpice, l'Un des Compagnons de Ce Voyage. Edited by John G. Shea. New York, 1858. No. 5 in the Cramoisy Series edited by Shea.

Relations des Jésuites Contenant Ce Qui S'Est Passé de Plus Remarquable dans les Missions des Pères de la Compagnie de Jésus dans la Nouvelle-France. Ouvrage Publié sous les Auspices du Gouvernement Canadien. 3 vols. Quebec, 1858. A reprint of the entire run of the seventeenth-century published Relations. The page numbering, beginning afresh for each annual, does not correspond with the originals.

Relations des Jésuites sur les Découvertes et les Autres Événements Arrivés en Canada et au Nord et à l'Ouest des États-Unis (1611–1672) par le Dr. E. B. O'Callaghan, Membre Correspondant de la Société Historique de New-York, et Membre Honoraire de la Société Historique de Connecticut. Traduit de l'Anglais avec Quelques Notes, Corrections et Additions. Translated and edited by Felix Martin. Montreal, 1850. The public announcement by Father Martin of the Marquette documents received from the Hôtel Dieu in Quebec.

Relations et Mémoires Inédites pour Servir à l'Histoire de la France dans les Pays de l'Outremer, Tirés des Archives du Ministère de Marines et des Colonies. Edited by Pierre Margry. Paris, 1867. Contains Henri de Tonti's second narrative of travels with de La Salle, Archives de la Bibliothèque Nationale, Paris, Mss.fr., n.a., 7485, 103–118. This was drawn on and added to, in the composition of the spurious *Derniere Decouvertes dans l'Amerique Septentrionale de Monsieur De La Salle*, Paris, 1697.

Relations Inédites de la Nouvelle-France, 1672–1679, pour Faire Suite aux Anciennes Relations, 1615–1672, Voyages et Travaux des Missionaires de la Compagnie de Jésus, Publiés par les Pères de la Même Compagnie pour Servir de Complément aux Lettres Édifiantes. Edited by Fortuné M. de Montézon. Published by Charles Douniol. Paris, 1861. The reprint of the manuscript Relations written by Father Dablon from 1673 to 1678.

Walter, Frank K. and Doneghy, Virginia M. *Jesuit Relations and Other Americana in the Library of James F. Bell.* Minneapolis, 1950. Lists and describes the whole run of the Relations printed in the seventeenth century.

SECTION III

The Published Sources

Vander Aa, Pieter, tr. [Melchisedech Thevenot]. *Ondekking van Eenige Landen en Volkeren in't Noorder Gedeelte van America door P. Marquette en Joliet Gedaan in Het Jaar 1673.* Leyden, 1707.

[Académie Françoise]. *Le Dictionnaire de l'Académie Françoise Dedié au Roy.* 2 vols. 1st edition, Paris, 1694; reprinted, ed., Paul Dupont, Lille, 1901.

Anderson, Melville B., tr. *Relation of Henry De Tonty.* Chicago, 1898.

————, ed. *Relation of the Discoveries and Voyages of Cavalier De La Salle from 1679 to 1681.* Chicago, 1901.

Antonelli, F., O.F.M., relator. *The POSITIO of the Historical Section of the Sacred Congregation of Rites on the Introduction of the Cause for the Beatification and Canonization and on the Virtues of the Servant of God Katherine Tekakwitha, the Lily of the Mohawks, Being the Original Documents First Published at the Vatican Polyglot Press, Now Done into English and Presented for the Edification of the Faithful.* New York, 1940.

Arnauld, Antoine. *La Morale Pratique des Jésuites, Histoire des Differens entre les Missionnaires Jésuites . . . et Ceux des Ordres de S. Dominique et de S. François les Cultes Chinois.* Cologne, 1692.

Arregui, Antonio M. *Summarium Theologiae Moralis.* Editio Septima, Bilbao, 1922.

Arth, Mary C. "Marquette Memorials." Mid-America, XIII (1930–31), 291–303.

Bancroft, George. *History of the United States from the Discovery of the American Continent.* 10 vols. Boston, 1834–74.

Barnhart, John D. *Valley of Democracy, The Frontier versus The Plantation in the Ohio Valley, 1775–1818.* Bloomington, Ind., 1953.

Bassett, John S., ed. "Letters of Francis Parkman to Pierre Margry." *Smith College Studies in History,* VIII (1923), 124–208.

De Beaumont, Christophe. *Instruction Pastorale de Monseigneur l'Archevêque de Paris sur les Atteintes Données à l'Autorité de l'Église par les Jugements des Tribunaux Séculiers dans l'Affaire des Jésuites.* Paris, 1763.

Beers, Henry P. *The French and British in the Old Northwest, a Bibliographical Guide to the Archives and Manuscript Sources.* Detroit, 1964.

————. *The French in North America, a Bibliographical Guide to French Archives, Reproductions and Research Missions.* Baton Rouge, 1957.

De Belmont, François. *Histoire du Canada, Collection de Mémoires et Relations sur l'Histoire Ancienne du Canada d'après des Manuscrits Récement Obtenus des Archives et Bureaux Publics en France Publiée sous la Direction de la Société Litteraire et Historique de Québec.* Quebec, 1840.

Beltrami, Giacomo C. *A Pilgrimage in Europe and America, Leading to the Discovery of the Sources of the Mississippi and Bloody River, with a Description of the Whole Course of the Former and of the Ohio.* 2 vols. London, 1828.

Bernard, Matthew A. "La Signature du Père Marquette." *Bulletin des Recherches Historiques* (Quebec), IV (1898), 286.

Bernou, Claude, tr. and ed. *Nouvelle Relation de la Chine Contenant la Description des Particularites les Plus Considerables de Ce Grand Empire. Composée en l'Année 1668, par le R. P. Gabriel De Magaillans . . . .* Paris, 1688.

Bigot, Jacques. *Cramoisy No. 2, Relation de Ce Qvi S'Est Passé Plvs Remarqvable dans la Mission Abnaquise de Sainct Joseph de Sillery l'Année 1684.* Edited by John G. Shea. New York, 1857.

Binius, Severinus, ed. *Concilia Generalia et Provincialia Graeca et Latina Qvotqvot Reperiri Potvervnt . . . .* 4 vols. Coloniae Agrippinae, 1618.

Blair, Emma H., ed. *The Indian Tribes of the Upper Mississippi Valley and Region of the Great Lakes as Described by Nicolas Perrot, French Commandant of the Northwest; Bacqueville De La Potherie, French Royal Commissioner to Canada; Morrell Marston, American Army Officer; and Thomas Forsythe, United States Agent at Fort Armstrong.* 2 vols. Cleveland, 1911.

Boimare, A. L. "Notes Bibliographiques et Raisonnées sur les Principaux Ouvrages Publiés sur la Floride et l'Ancienne Louisiane . . . ." *Louisiana Historical Quarterly,* I (1917), 9–78.

De Boislisle, A., ed. *Mémoires de Saint-Simon.* 41 vols. Paris, 1923–30.

Boucher, Pierre. *Histoire Veritable et Natvrelle des Moevrs et Prodvctions du Pays de la Novvelle-France.* Paris, 1663. Reprinted, ed., G. Coffin, Montreal, 1882.

—————. "Mémoires de Feu Monsieur Boucher, Seigneur de Boucherville et Ancien Gouverneur de Trois-Rivières." *Bulletin des Recherches Historiques* (Quebec), XXXII (1926), 398–404.

Bowden, Henry W. "John Gilmary Shea: A Study of Method and Goals in Historiography." *The Catholic Historical Review,* LIV (1968), 235–60.

Bradbury, John. *Travels in the Interior of America, 1809, 1810, 1811, Including a Description of Upper Louisiana, with the States of Ohio, Kentucky, Indiana and Tennessee, with Illinois and Western Territories and Containing Remarks and Observations Useful to Persons Emigrating to Those Countries.* Vol. V in *Early Western Travels, 1748–1846.* Edited by Reuben G. Thwaites. 32 vols. Cleveland, 1904.

Briquet, Charles M. *Les Filigranes, Dictionnaire Historique des Marques du Papier dès Leur Apparition vers 1282 jusqu'en 1600.* 4 vols. Leipzig, 1923.

Brucker, Joseph. "Vie de Mgr. de Laval Premier Évêque de Québec et Apôtre du Canada (1622–1708), par l'abbé Auguste Gosselin, Québec, 1890." *Études Religeuses,* LIII [should be LII] (1891), 510–15.

Bullarum, Priviligiorum ac Diplomatum Romanorum Pontificum Amplissima Collectio Cui Accessere Pontificum Omnium Vitae, Notae et Indices Opportuni. Edited by Carolus Coquelines. 14 vols. Romae, 1739–62.

Burpee, Lawrence J. *The Search for the Western Sea, the Story of the Exploration of Northwestern America.* 2 vols. Toronto, 1935.

Burrus, Ernest J. "Father Jacques Marquette, S.J., His Priesthood in the Light of the Jesuit Roman Archives." *The Catholic Historical Review,* XLI (1955), 257–71.

—————. "Monumenta Historica Societatis Jesu." *Woodstock Letters,* LXXXIII (1954), 158–68.

Butler, Ruth F. *A Checklist of Manuscripts in the Edward E. Ayer Collection.* Chicago, 1937.

"Calendar of Manuscripts in the Archives of the Chicago Historical Society." *Report Concerning the Canadian Archives, 1905* (Ottawa, 1906), xxii–xlvii.

Carayon, Auguste, ed. *Bibliographie Historique de la Compagnie de Jésus ou Catalogue des Ouvrages Relatifs à l'Histoire des Jésuites depuis Leur Origines jusqu'à Nos Jours.* Paris, 1864.

——. *Documents Inédits Concernant la Compagnie de Jésus.* 23 vols. Poitiers, 1863–86.

——. *Voyages et Missions du Père Alexandre De Rhodes de la Compagnie de Jésus en la Chine et Autres Royaumes de l'Orient.* Paris, 1854.

Caron, Ivanhöe. "Inventaire des Documents concernant L'Église du Canada sous le Régime Français." *Rapport de l'Archiviste de la Province de Québec, 1939–1940* (1941), pp. 155–353.

Carrez, Ludovicus. *Atlas Geographicus Societatis Jesu in Quo Delineantur Quinque Ejus Modernae Assistentiae . . . Necnon et Veteres Ejusdem Societatis Provinciae Quadraginta-tres cum Earum Domiciliis Quantum Fieri Licuit.* Paris, 1900.

——. *Documenta ad Historiam Societatis Jesu in Gallia Concinnandam, Catalogi Sociorum et Officiorum Provinciae Campaniae Societatis Jesu.* 10 vols. v.p., 1897–1914.

Carrier, J. M. "L'oeuvre de la France dans la Vallée du Mississippi." *Canada Français,* XXVIII (1941), 457–76.

Caruso, John A. *Great Lakes Frontier, An Epic of the Old Northwest.* Indianapolis, 1961.

——. *The Mississippi Valley Frontier.* Indianapolis, 1966.

[De Casson, François D.] *A History of Montreal, 1640–1670, from the French of Dollier De Casson.* Translated and edited by Ralph Flenley. New York, 1928.

Catalogue des Livres de la Bibliotheque de la Maison Professe des Ci-Devant Soi-Disans Jesuites. Paris, 1763.

Catalogue Général des Manuscrits des Bibliothèques Publiques de France, Départements. 51 vols. Paris, 1886–1956.

[Cavelier, Jean]. *Cramoisy No. 5, Relation du Voyage Entrepris par Feu M. Robert Cavelier, Sieur De La Salle, pour Découvrir dans le Golfe de Mexique l'Embouchure du Fleuve Mississipy, par Son Frère M. Cavelier, Prêtre de St. Sulpice l'Un des Compagnons de Ce Voyage.* Edited by John G. Shea. New York, 1858.

[De Chambout, Sébastien J.]. *La Morale Pratique des Jésuites ou Elle Est Representée en Pleusieurs Histoires Arrivées dans Toutes les Parties du Monde.* Cologne, 1683.

Chapais, Thomas. *Jean Talon Intendant de la Nouvelle-France, 1665–1672.* Quebec, 1904.

Chappoulie, Henri. *Aux Origines d'Une Église, Rome et les Missions d'Indochine au XVIIᵉ Siècle.* 2 vols. Paris, 1948.

De Charlevoix, Pierre F.-X. *Histoire et Description Generale de la Nouvelle-France avec le Journal Historique d'Un Voyage Fait par Ordre de Roi dans l'Amerique Septentrionale.* 6 vols. Paris, 1744.

————. *History and General Description of New France by the Rev. P. F. X. De Charlevoix, S.J.* 6 vols. Translated and edited by John G. Shea. New York, 1866–72.

————. *Journal of a Voyage to North America Translated from the French of Pierre François Xavier De Charlevoix.* 2 vols. Edited by Louise P. Kellogg. Chicago, 1923.

————. *Journal of a Voyage to North America Undertaken by Order of the French King, Containing the Geographical Description and Natural History of That Country, Particularly Canada together with an Account of the Customs, Characters, Religion, Manners and Traditions of the Original Inhabitants, in a Series of Letters from the French of P. De Charlevoix.* 2 vols. London, 1761.

Chesnel, Paul. *History of Cavelier De La Salle, 1643–1687; Explorations in the Valley of the Ohio, Illinois and Mississippi, Taken from His Letters, Reports to King Louis XIV, also the Reports of Several of His Associates . . . .* New York, 1932.

Chinard, Gilbert. *Baron De Lahontan, Dialogues Curieux entre l'Auteur et Un Sauvage de Bon Sens Qui a Voyagé.* London, 1931.

Churchill, William A. *Watermarks in Paper in Holland, England, France, etc., in XVII and XVIII Centuries and Their Interconnection.* Amsterdam, 1935.

[La Clercq, Chrestien]. *First Establishment of the Faith in New France by Father Christian Le Clercq, Recollect Missionary, Now First Translated with Notes.* 2 vols. Translated and edited by John G. Shea. New York, 1881.

————. *Premier Etablissement de la Foy dans La Nouvelle France, Contenant la Publication de l'Evangile, l'Histoire des Colonies Francoises, & les Fameuses Découvertes depuis le Fleuve de Saint Laurent, la Louisiane & le Fleuve Colbert jusqu'au Golphe Mexique Achevées sous la Conduite de Feu Monsieur De La Salle, par Ordre du Roy avec les Victoires Resportées en Canada par les Armes de Sa Majesté sur les Anglois & les Iroquois en 1690.* 2 vols. Paris, 1691.

Codex Juris Canonici Pii X Pontificis Maximi Iussu Digestus, Benedicti Papae XV Auctoritate Promulgatus. Westminster, Md., 1944.

Coffin, G., ed. *Histoire Veritable et Natvrelle des Moevrs et Prodvctions du Pays de la Novvelle-France par Pierre Boucher.* Montreal, 1882.

Collectanea S. Congregationis de Propaganda Fide, Seu Decreta, Instructiones, Rescripta pro Apostolicis Missionibus. 2 vols. Romae, 1907.

Collection de Manuscrits Contenant Lettres, Mémoires et Autres Documents Historiques Relatifs a la Nouvelle France Recueillis aux Archives de la Province de Québec, ou Copiés a l'Étranger. 4 vols. Edited by Benjamin Sulté. Quebec, 1883–85.

La Compagnie de Jésus au Canada, 1842–1942, l'Oeuvre d'Un Siècle. Montreal, 1942.

Constitutiones Societatis Jesu Latinae et Hispanicae cum Earum Declarationibus. Matriti, 1892.

Constitutiones Societatis Jesu. Vols. LXIII–LXV in *Monumenta Historica Societatis Jesu.* Romae, 1934–38.

Cordier, Henri. *Mélanges Américains.* Paris, 1913.

Corrigan, William R. "Propaganda and the Suppression of the Jesuit Relations." *Mid-America*, XII (1929–30), 306–10.

Cox, Isaac J., ed. *The Journey of René Robert Cavelier, Sieur De La Salle, as Related by His Faithful Lieutenant Henri De Tonty; His Missionary Colleagues, Fathers Zenobius Membré, Louis Hennepin and Anastasius Douay; His Early Biographer, Father Christian Le Clercq; His Trusted Subordinate Henri Joutel . . . .* 2 vols. New York, 1905.

Coyne, James H., tr. and ed. *Exploration of the Great Lakes 1669–1670, by Dollier De Casson and De Bréhant De Galinée, Gal-*

inée's Narrative. Ontario Historical Society Papers and Records,
IV, pt. 1. Toronto, 1903.

Cronin, Vincent. *The Wise Man from the West.* New York, 1955.

Cross, Marion E., tr. *Father Louis Hennepin's Description of
Louisiana Newly Discovered to the Southwest of New France by
Order of the King.* Minneapolis, 1938.

Crouse, Nellis M. *Contributions of the Canadian Jesuits to the Geographical Knowledge of New France, 1632–1675.* Ithica, 1924.

———. *Lemoyne D'Iberville, Soldier of New France.* Ithica, 1954.

Cummins, J. S., ed. *The Travels and Controversies of Friar Domingo Navarrete 1618–68.* 2 vols. New York, 1962.

[Dablon, Claude]. *Cramoisy No. 12, Relation de Ce Qui S'Est
Passé de Plus Remarquable aux Missions des Peres de la Compagnie de Jesus en la Nouvelle-France les Années 1673 à 1679
par R.P. Claude Dablon Recteur du College de Quebec & Superieur des Missions de la Compagnie de Jesus en la Nouvelle-
France.* Edited by John G. Shea and Felix Martin. New York,
1860.

———. *Cramoisy No. 13, Relation de Ce Qui S'Est Passé de Plus
Remarquable aux Missions des Pères de la Compagnie de Jésus
en la Nouvelle-France Pendant les Années 1672 et 1673.* Edited
by John G. Shea. New York, 1861.

———. *Relation de Ce Qui S'Est Passé de Plus Remarquable aux
Missions des Pères de la Compagnie de Jesus en la Nouvelle
France les Années 1670. & 1671.* Paris, 1672.

———. *Relation de Ce Qui S'Est Passé . . . les Années 1671. &
1672.* Paris, 1673.

———. *Relation de Ce Qui S'Est Passé de Plvs Remarqvable avx
Missions des Peres de la Compagnie de Iesvs en la Novvelle
France és Années 1676 & 1677.* Edited by James Lenox. Albany,
1854.

Delanglez, Jean. "The Authorship of the Journal of Jean Cavelier."
Mid-America, XXV (1943), 220–23.

———. "A Calendar of La Salle's Travels, 1643–1683." *Mid-
America,* XXII (1940), 278–305.

———. "The Cartography of the Mississippi." *Mid-America,* XXX
(1948), 257–84; XXXI (1949), 29–52.

————. "Claude Dablon, S.J., 1619–1697." *Mid-America,* XXVI (1944), 91–110.

————. "The Discovery of the Mississippi, Primary Sources." *Mid-America,* XXVII (1945), 219–31.

————. "The Discovery of the Mississippi, Secondary Sources." *Mid-America,* XXVIII (1946), 3–22.

————. "The First Establishment of the Faith in New France, Chapters XXI to XXV." *Mid-America,* XXX (1948), 187–214.

————. "Franquelin, Mapmaker." *Mid-America,* XXV (1943), 29–74.

————. *Frontenac and the Jesuits.* Chicago, 1939.

————. *Hennepin's "Description of Louisiana" a Critical Essay.* Chicago, 1941.

————. "Hennepin's Voyage to the Gulf of Mexico 1680." *Mid-America,* XXI (1939), 32–81.

————. "Jacques Marquette était-il Prêtre?" *Revue d'Histoire de l'Amérique Française,* III (1949), 73–74.

————. "The Jolliet Lost Map of the Mississippi." *Mid-America,* XXVIII (1946), 67–144.

————. *The Journal of Jean Cavelier, the Account of a Survivor of La Salle's Texas Expedition, 1684–1688.* Chicago, 1938.

————. "La Salle, 1669–1673." *Mid-America,* XIX (1937), 197–216, 237–53.

————. "La Salle's Expedition of 1682." *Mid-America,* XXII (1940), 3–35.

————. *Life and Voyages of Louis Jolliet, 1645–1700.* Chicago, 1948.

————. "Louis Jolliet, Early Years, 1645–1674." *Mid-America,* XXVII (1945), 3–29.

————. "Louis Jolliet, the Middle Years, 1674–1686." *Mid-America,* XXVII (1945), 67–96.

————. "Marquette's Autograph Map of the Mississippi River." *Mid-America,* XXVII (1945), 30–53.

————. "A Mirage: The Sea of the West." *Revue d'Histoire de l'Amérique Française,* I (1947–48), 346–81, 541–68.

————. "The 'Recit des voyages et des decouvertes du Pere Jacques Marquette.'" *Mid-America,* XXVIII (1946), 173–94, 211–58.

————. "Le Révérend Père Jacques Marquette, S.J., était-il Prêtre?" *Revue d'Histoire de l'Amérique Française*, II (1949), 581–83.

————. "The 1674 Account of the Discovery of the Mississippi." *Mid-America*, XXVI (1944), 301–24.

————. *Some La Salle Journeys*. Chicago, 1938.

————. "Tonti Letters." *Mid-America*, XXI (1939), 209–38.

————. "The Voyage of Louis Jolliet to Hudson Bay in 1679." *Mid-America*, XXVI (1944), 221–50.

Delattre, Pierre, ed. *Les Établissements des Jésuites en France depuis Quatre Siècles*. 5 vols. Enghien, Belgium, 1940–57.

Dernieres Decouvertes dans l'Amerique Septentrionale de M. De La Salle; Mises au Jour par M. le Chevalier Tonti Gouverneur de Fort Saint Louis, aux Islinois. Paris, 1697.

Desjardins, Paul. *Le Collège Sainte-Marie de Montréal*. 2 vols. Montreal, 1940–45.

————. "Jacques Marquette était-il prêtre?" *La Revue de l'Université Laval* (Quebec), III (1949), 634–39.

Dictionary Catalog of the History of the Americas Collection, The New York Public Library. 25 vols. Boston, 1961.

Dillon, Richard H. *Meriwether Lewis, a Biography*. New York, 1965.

Domenech, L'abbé, ed. *Histoire du Jansénisme, depuis Son Origine jusqu'en 1644 par René Rapin*. Paris, n.d. [1861].

Donnelly, Joseph P. *Jacques Marquette, S.J., 1637–1675*. Chicago, 1968.

————. *The Parish of the Holy Family, Cahokia, Illinois, 1699–1949*. n.p., 1949.

————. *Thwaites' Jesuit Relations Errata and Addenda*. Chicago, 1967.

Drolet, A. "La bibliothèque de collège des Jésuites." *Revue d'Histoire de l'Amérique Française*, XIV (1961), 487–544.

Dumont, Georges H. *Louis Hennepin Explorateur du Mississippi*. Bruxelles, 1957.

Dunne, George H. "What Happened to the Chinese Liturgy." *The Catholic Historical Review*, LXVII (1961), 1–14.

Dupont, Paul, ed. *Le Dictionnaire de l'Académie Françoise Dedié au Roy*. Reprinted, Lille, 1901.

Eccles, William J. *Canada under Louis XIV, 1663–1701. The Canadian Centenary Series.* New York, 1964.

———. *Frontenac the Courtier Governor.* Toronto, 1959.

M. l'Évêque de Québec [Jean-Baptiste St. Vallier]. *Estat Present de l'Eglise et de la Colonie Française dans la Nouvelle-France.* Paris, 1688.

Faillon, Étienne M. *Histoire de la Colonie Française en Canada.* 3 vols. Montreal, 1865–66.

Faribault, George B., ed. *Catalogue d'Ouvrages sur l'Histoire de l'Amérique et en Particulier sur Celle du Canada de la Louisiane de l'Acadie et Autres Lieux Ci-Devant Connus sous le Nom de Nouvelle-France . . . .* Quebec, 1837.

"Father Marquette, S.J., Discovery of His Remains." *Woodstock Letters,* VI (1877), 164–70.

"Father Marquette's Grave." *Chicago Province Chronicle,* XVI (1952), 51–52.

Faux, Jean M. "La Fondation et les Premières Rédacteurs des Mémoires de Trévoux, 1701–1739, d'après Quelques Documents Inédits." *Archivum Historicum Societatis Jesu* (Rome), XXIII (1954), 131–51.

Ferland, J.B.A. *Course d'Histoire du Canada.* 2 vols. Quebec, 1861–65.

Fine, Edouard. *Juris Regularia Tum Communis Tum Particularis Quo Regitur Societas Iesu Declaratio.* Prati, 1909.

Flenley, Ralph, ed. *A History of Montreal, 1640–1670, from the French of Dollier De Casson.* New York, 1928.

Flint, Timothy. *Recollections of the Last Ten Years Passed in Occasional Residences and Journeys in the Valley of the Mississippi from Pittsburg and the Missouri to the Gulf of Mexico and from Florida to the Spanish Frontier . . . .* Boston, 1826.

Frégault, Guy. "Jean Delanglez, S.J. (1894–1949)." *Revue d'Histoire de l'Amérique Française,* III (1949), 165–71.

French, Benjamin F., ed. *Historical Collections of Louisiana Embracing Many Rare and Valuable Documents Relating to the Natural Civil Political History of That State, Compiled with Historical and Biographical Notes and an Introduction.* 5 vols. New York, 1846–53.

[De Freytas, Nicholas]. *The Expedition of Dom Diego Dionisio*

De Peñalosa, Governor of New Mexico from Santa Fe to the River Mischipi & Quivira in 1662 Described by Father Nicholas De Freytas. Translated and edited by John G. Shea. New York, 1882.

Gagnon, Ernest. " 'Jolliet' ou 'Joliet?' Faut-il écrire." *Bulletin des Recherches Historiques* (Quebec), XII (1906), 306–10.

———. *Louis Jolliet Découvreur de Mississippi et du Pays des Illinois, Premier Seigneur de l'Ile d'Anticosti.* 2nd ed. Montreal, 1913.

———. "Ou est mort Louis Jolliet?" *Bulletin des Recherches Historiques* (Quebec), VIII (1902), 277–79.

Gagnon, Phileas. *Essai de Bibliographie Canadienne.* 2 vols., Quebec, 1895, 1913.

———. "Noms Propres au Canada-Français." *Bulletin des Recherches Historique* (Quebec), XV (1909), 148.

[De Galinée, de Bréhant]. *Exploration of the Great Lakes, 1669–1670 by Dollier De Casson and De Bréhant De Galinée, Galinée's Narrative and Map with an English Version, Including All the Map Legends.* Translated and edited by James H. Coyne. *Ontario Historical Society Papers and Records,* IV, pt. 1. Toronto, 1903.

Ganong, William F., ed. *New Relation of Gaspesia with the Customs and Religion of the Gaspesian Indians, by Father Chrestien Le Clercq . . . with a Reprint of the Original.* Toronto, 1910.

Garraghan, Gilbert J. *Chapters in Frontier History.* Milwaukee, 1933.

———. "The Great Village of the Illinois, A Topographical Problem." *Mid-America,* XIV (1931–32), 141–51.

———. *A Guide to Historical Method.* New York, 1948.

———. *The Jesuits of the Middle United States.* 3 vols. New York, 1938.

———. "The Jolliet-Marquette Expedition of 1673." *Thought,* IV (1929), 32–71.

———. "La Salle's Jesuit Days." *Mid-America,* XIX (1937), 93–103.

———. *Marquette, Ardent Missioner, Daring Explorer.* New York, 1937.

———. "Marquette's Titles to Fame." *Mid-America,* XX (1938), 30–36.

————. "Some Hitherto Unpublished Marquettiana." *Mid-America,* XVIII (1936), 15–26.

————. "Some Newly Discovered Marquette and La Salle Letters." *Archivum Historicum Societatis Jesu* (Rome), IV (1935), 268–90.

Gazette de France. 8 decembre, 1674 to 28 decembre, 1675.

Gazier, Augustin. *Histoire Générale du Mouvement Janséniste depuis Ses Origines jusqu'à Nos Jours.* 2 vols. Paris, 1923–24.

Gerin, Charles. *Recherches Historiques sur l'Assemblée du Clergé en France de 1682.* Paris, 1869.

Glazier, Willard. *Down the Great River, Embracing an Account of the Discovery of the True Source of the Mississippi.* Philadelphia, 1891.

Godbout, Archange. "Nos Ancêtres au XVII Siècle." *Rapport de l'Archiviste de la Province de Québec, 1959–1960,* pp. 277–354.

Gosselin Amedée. "Jean Jolliet et ses enfants." *Proceedings and Transactions of the Royal Society of Canada,* XIV (sec. 1, 1921), 65–81.

Gosselin, Auguste H. *L'Église du Canada depuis Monseigneur de Laval jusqu'à la Conquête.* 3 vols. Quebec, 1911–14.

————. *Vie de Mgr. De Laval Premier Évêque de Québec et Apôtre du Canada, 1622–1708.* 2 vols. Quebec, 1890.

La Grande Encyclopedie Inventaire Raisonné des Sciences des Lettres et des Artes . . . . 31 vols. Paris, 1887–1902.

De Granges, de Surgères. *Répertoire Historique et Biographique de la Gazette de France depuis l'Origine jusqu'à la Revolution, 1631–1790.* 4 vols. Paris, 1902–6.

Gravier, Gabriel. *Cavelier De La Salle de Rouen.* Paris 1871.

————. *Etude sur Une Carte Inconnue, le Primière Dressée par Louis Joliet en 1674, après Son Exploration du Mississippi avec le P. Jacques Marquette en 1673.* Paris, 1880.

[Gravier, Jacques]. *Cramoisy No. 1, Relation de la Mission des Illinois, 1693.* Edited by John G. Shea. New York, 1857.

Griffin, Appleton P. G. *The Discovery of the Mississippi, a Bibliographical Account with a Fac-Simile of the Map of Louis Joliet, 1674.* New York, 1883.

Groulx, Lionel A. *L'Histoire du Canada Français depuis la Découverte.* 2 vols. Montreal, 1963.

————. "Colonisation au Canada sous Talon." *Revue de l'Histoire de l'Amerique Française,* IV (1950), 61–73.

Guilday, Peter. *John Gilmary Shea, Father of American Catholic History, 1824–1892.* New York, 1926.

Guy, Francis S. *Edmund Bailey O'Callaghan, a Study in American Historiography, 1797–1880.* Washington, 1934.

Habig, Marion A. *The Franciscan Père Marquette, a Critical Biography of Father Zénobe Membré, O.F.M. Franciscan Studies,* no. 13, New York, 1934.

————. "The Site of the Great Illinois Village." *Mid-America,* XVI (1933), 3–13.

Hackett, Charles W. "New Light on Don Diego Peñalosa: Proof That He Never Made an Expedition from Santa Fe to Quivira and the Mississippi River in 1662." *Mississippi Valley Historical Review,* VI (1919), 313–35.

Hamilton, Raphael N. "The Early Cartography of the Missouri Valley." *American Historical Review,* XXXIX (1934), 645–62.

————. "Father Jacques Marquette, S.J., Priest." *La Revue de l'Université Laval* (Quebec), III (1949), 640–42.

————. "Father Marquette's Visit to Milwaukee." *Historical Messenger of the Milwaukee County Historical Society,* XXIII (1967), 44–47.

————. *Great Men of Michigan: Father Marquette.* Grand Rapids, Mich., 1970.

————. "Jesuit Mission at Sault Ste. Marie." *Michigan History,* LII (1968), 123–32.

————. "The Location of the Mission of St. Ignace from 1670 to 1673." *Michigan History,* XLII (1958), 260–66.

————. "The Marquette Death Site: The Case for Ludington." *Michigan History,* XLIX (1965), 228–48.

————. "Marquette, Jacques (Pere Marquette)." *Encyclopaedia Britannica.* Chicago, 1967.

————. *The Story of Marquette University, an Object Lesson in the Development of Catholic Higher Education.* Milwaukee, 1953.

————. "To the Editor of the Wisconsin Magazine of History." *Wisconsin Magazine of History,* XXXII (1949), 472–73.

Hamy, Alfred. *Au Mississippi la Première Exploration, 1673. Le Père Jacques Marquette de Laon Prêtre de la Compagnie de Jésus,*

1637–1675 et Louis Jolliet, d'après M. Ernest Gagnon. Paris, 1903.

Hanke, Lewis. *Bartolomé De Las Casas Historian, an Essay in Spanish Historiography.* Gainesville, Fla., 1952.

Hansen, H. *The Chicago River.* New York, 1942.

Harris, Richard C. *The Seigneural System in Early Canada, A Geographical Study.* Madison, Wis., 1966.

Harrisse, Henry. *Notes pour Servir à l'Histoire, à la Bibliographie et à la Cartographie de la Nouvelle-France et des Pays Adjacents, 1545–1700.* Paris, 1872.

Havighurst, Walter. *Voices on the River, the Story of the Mississippi Waterway.* New York, 1964.

Hay, Malcom. *Failure in the Far East, Why and How the Breach between the Western World and China First Began.* Philadelphia, 1957.

Hedges, Samuel. *Father Marquette Jesuit Missionary and Explorer, the Discoverer of the Mississippi, His Place of Burial at St. Ignace, Michigan.* New York, 1903.

Heming, Harry H. *The Catholic Church in Wisconsin.* Milwaukee, 1895–98.

Hennepin, Ludwig. *Beschreibung der Landschafft Lovisiana Welche auf Befehl des Koenigs in Frankreich, Neulich Gegen Sudwestern Neu-Frankreichs in Amerika Entdeket Worden.* Nurenberg, 1689.

———. *Description de la Louisiane Nouvellement Decouverte au Sud Oüest de la Nouvelle France, par Ordre du Roy. Avec la Carte du Pays: les Moevrs & la Maniere de Vivre des Sauvages.* Paris, 1683.

———. *Father Louis Hennepin's Description of Louisiana Newly Discovered to the Southwest of New France by Order of the King.* Translated by Marion E. Cross. Minneapolis, 1938.

———. *Father Louis Hennepin's "A Description of Louisiana," Translated from the Edition of 1683, and Compared with the "Nouvelle Decouverte" the La Salle Documents and Other Contemporaneous Papers.* Translated and edited by John G. Shea. New York, 1880.

———. *A New Discovery of a Vast Country in America Extending*

Over Four Thousand Miles, between New France and New Mexico . . . . London, 1698.

———. *A New Discovery of a Vast Country in America by Father Louis Hennepin.* Edited by Reuben G. Thwaites. 2 vols. Chicago, 1903.

———. *Nouveau Voyage d'Un Pais Plus Grand que l'Europe avec les Reflections des Entreprises du Sieur De La Salle, sur les Mines de St. Barbe &c* . . . . Utrecht, 1698.

———. *Nouvelle Decouverte d'Un Tres Grand Pays Situé dans l'Amerique, entre le Nouveau Mexique, et la Mer Glaciale, avec, les Cartes, & les Figures Necessaires, & de Plus l'Histoire Naturelle & Morale, & les Avantages, Qu'On en Peut Tirer par l'Etablissement des Colonies.* Utrecht, 1697.

Hock, Conrad. *The Four Temperaments.* Milwaukee, 1934.

Hodge, Frederick W., ed. *Handbook of American Indians North of Mexico.* 2 vols. Washington, 1907–10.

Howe, M. A. De Wolfe. *The Life and Letters of George Bancroft.* 2 vols. New York, 1908.

Iansenii, Cornelii, Episcopi Iprensis. *Avgvstinvs.* 3 vols. Lovanii, 1640. Facsimile reprint. Frankfurt/Main, 1964.

Institutum Societatis Iesu. 3 vols. Florentiae, 1892–93.

Jacker, Edward. "Father Marquete, S.J., Discovery of His Remains." *Woodstock Letters,* VI (1877), 167–70.

Jacobs, Wilbur R., ed. *The Letters of Francis Parkman.* 2 vols. Norman, Okla., 1960.

Jacobsen, Jerome V. "Attempted Mayhem on Père Marquette." *Mid-America,* XXXI (1949), 109–15.

———. "Documents: Marquette's Ordination." *Mid-America,* XXXII (1950), 46–54.

———. "Jean Delanglez—In Memoriam." *Mid-America,* XXXI (1949), 208–12.

Jansenius, Cornelius. See "Iansenii."

Jensen, George P. *Historic Chicago Sites.* Chicago, 1953.

Le Jeune, Louis. *Le Chevalier Pierre Le Moyne, Sieur D'Iberville.* Ottawa, 1937.

Jones, Arthur E. "Catalogue of the Jesuit Missionaries to New France and Louisiana, 1611–1800." In *Jesuit Relations and Allied*

Documents, edited by Reuben G. Thwaites, Vol. LXXI, 120–81. Cleveland, 1901.

―――. "The Site of the Mascoutin." *Proceedings of the State Historical Society of Wisconsin, 1906,* LIV (1907), 175–83.

[Joutel, Henri]. *Joutel's Journal of La Salle's Last Voyage, 1684–7* . . . . Translated and edited by Henry R. Stiles. Albany, 1906.

Jugements et Deliberations du Conseil Souverain de la Nouvelle France, 1663–1704 et du Conseil Superieur, 1705–1716. 6 vols. Quebec, 1885–91.

Kane, William. "The End of a Jesuit Library." *Mid-America,* XXIII (1941), 190–213.

Karpinski, Louis C. *Bibliography of Printed Maps of Michigan with a Series of over One Hundred Reproductions of Maps Constituting an Historical Atlas of the Great Lakes and Michigan.* Lansing, Mich., 1931.

Kellogg, Louise P. *Early Narratives of the Northwest, 1634–1699.* New York, 1917.

―――. "Father Jacques Marquette, a Tercentenary Tribute." *The Catholic World,* CXLV (1937), 265–73.

―――. *The French Regime in Wisconsin and the Northwest.* Madison, Wis., 1925.

―――. *Journal of a Voyage to North America. Translated from the French of Pierre Francois Xavier De Charlevoix.* 2 vols. Chicago, 1923.

―――. "Marquette's Authentic Map Possibly Identified." *Proceedings of the State Historical Society of Wisconsin, 1906,* LIV (1907), 183–93.

Kennedy, John H. *Jesuit and Savage in New France.* New Haven, 1950.

Kenny, Lawrence. "A New Marquette Document." *America,* XXIV (1920), 59–60.

Kenton, Edna, ed. *The Jesuit Relations and Allied Documents, Travels and Explorations of Jesuit Missionaries in North America 1610–1791, Selected and Edited,* New York, 1925.

Knight, Robert and Zeuch, Lucius H. *The Location of the Chicago Portage Route of the Seventeenth Century.* Chicago, 1928.

Koch, Ludwig. *Jesuiten-Lexikon Die Gesellschaft Jesu Einst und Jetzt.* Paderborn, 1934.

Lafitau, Joseph F. *Moeurs des Sauvages Amériquaine Comparées aux Moeurs des Premiers Temps.* 2 vols. Paris, 1724.

De Lahontan, Louis Armand de Lorn d'Arce, Baron. *New Voyages to North-America. Containing an Account of the Several Nations of That Vast Continent; Their Customs, Commerce and Way of Navigation upon the Lakes and Rivers; the Several Attempts of the English and French to Dispossess One Another; with the Reasons of the Miscarriage of the Former; and the Various Adventures between the French, and the Iroquese Confederates of England, from 1683 to 1694* . . . . 2 vols. London, 1703.

——. *New Voyages to North America by Baron Lahontan.* Edited by Reuben G. Thwaites. 2 vols. Chicago, 1905.

[Lalande, Louis]. *Une Vieille Seigneurie: Boucherville.* Montreal, 1890.

Lamalle, Edmond. "Les Catalogues des Provinces et les Domiciles de la Compagnie de Jésus." *Archivum Historicum Societatis Jesu,* XIII (1944), 77–101.

——, and Polgar, Ladislas. "Bibliographie periodique de l'histoire des Jésuites." *Archivum Historicum Societatis Jesu,* I (1932), 123–88, continued in each volume to the present.

Lanctot, Gustave. *Histoire du Canada des Origines au Régime Royal.* Montreal, 1960.

Langlois, Charles V. and Signobos, Ch. *Introduction aux Études Historiques.* Paris, 1899.

Laon, Société Académique de. *Jacques Marquette et l'Inauguration de Son Monument à Laon le 13 juin 1937.* Laon, 1937.

Laverdière, C. H. and Casgrain, H. R., eds. *Le Journal des Jésuites Publié d'après le Manuscrit Original Conservé aux Archives de Séminaire de Québec.* Quebec, 1871.

Lefebvre, Fernand. "Introduction à la paleographie canadienne." *Revue de l'Université d'Ottawa,* XXVIII (1958), 490–521.

Leland, Waldo G. *Guide to Materials for American History in the Libraries of Paris.* The Carnegie Institution of Washington, Publications, No. 392, 2 vols. Washington, 1932, 1943.

——. "Notes on Material in the French Archives Relating to the

Mississippi Valley." *Proceedings of the State Historical Society of Wisconsin,* LVI (1909), 41–46.

Lemay, Hugolin. *Bibliographie du Père Louis Hennepin, Récollet, les Pièces Documentaires.* Montreal, 1937.

Lenox, James, ed. *Relation de Ce Qvi S'Est Passé du Plvs Remarqvable aux Missions des Peres de la Compagnie de Iesus en la Novvelle France es Années 1676 & 1677.* Albany, 1854.

———— and Shea, John G. *Recit des Voyages et des Decouvertes de R. Père Jacques Marquette de la Compagnie de Jésus, en l'Année 1673 et aux Suivantes; La Continuation de Ses Voyages par le R. P. Claude Alloüez, et le Journal Autographe du P. Marquette en 1674 & 1675. Avec la Carte de Son Voyage Tracée de Sa Main. Imprimé d'après le Manuscrit Original Restant au Collège Ste. Marie à Montreal.* Albany, 1855.

Leymaire, A. Léon. *Analyse des Documents Exposés par la Compagnie de Jésus et sur les Jésuites, Exposition Retrospective des Colonies Françaises de l'Amerique du Nord, Paris, avril–juin, 1929.* Paris, 1929.

Littré, E., ed. *Dictionnaire de la Langue Française.* 4 vols. Paris, 1889.

Lomasney, Patrick J. "The Canadian Jesuits and the Fur Trade." *Mid-America,* XV (1933), 139–50.

————. "Marquette's Burial Site Located." *Illinois Catholic Historical Review,* IX (1926–27), 348–62.

Longnon, Jean, ed. *Mémoires de Louis XIV.* Paris, 1933.

Lorin, H. *Le Comte De Frontenac.* Paris, 1897.

Magaillans, Gabriel [de Magalhães, Gabriel] *Nouvelle Relation de la Chine Contenant la Description des Particularitez les Plus Considerables de Ce Grand Empire. Composée en l'Année 1668, par le R. P. Gabriel De Magaillans de la Compagnie de Jesus, Missionaire Apostolique. Et Traduite de Portugais en François par le Sr. B. [Bernou].* Paris, 1688.

Marcel, Gabriel. *Cartographie de la Nouvelle France, Supplement à l'Ouvrage de M. Harrisse Publié avec des Documents Inédits Extrait de la Revue de Geographie.* Paris, 1885.

————. *Reproductions de Cartes & de Globes Relatifs à la Découverte de l'Amerique du XVIe au XVIIIe Siècle avec Texte Explicatif, Atlas.* Paris, 1893–94.

Margry, Pierre. Letter to Lyman C. Draper, "July 4, 1879." *Collections of the State Historical Society of Wisconsin,* IX (1882. Reprint 1909), 109–12.

———. *Mémoires et Documents pour Servir à l'Histoire des Origines Françaises des Pays d'Outre-Mer. Découvertes et Établissements des Français dans l'Ouest et dans la Sud de l'Amérique Septentrionale, 1614–1754.* 6 vols. Paris, 1879–88.

———. "Les Normands dans les Vallés de l'Ohio et du Mississippi." *Journal Général de l'Instruction Publique* (1862).

———. *Relations et Mémoires Inédites pour Servir à l'Histoire de la France dans les Pays d'Outre-Mer Tirés des Archives du Minstère de Marines et des Colonies.* Paris, 1867.

[Marie de L'Incarnation]. *Lettres de la Révérende Mère Marie De L'Incarnation (née Marie Guyard) Première Supérieure du Monastère des Ursulines de Québec. Nouvelle Édition.* Edited by l'abbé Richaudeau. Paris, 1876.

Marion, Seraphin. *Un Pionnier Canadien: Pierre Boucher.* Quebec, 1927.

The Marquette Tribune. XI (1926–27).

Marsden, Gerald K. "Father Marquette and the A.P.A.: An Incident in American Nativism." *The Catholic Historical Review,* XLVI (1960), 1–21.

Martin, Felix, tr. and ed. *Relation Abrégée de Quelques Missions des Pères de la Compagnie de Jésus dans la Nouvelle-France par le R.P. F-J. Bressany.* Montreal, 1852.

———. *Relations des Jésuites sur les Découvertes et les Autres Evènements Arrivés en Canada, et au Nord et à l'Ouest des États-Unis (1611–1672) par le Dr. E. B. O'Callaghan, Membre Correspondent de la Société Historique de New-York, et Membre Honoraire de la Société Historique de Connecticut. Traduit de l'Anglais avec Quelques Notes, Corrections et Additions.* Montreal, 1850.

Martin, Francois X. *History of Louisiana from the Earliest Period.* 2 vols. New Orleans, 1827–29.

Masseron, Alexander. *The Franciscans.* London, 1931.

May, George S. "The Discovery of Father Marquette's Grave at St. Ignace in 1877 as Related by Father Edward Jacker." *Michigan History,* XLII (1958), 267–87.

Maynard, Ernest. "M. et Madame De Frontenac." *Bulletin des Recherches Historiques* (Quebec), VIII (1902), 97–110, 129–36.

McCoy, James C. *Jesuit Relations of Canada, 1632–1673, a Bibliography.* Paris, 1937.

McKenty, Neil. "Journey's End." *Martyr's Shrine Messenger,* XVIII (1954), 102–3.

McWilliams, Richebourg G., ed. *Fleur de Lys and Calumet, Being the Pénicaut Narrative of French Adventure in Louisiana.* Baton Rouge, 1953.

[Melançon, Arthur]. *Liste des Missionnaires Jésuites, Nouvelle-France et Louisiane, 1611–1800.* Montreal, 1929.

[Le Mercier, François]. *Relation de Ce Qvi S'Est Passé de Plvs Remarqvable avx Missions des Pères de la Compagnie de Iesvs en la Novvelle France aux Années Mil Six Cens Soixante-Sept & Mil Six Cens Soixante-Huit.* Paris, 1669.

————. *Relation de Ce Qvi S'Est Passé . . . les Années 1668. & 1669.* Paris, 1670.

————. *Relation de Ce Qvi S'Est Passé . . . les Années 1669. & 1670.* Paris, 1671.

Michaud, L. C., ed. *Biographie Universelle Ancienne et Moderne ou Histoire, par Ordre Alphabetique, de la Vie Publique et Privée de Tous les Hommes Qui Se Sont Fait Remarquer par Leurs Écrits, Leurs Actions, Leurs Talents, Leurs Vertus et Leurs Crimes.* 52 vols. Paris, 1811–45.

De Michel, M. *Journal Historique du Dernier Voyage que Feu M. De La Salle Fit dans le Golfe de Mexique, pour Trouver l'Embouchure, & le Course de la Riviere de Missicipi, Nommée à Present la Riviere de Saint Loüis, Qui Traverse la Louisiane. Ou l'On Voit l'Histoire Tragique de Sa Mort, & Plusieurs Choses Curieuses du Nouveau Monde par Monsieur Jovtel, l'Un des Compagnons de Ce Voyage, Redigé & Mis en Ordre.* Paris, 1713.

Moniteur Bibliographique de la Compagnie de Jésus. 4 vols. Paris, 1889–1914.

[De Montézon, Fortuné M. and Douniol, Charles], eds. *Mission du Canada, Relations Inédites de la Nouvelle-France, 1672–1679, pour Faire Suite aux Anciennes Relations, 1615–1672.* In "Voyages et Travaux des Missionnaires de la Compagnie de Jésus Publiés par les Pères de la Même Compagnie pour Servir de

Complément aux Lettres Édifiantes," vol. III in 2 parts. Paris, 1861.

Moore, G. H., ed., *The Jesuit Relations etc.* In Contributions to a Catalogue of the Lenox Library, no. II. New York, 1879.

[De Navarrete, Domingo]. *The Travels and Controversies of Friar Domingo Navarrete (1618–68).* Edited by J. S. Cummins. 2 vols. New York, 1962.

De Navarrete, Martin F., ed. *Coleccion de los Viages y Descubrimientos que Hicieron por Mar los Españoles desde Fines del Siglo XV, con Varios Documentos Ineditos Concernientes a la Historia de la Marina Castellana y de los Establecimientos Españoles en Indias.* 3 vols. Buenos Aires, 1945.

Neilson, J. L. Hubert. *Facsimile of Pere Marquette's Illinois Prayer Book, It's* [*sic*] *History by the Owner.* Quebec, 1908.

Nute, Grace L. *Caesars of the Wilderness, Médard Chouart Sieur Des Groseilliers and Pierre Esprit Radisson, 1618–1710.* New York, 1943.

———. "Father Hennepin's Later Years." *Minnesota History,* XIX (1938), 393–98.

O'Callaghan, Edmund B., ed. *The Documentary History of the State of New York, Arranged under Direction of the Hon. Christopher Morgan Secretary of State.* 4 vols. Albany, 1849–51.

———. *Documents Relative to the Colonial History of the State of New York, Procured in Holland, England, and France by John Romeyn Brodhead.* 11 vols. Albany, 1853–61.

———. *The History of New Netherlands; or New York under the Dutch.* 2 vols. New York, 1846–48.

———. *Jesuit Relations of Discoveries and Other Occurrences in Canada and the Northern and Western States of the Union, 1632–1672, from the Proceedings of the New York Historical Society.* New York, 1747 [should be 1847].

O'Dea, Arthur J. "The Observance of the Marquette Tercentenary." *Mid-America,* XX (1938), 15–29.

O'Neill, James E. "Copies of French Manuscripts for American History in the Library of Congress." *Journal of American History,* LI (1965), 674–89.

Orcibal, Jean. *Les Origines du Jansénisme.* 5 vols. Paris, 1947–48.

————. *Louis XIV contre Innocent XI, les Appels au Future Concile de 1688 et l'Opinion Française.* Paris, 1949.

————. *Louis XIV et les Protestants.* "*La Cabale des Accommodeurs de Religion,*" *la Caisse des Conversions, la Revocation de l'Édit de Nantes.* Paris, 1951.

D'Orleans, F. J. *The History of the Revolutions in England and under the Family of the Stuarts from 1603, to 1690, in Three Books; wherein Are Contained Many Secret Memoirs Relating to That Family and the Last Great Revolution, Anno 1688.* London, 1722.

Ouellet, Ferdinand, ed. "Inventaire de la *Saberdache* de Jacques Viger." *Rapport de l'Archiviste de la Province de Québec, 1955–1956 and 1956–1957,* pp. 31–176.

Parkman, Francis. *Count Frontenac and New France under Louis XIV.* Boston, 1898.

————. *La Salle and the Discovery of the Great West.* Boston, 1898.

————. *The Letters of Francis Parkman.* 2 vols. Edited by Wilbur R. Jacobs. Norman, Okla., 1960.

————. *The Old Regime in Canada.* Boston, 1898.

Von Pastor, Ludwig Freiherr. *The History of the Popes from the Close of the Middle Ages, Drawn from Secret Archives of the Vatican and Other Original Sources.* 39 vols. London, 1891–1952.

Paullin, Charles O. *Atlas of the Historical Geography of the United States.* Washington, 1932.

Pauly, Marie-Helene. *Fleur-de-Lys, Castors et Calumets, l'Épopée Française du Ouisconsin.* Montreal, 1958.

Pease, Theodore C. and Werner, Raymond C. eds. *The French Foundations 1660–1693.* In French Series, vol. 1. *Collections of the Illinois State Historical Library,* XXIII (1934).

[Perrot, Nicholas]. *Memoire sur les Moeurs, Coustumes et Religion des Sauvages de l'Amerique Septentrionale par Nicolas Perrot.* Edited by Jules Tailhan. Leipzig, 1864.

Phillips, P. Lee. *The Rare Map of the Northwest, 1785, by John Fitch Inventor of the Steamboat, a Bibliographical Account with a Facsimile Reproduction Including Some Account of Thomas Hutchins and William McMurray.* Washington, 1916.

Pierce, Bessie L. *A History of Chicago.* 3 vols. New York, 1937–57.

Pinart, Alphonse. *Recueil de Cartes, Plans et Vues Relatifs aux États-Unis et au Canada, New York, Boston, Montréal, Québec, Louisbourg, 1651–1731.* Paris, 1893.

De La Potherie, Claude C. de Bacqueville. *Voyage de l'Amerique, Contenant Ce Qui S'Est Passé de Plus Remarquable dans l'Amerique Septentrionale depuis 1534 jusqu'à Present.* 4 vols. Amsterdam, 1723.

Pouliot, Léon. *Étude sur les Relations des Jésuites de la Nouvelle-France (1632–1672).* Montreal, 1940.

Preston, Richard A. and Lamontagne, Leopold. *Royal Fort Frontenac, Texts Selected and Translated from the French.* Toronto, 1958.

Provost, Antoine F. *Histoire Général des Voyages ou Nouvelle Collection de Toutes les Relations de Voyages par Mer et par Terre Qui Ont Été Publiées jusq'à Present . . . .* 20 vols. Paris, 1746–89.

[Radisson, Pierre E.]. *Voyages of Peter Esprit Radisson, Being an Account of His Travels and Experiences among the North American Indians from 1652–1684.* Edited by Gideon D. Scull. London, 1853. Reprint New York, 1943.

Rapin, René. *Histoire du Jansénisme, depuis Son Origine jusqu'en 1644.* Edited by L'Abbé Domenech. Paris, n.d. [1861].

Recueil Dit de Maurepas, Pieces Libres, Chansons, Epigrammes et Autres Vers Satiriques . . . des Siècles de Louis XIV et Louis XV . . . . 6 vols. Leyde, 1865.

[Regnaut, Christophe]. "A true account of the martyrdom of Fathers Breboeuf and L'Alemant by the Iroquois, 16th March, 1649, written by Christophe Regnaut." *Report Concerning the Canadian Archives, 1884,* n. E, pp. lxiii–lxvii.

———. "The Martyrdom of FF. Breboeuf and L'Alemant by an Eye-Witness." *Woodstock Letters,* XIV (1885), 331–40.

Relations des Jésuites Contenant Ce Qui S'Est Passé de Plus Remarquable dans les Missions des Pères de la Compagnie de Jésus dans la Nouvelle-France. Ouvrage Publié sous les Auspices du Gouvernement Canadien. 3 vols. Quebec, 1858.

Repplier, Agnes. *Père Marquette, Priest, Pioneer and Adventurer.* Garden City, N.Y., 1929.

Rezek, Antoine I. *History of the Diocese of Sault Ste. Marie and Marquette.* 2 vols. Houghton, Mich., 1907.

De Rhodes, Alexandre. *Voyages et missions du Père Alexandre De Rhodes de la Compagnie de Jésus en la Chine et Autres Royaumes de l'Orient.* Paris, 1653. Nouvelle édition par un père de la même Compagnie [August Carayon]. Paris, 1854.

Rich, Edwin E. *The History of the Hudson's Bay Company, 1670–1870,* 2 vols. London, 1958–59.

————. *Minutes of the Hudson's Bay Company, 1671–1674.* London, 1942.

Rich, Obadiah, ed. *Voyage et Découverte de Quelques Pays et Nations de l'Amerique Septentrionale par le P. Marquette et Sr. Joliet, [par Melchisedech Thevenot].* Paris, 1845.

[Richard, Gabriel]. "Lettre de M. Richard, Missionnaire au Detroit à M. ***." *Annales de l'Association de la Propagation de la Foi,* Lyon, III (1827–29), 336–49.

Richaudeau, L'abbé, ed. *Lettres de la Révérende Mère Marie De L'Incarnation (née Marie Guyard) Première Supérieure du Monastère des Ursulines de Québec.* 2 vols. Reprinted, Paris, 1876.

Rituale Romanum, Pauli V Pontificis Maximi Jussu Editum. Ratisbonae, 1926.

Robinson, Percy J., tr. and Conacher, James B. ed. *The History of Canada or New France by Father Francois Du Creux, S.J.,* 2 vols. Toronto, 1951–52.

De Rochemonteix, Camille. *Les Jésuites et la Nouvelle-France au XVIIᵉ Siècle, d'après Beaucoup de Documents Inédits.* 3 vols. Paris 1895–96.

De La Roncière, Charles G. *Au Fil du Mississipi avec le Père Marquette.* Paris, 1935.

Roustang, Francois. *Documents Jésuites de la Nouvelle France.* Paris, 1960.

Roy, Antoine. *L'Oeuvre Historique de Pierre-Georges Roy, Bibliographie Analytique.* Paris, 1928.

Roy, Joseph E. *Rapport sur les Archives de France Relatives a l'Histoire du Canada.* Ottawa, 1911.

Roy, Pierre-Georges, ed. *Inventaire des Concessions en Fief Seig-*

neurie Fois et Hommages et Aveux et Dénombrements Conservés aux Archives de la Province de Québec. 6 vols. Beauceville, 1927–29.

————. *Inventaire d'Un Collection des Pièces Judiciaires, Notoriales, etc. etc. Conservées aux Archives Judiciaires de Québec.* 2 vols. Beauceville, 1917.

————. "Le Projet de conquête de la Nouvelle York de M. de Callières en 1689." *Bulletin des Recherches Historiques* (Quebec), XXIV (1918), 289–302; continuing to XXV (1919), 33–49.

————. "Les ordonnances des Six Premiers Intendants de la Nouvelle-France." *Bulletin des Recherches Historiques* (Quebec), XXV (1919), 161–173 and 193–205.

————. *Ordonnances, Commissions, etc., etc. des Gouverneurs et Intendants de la Nouvelle-France, 1639–1706.* 2 vols. Beauceville, 1924.

————. *Toutes Petites Choses du Régime Francaise, Première Série.* Quebec, 1944.

———— and Roy, Antoine. *Inventaire des Greffes des Notaires du Régime Français.* 2 vols. Quebec, 1942.

Roy, Regis. "Frontenac, encore." *Bulletin des Recherches Historiques* (Quebec), XX (1914), 322–27.

Sabin, Joseph. *A Dictionary of Books Relating to America, from Its Discovery to the Present Time.* 29 vols. New York, 1868–1936.

Sagard-Theodat, F. Gabriel. *Le Grand Voyage dv Pays des Hvrons, Situé en l'Amerique vers la Mer Douce, és Derniers Confins de la Nouvelle France . . . auec vn Dictionnaire de la Langue Huronne . . .* 2 vols. Paris, 1632. Reprinted, ed., Emile Chevalier, Paris, 1865.

————. *Histoire du Canada et Voyages que les Freres Mineurs Recollets y Ont Faicts pour la Conversion des Infidelles Diuisez en Quatre Liures ou Est Amplement Traicte des Choses Principales Arriuées dans le Pays depuis l'An 1615 . . . .* 4 vols. Paris, 1636. Reprinted, Paris, 1866.

[De Sainte-Simon, Louis de Rouvroy, Duc]. *Mémoires de Saint-Simon, Nouvelle Édition Collationnée sur le Manuscrit Autographe Augmentée des Additions de Saint-Simon au Journal de*

Dangeau et de Notes et Appendices. 41 vols. Edited by A. de. Boislisle. Paris, 1923–30.

Schoolcraft, Henry R. *Narrative Journal of Travels through the Northwestern Regions of the United States, Extending from Detroit through the Great Chain of American Lakes to the Sources of the Mississippi River in the Year 1820.* Edited by Mentor L. Williams. East Lansing, Mich., 1953.

Schroeder, H. J. *Canons and Decrees of the Council of Trent, Original Text with English Translation.* St. Louis, 1950.

Scull, Gideon D., ed. *Voyages of Peter Esprit Radisson, Being an Account of His Travels and Experiences among the North American Indians from 1652–1684.* New York, 1943.

Semedo, Alvarez and Martini, Martin. *Histoire Vniverselle de la Chine.* Lyon, 1667.

Severin, Timothy. *Explorers of the Mississippi.* New York, 1967.

Shea, John G. "The Bursting of Pierre Margry's La Salle Bubble." *Collections of the State Historical Society of Wisconsin,* VII (1873–76), 111–22.

——, ed. *Cramoisy No. 1, Relation de la Mission des Illinois, 1693.* New York, 1857.

——. *Cramoisy No. 2, Relation de Ce Qvi S'Est Passé de Plvs Remarqvable dans la Mission Abnaquise de Sainct Joseph de Sillery . . . l'Année 1684.* New York, 1857.

——. *Cramoisy No. 5, Relation du Voyage Entrepris par Feu M. Robert Cavelier, Sieur De La Salle, pour Découvrir dans le Golfe de Mexique l'Embouchure du Fleuve Mississipy, par son Frère M. Cavelier, Prêtre de St. Sulpice, l'Un des Compagnons de Ce Voyage.* New York, 1858.

——. *Cramoisy No. 13, Relation de Ce Qui S'Est Passé de Plus Remarquable aux Missions des Pères de la Compagnie de Jésus en la Nouvelle-France Pendant les Années 1672 et 1673.* New York, 1861.

——. *Discovery and Exploration of the Mississippi Valley: with the Original Narratives of Marquette, Allouez, Membré, Hennepin, and Anastase Douay.* New York, 1853.

——. *Early Voyages Up and Down the Mississippi by Cavelier, St. Cosme, La Sueur, Gravier and Guignas, with an Introduction and an Index.* Albany, 1861. Reprinted 1902.

————. *The Expedition of Dom Diego Dionisio De Peñalosa, Governor of New Mexico from Santa Fe to the River Mischipi & Quivira in 1662 Described by Father Nicholas De Freytas.* New York, 1882.

————. *Father Louis Hennepin's "A Description of Louisiana," Translated from the Edition of 1683, and Compared with the "Nouvelle Decouverte," the La Salle Documents and Other Contemporaneous Papers.* New York, 1880.

————. *First Establishment of the Faith in New France by Father Christian Le Clercq, Recollect Missionary.* 2 vols. New York, 1881.

————. *History and General Description of New France by the Rev. P. F. X. De Charlevoix, S.J.* 6 vols. New York, 1866–72.

————. *The History of the Catholic Church in the United States.* 4 vols. New York, 1886–92.

————. *History of the Catholic Missions among the Indian Tribes of the United States, 1529–1854.* New York, 1855.

————. "Romance and Reality of the Death of Marquette and the Recent Discovery of His Remains." *The Catholic World,* XXVI (1877), 267–81.

———— and Martin, Felix. *Cramoisy No. 12, Relation de Ce Qui S'Est Passé de Plus Remarquable aux Missions des Peres de la Compagnie de Jesus en la Nouvelle France les Années 1673 à 1679 par R.P. Claude Dablon Recteur du College de Quebec & Superieur des Missions de la Compagnie de Jesus en la Nouvelle France.* New York, 1860.

Shiels, W. Eugene. *King and Church.* Chicago, 1961.

Short, Joseph C. "Communication." *Wisconsin Magazine of History,* XXXIII (1949), 92–95.

————. "Jacques Marquette, s.j. catechist." *La Revue de l'Université Laval* (Quebec), III (1949), 436–41.

————. *Reprint from the Sheboygan (Wis.) Press,* Thursday, February 15, 1951.

[Smith, Emerson R.]. *Before the Bridge, a History and a Directory of St. Ignace and Nearby Localities.* St. Ignace, Mich., 1957.

Smith, Sydney F. "The Suppression of the Society of Jesus." *The Month,* XCIX (1902), 113–30; continued Vols. C to CII.

Société Academique de Laon. *Jacques Marquette et l'Inauguration de Son Monument à Laon, le 13 juin, 1937.* Laon, 1937.

Sommervogel, Carlos, ed. *Bibliothèque de la Compagnie de Jésus, Première Partie: Bibliographie par les Pères Augustin et Aloys Backer, Second Partie: Histoire par le Père August Carayon.* 12 vols. Bruxelles, 1890–1932.

Spalding, Henry S. "The History of the Marquette Statue Presented to Statuary Hall, in the Capitol, by the State of Wisconsin." *Historical Records and Studies,* III (1904), 360–439.

Sparks, Jared. *Life of Father Marquette.* In Library of American Biography, vol. X. Edited by Jared Sparks. New York, 1839. Reprint, New York, 1865.

Spillane, Edward. "Bibliography of John Gilmary Shea." *Historical Records and Studies,* VI (pt. 2, 1912), 249–72.

Stanley, George F. G. "The Policy of Francisation as Applied to the Indians During the Ancien Regime." *Revue de Histoire de l'Amérique Francaise,* III (1949), 333–48.

Steck, Francis B. "Essays Relating to the Jolliet-Marquette Expedition 1673." Edited by August Reyling. 2 vols. Mimeographed, 1953.

––––––. "Father Garraghan and the Jolliet-Marquette Expedition, 1673." *Fortnightly Review,* XXXVI (1929) ; XXXVII (1930).

––––––. *The Jolliet-Marquette Expedition, 1673, Revised and Enriched with Maps and Documents.* Quincy, Ill., 1928.

––––––. *Marquette Legends.* Edited by August Reyling. New York, 1960.

––––––. "Miss Repplier's Père Marquette." *Fortnightly Review,* XXXVI (1929).

Stevenson, Edward L. *Terrestrial and Celestial Globes, Their History and Construction Including a Consideration of Their Value as Aids in the Study of Geography and Astronomy.* 2 vols. New Haven, 1921.

Stiles, Henry R., tr. and ed. *Joutel's Journal of La Salle's Last Voyage, 1684–7* . . . . Albany, 1906.

Stoddard, Amos. *Sketches Historical and Descriptive of Louisiana.* Philadelphia, 1812.

Stone, W. D. *Map of Wisconsin.* Washington, n.d. [c.a. 1840].

Strickland, W. P. *Old Mackinaw, or the Fortress of the Lakes and Its Surroundings.* Philadelphia, 1860.

Sulté, Benjamin. "Pierre Boucher et Son Livre." *Memoirs de la Société Royale du Canada,* II (s. 2, 1890), 99–168.

De Surgères, de Grange. *Répertoire Historique et Bibliographique de la Gazette de France depuis l'Origine jusqu'à la Revolution, 1631–1790.* 4 vols. Paris, 1902–6.

Surrey, Nancy M., ed. *Calendar of Manuscripts in Paris Archives and Libraries Relating to the History of the Mississippi Valley to 1803.* 2 vols. Washington, 1926–28.

Tailhan, Jules, ed. *Memoire sur les Moeurs, Coustumes et Religion des Sauvages de l'Amerique Septentrionale par Nicolas Perrot.* Leipzig, 1864.

Tanguay, Cyprien. *Dictionnaire Généalogique des Familles Canadiennes.* 7 vols. Montreal, 1871–90.

———. *Répertoire Général du Clergé Canadien par Ordre Chronologique depuis la Fondation de la Colonie jusqu'à Nos Jours.* Montreal, 1893.

[Le Tellier, Michel]. *Défense des Nouveaux Chretiens et des Missionnaires de la Chine, du Japon & des Indes contre Deux Livres Intitulez la Morale Pratique des Jésuites et l'Esprit de M. Arnauld.* Paris, 1687.

[Thevenot, Melchisedech]. *Ontdekking van Eenige Landen en Volkeren in't Noorder Gedeelte van America door P. Marquette en Joliet Gedaan in Het Jaar 1673.* Translated by Pieter Vander Aa. Leyden, 1707.

———. *Recueil de Voyages de Mr. Thevenot. Dedié au Roy.* Paris, 1681.

———. *Voyage et Découverte de Quelques Pays et Nations de l'Amerique Septentrionale par le P. Marquette et Sr. Joliet.* Edited by Obadiah Rich. Paris, 1845.

Thomassy, Raymond. *Geologie Pratique de la Louisiane.* New Orleans, 1860.

Thwaites, Reuben G., *Father Marquette.* New York, 1902.

———. *The Jesuit Relations and Allied Documents Travels and Explorations of the Jesuit Missionaries in New France, 1610–1791.* 73 vols. Cleveland, 1896–1901.

——. *A New Discovery of a Vast Country in America by Father Louis Hennepin.* 2 vols. Chicago, 1903.

——. *New Voyages to North America by Baron Lahontan.* 2 vols. Chicago, 1905.

——. *Wisconsin as a Province.* In Wisconsin in Three Centuries, vol. 1. Edited by Henry C. Campbell. 4 vols. New York, 1906.

De Tonti, Henri. *Derniers Découvertes dans l'Amerique Septentrionale De M. De La Salle; Mises en Jour par M. le Chevalier Tonti Gouverneur de Fort Saint Louis, aux Islinois.* Paris, 1697.

——. *Relation of Henry Tonty.* Translated by Melville B. Anderson. Chicago, 1898.

Toss, Edwin, ed. *Histoire de la Novvelle-France . . . par Marc Lescarbot.* 3 vols. Paris, 1866.

De La Tour, Bertrand. *Mémoires sur la Vie de M. De Laval, Première Évêque de Québec.* Cologne, 1761.

Tucker, Sara J. *Indian Villages of the Illinois Country.* Part 1, *Atlas.* Springfield, Ill., 1942.

De La Vega, Garcilaso. *La Florida del Inca.* In Biblioteca de Autores Españoles desde la Formacion de Lenguaje hasta Nuestro Dias, vol. CXXXII. Many editors. 208 vols. Madrid, 1960.

Verwyst, Chrysostom. *Missionary Labors of Father Marquette, Ménard and Allouez in the Lake Superior Region.* Milwaukee, 1886.

De Villiers du Terrage, Marc. *L'Expedition de Cavelier De La Salle dans le Golfe du Mexique, 1684–1687.* Paris, 1931.

——. *La Louisiane, Histoire de Son Nom et de Ses Frontières Successives, 1681–1819.* Paris, 1929.

——. *Les Raretés des Indes, "Codex Canadiensis," Album Manuscrit de la Fin du XVIIIe Siècle Contenant 180 Dessins.* Paris, 1930.

De Vorst, C. Van and Goetstouwers, J. B., eds. *Synopsis Historiae Societatis Jesu.* Lovanii, 1959.

Walter, Frank K. and Doneghy, Virginia. *Jesuit Relations and Other Americana in the Library of James F. Bell.* Minneapolis, 1950.

Washburn, Wilcomb E. "The Meaning of 'Discovery' in the Fifteenth and Sixteenth Centuries." *American Historical Review,* LXVIII (1962), 1–21.

Watrous, Jerome A. *Memoirs of Milwaukee County.* 3 vols. Madison, Wis., 1909.

Weld, Laenas G. "Jolliet and Marquette in Iowa." *Iowa Journal of History and Politics,* I (1903), 3–16.

Willaert, Leopold. *Bibliotheca Janseniana Belgica, Répertoire des Imprimés Concernant les Controverses Théologiques en Relation avec le Jansénisme dans les Pays-Bas Catholiques et le Pays de Liège aux XVIIᵉ Siècle.* 3 vols. Namur, 1947–51.

Winsor, Justin. *Cartier to Frontenac, Geographical Discovery of the Interior of North America in Its Historical Relations, 1534–1700.* Boston, 1894.

———. *Narrative and Critical History of America.* 8 vols. Boston, 1884–89.

Wood, John J. "The Mascoutin Village." *Proceedings of the State Historical Society of Wisconsin, 1906,* LIV (1907), 167–74.

Wrong, George M. *The Rise and Fall of New France.* 2 vols. Toronto, 1928.

Den Wyngaert, Anastasius Van, ed. *Sinica Franciscana, Relationes et Epistolae Fratrum Minorum Saeculi XVI et XVII . . . Adnotavit.* 5 vols. Florentiae, 1933–54.

INDEX

Hamy, Alfred (biographer of Marquette), 42

Handwriting. *See* Bibliotics; Harrisse, Henry

Harrisse, Henry: comments on Jolliet's handwriting, 93–94

Hennepin, Louis (Recollect missionary), 28, 153–54, 170–75

Holy Spirit Mission, 17

Hôtel Dieu (Quebec hospital), 31–32

Howe, M. A. De Wolfe (biographer of Bancroft), 29

Hudson Bay: Jolliet's trip to, 74; Albanel sent to, 166–67

Huron, Lake, 16, 147

Ignatius Loyola. *See* Loyola, Saint Ignatius of

Illinois River, 179, 184

Immaculate Conception, 140

Imprimatur, 61

Indians, 51, 84, 124, 142–43

—Algonquin, 16

—Chippewa, 16

—Huron, 17

—Illinois: Marquette works with, 18, 46, 84; Marquette's first encounter with, 134; Marquette travels with, 144; and Conception Mission, 145–46, 151–52; and Fr. Allouez, 160; at Chequamegon Bay, 161

—Kaskaskia, 181

—Kiskakon Ottawa, 149

—Miami, 178

—Misissaki, 149

—Mohawk, 138

—Montagni. *See* Indians: Algonquin

—Nipissirinien, 148–49

—Ottawa, 14, 16, 17, 164, 190–92

—Potawatomi, 144

—Sioux, 17, 108, 164, 175

—Wild Rice, 56

Institute of Jesuit history: origin of, 44–45

Institutum Societatis Jesu, 4, 13, 205–6. *See also Constitutiones Societatis Jesu*

Iowa: Marquette visits, 179

Jacker, Edward (pastor of St. Ignace), 192–94

Jansenism: teachings opposed by Jesuits, 76, 123; and *The Augustinus,* 76; promoted by Eusèbe Renaudot, 76; popularized by Arnauld, 99

Jansenius, Cornelius (founder of Jansenism), 76, 99

Jefferson, Thomas, 22

Jesuits. *See* Society of Jesus

Jolliet, Adrien (older brother of Louis), 103–4

Jolliet, Louis: explorations of, with Marquette, 27, 115, 158, 165, 176; Bancroft neglects, 29; Steck's conjecture about, 43; narratives about, 46–50, 56, 57–58, 59, 74; writes dedicatory letter on maps, 59, 79; documents in French National Archives pertaining to, 74; travels to Hudson Bay and Labrador, 74; writes preface to the "Relation . . . les Années 1672–1673," 77–79; handwriting of, 79–80; friendship of, with Bishop Laval, 93; correct spelling of, 94; engages in fur trade, 103–7; friendship of, with Jesuits, 111; and the Relations, 116, 163–64; companions of, 117–18; at Wisconsin River, 133; partnership of, with Marquette, 158–65; meets Marquette, 159, 160, 163–65; musical talent of, 163; and Hennepin, 170–72; log of discovery by, 172–75; and Illinois River, 179; returns from Mississippi River, 180–